Don't Touch!

The educational story of a panic

Don't Tou___ the first book in the UK to explore the problems involved in 'touching___t ___dren in an educational environment. The book uses real-life examples ___ from ground-breaking research into the mentality of today's risk cult___a___d highlights a maddening state of affairs in which ordinary well-mea___ professionals feel they cannot offer even very young children basic leve___ ___omforting or affection.

This fasc___ ___ and long-overdue book examines the 'no-touch' pandemic in early yea___ ___ngs, primary and secondary schools today by use of extensive interview___ ___ practitioners, parents and pupils, which:

- ——___ the confusion experienced by many in knowing if, when and ___ touch and the more recent backlash by those who attempted ___ck the trend;

- ___est why this issue is important now (for example, at a time when ——___ are being encouraged to work in early years settings);

- ___der explanations such as panic, risk, society and fear.

Don't T___ also examines and explains where the law stands on these issues, a___ keep___ its key focus on practice throughout, representing an unsensationali___ and sensible approach to an issue that causes so much professional anxiety ___ ___i___ be welcomed by the entire teaching profession and child-care profes___ ___ ___ls, ___ng with researchers and other academics within education and th___ ___ci___ sciences.

Heathe___ ___per is Senior Research Fellow in the Education and Social Research institute of Manchester Metropolitan University, UK.

Ian Stronach is Research Professor of Education in the Education and Social Research Institute of Manchester Metropolitan University, UK.

Don't Touch!

The educational story of a panic

Heather Piper and Ian Stronach

LONDON AND NEW YORK

First published 2008 by Routledge
2 Park Square, Milton Park, Abingdon, Oxon OX14 4RN

Simultaneously published in the USA and Canada
by Routledge
270 Madison Ave., New York, NY 10016

Routledge is an imprint of the Taylor & Francis Group, an informa business

© 2008 Heather Piper and Ian Stronach

Typeset in Garamond by
Saxon Graphics Ltd, Derby
Printed and bound in Great Britain by
TJ International Ltd, Padstow, Cornwall

British Library Cataloguing in Publication Data
A catalogue record for this book is available from the British Library

Library of Congress Cataloging in Publication Data
Piper, Heather.
Don't touch! : the educational story of a panic / Heather Piper and
Ian Stronach
p. cm.
Includes bibliographical references and index.
1. Teacher-student relationships—Great Britain. 2. Early childhood
education—Social aspects—Great Britain. 3. Touch—Social aspects—
Great Britain. 4. Child sexual abuse—Great Britain—Prevention.
I. Stronach, Ian. II. Title.
LB1033.P59 2008
371.102'30941—dc22
                                      2007036114

ISBN 10: 0–415–42007–5 (hbk)
ISBN 10: 0–415–42008–3 (pbk)
ISBN 10: 0–203–93049–5 (ebk)

ISBN 13: 978–0–415–42007–5 (hbk)
ISBN 13: 978–0–415–42008–2 (pbk)
ISBN 13: 978–0–203–93049–6 (ebk)

Contents

Notes on contributors

Dr Helen Bowen (Manager, South Manchester Women's Aid, UK, helperry@yahoo.com) has a PhD in Education from Manchester Metropolitan University, UK, which focused on domestic violence and communities of practice. In addition to working on the Touchlines research project she has worked for many years as a multi-agency domestic violence coordinator, and currently works for South Manchester Women's Aid which provides refuge and outreach support to women and children experiencing domestic violence. Her research interests continue to focus on social action, education, and in particular violence against women.

Helen Lawson (PhD student Institute of Education Manchester Metropolitan University, UK, helen@lawson58.freeserve.co.uk), in addition to her PhD studies and working on the Touchlines research project, also works as a freelance researcher based in the South West of England. While her research interests are varied her particular research focus lies within the area of globalisation, citizenship and inclusion.

Dr Heather Piper (Senior Research Fellow, Manchester Metropolitan University, UK, h.j.piper@mmu.ac.uk) is a qualitative researcher and her interests span a broad range of educational and social issues. She has co-edited *Difference and Diversity* with Ian Stronach, has published widely and been involved in more than 20 research projects. Her 'voice' in research practice and academic writing is typified by a contrarian approach, a broad-based and eclectic intellectual territory in sociology, philosophy, social policy, and a sensitivity to interprofessional concerns informed by her own experiences outwith the academy.

Dr John Powell (Senior Lecturer Institute of Education Manchester Metropolitan University, UK, j.powell@mmu.ac.uk) is a qualified social worker and has a particular interest in early childhood studies, equal opportunities, children's rights, multiprofessional issues and professional development. In addition to his teaching role he has been involved in several research projects including the Evaluation of Early Years Excellence

Centres (1999–2002), a Teenage Parents Project (2001–2004), and more recently a Sure Start evaluation.

Dr Catherine Scott (Centre for Educational Leadership, Faculty of Education, University of Wollongong, Australia, cscott@uow.edu.au) has a PhD in psychology from Macquarie University, Australia, and is also a qualified school teacher. She has taught in secondary and primary schools and since 1989 in universities, where she has taught educational and developmental psychology and research methods. Her research interests include teachers' occupational identity; satisfaction and well-being; classroom communication; and contemporary perceptions of risk and their consequences for professionals and their clients.

Professor Ian Stronach (Research Professor of Education, Institute of Education, Manchester Metropolitan University, UK, i.m.stronach@ mmu.ac.uk) was Editor of the *British Educational Research Journal* for 12 years (1996–2007), and has published widely in international journals. His research interests are in postmodernist methodology and theory, as well as in areas such as evaluation, research epistemology and professionalism. Appointed 'expert witness' at the Summerhill Tribunal case (2000), he has since done ESRC-sponsored research there, including 'inspecting the inspectors'.

Preface and acknowledgements

Our interest in the problematics of touching between professionals and children in their care developed over a number of years. Early conversations between ourselves and Hannah Smith (a former Manchester Metropolitan University undergraduate whose honours dissertation had prompted our interest) resulted in some small-scale pilot research which confirmed the impression that the touching of children in professional settings had increasingly stopped being relaxed, or instinctive, or primarily concerned with responding to the needs of the child. It was becoming a self-conscious negative act, requiring a mind–body split for both children and adults, the latter being controlled more by fear than a commitment to caring. We were able to consider these issues in more depth as a result of a successful research proposal to the Economic Social Research Council (ESRC RES-000–22–0815, 2006). It is this research which provides much of the data we refer to throughout this book. Although the research focused on the UK context, available literature suggests that the same issues are pertinent to many other countries worldwide, particularly the US, Canada, Australia and New Zealand. A full comparative study of discourse and practice in non-Anglophone cultures would obviously be of great interest, but was beyond the scope of our project.

Our research design for the ESRC was substantially qualitative and case-based as we sought depth of insight into the sociocultural practices, beliefs and meaning invested in touch between children and adults/professionals in the chosen settings. Adopting case study as a method of data collection (Stake 1978) allowed us to work closely with the participants, both adults and children, building the trust and confidence necessary for addressing complex issues. We initially adopted the 'grounded' approach of Glaser and Strauss (1967) and Strauss and Corbin (1998) as our main form of analysis, and subsequently augmented that approach with both narrative and discourse analysis, as well as deconstruction.

Our research addressed children and young people of all ages and across a range of educational settings. The process began with a questionnaire in which we requested copies of any existing guidelines on touching practices between adults and children from a range of public and private bodies. In addition we invited involvement in the later research processes. We received more than 400 replies, many including documentation which on closer consideration confirmed how the problematics of touch have been addressed in official discourses (see Chapter 4), along with many offers from those keen to be involved with later stages of the research. Some of our case study sites emerged as a result of this process, others being identified through personal contacts as we sought to ensure we involved children and young people from a variety of educational settings. These included preschool, primary/junior school, secondary school, school for those experiencing severe physical and emotional difficulties, residential school, and Summerhill School as a setting which previous research experience had led us to intuit would be relatively unaffected by the moral panic discussed throughout. Our sample also included schools from both the state and public (private) sector, so children and young people from less to more privileged backgrounds were involved in the process.

In spite of many early offers to be included in the research, the secondary school case study site still proved difficult to recruit (see Chapter 8), and *all* settings except Summerhill School requested confidentiality. Consequently the names of all establishments, staff, children and young people have either been removed or fictionalised and the reasons for this sensitivity will become apparent. The choice of settings deliberately included some which took explicit pride in being 'touchy feely'. For example:

> We are a nursery school. As such it is vitally necessary to establish warm, supportive relationships with young children – so staff are encouraged to touch, cuddle, and hug our children. If the day ever dawned when we were not allowed to be affectionate and give physical support to our under fives, I would definitely close the nursery and it would be a day of great sadness, and portend ill for the development of these children.

Others claimed to be more defensive (even in early years' settings) and were also included as we attempted to identify a balanced sample:

> All members of staff are instructed not to be alone with a child. Key members of staff are sent on restraint training [you] must have an open door, adult witness. When restraining, do not touch with thumb, lead more than 'push'. Calm the children verbally, calm using body language. Do not allow the child to sit on your lap or lean against you.

In all settings we were able to observe interactions between the adults and children/young people, and conduct semi-structured or unstructured individual and group interviews with young people and various appropriate adults (including parents in most settings). In total 20 detailed observations of situations involving professionals with children were recorded and 45 interviews with children and young people were taped and later transcribed. In addition 48 teachers and other professionals and/or interested parties were interviewed, as were six parents (although the majority of those in the former group were parents in addition to their professional role). The majority of our case study sites are in the North of England, except for Summerhill, which is in the South East, and the primary/junior school which is in the South West. It is these data which provide the substance for Chapters 6 to 10.

Originally we had intended helping our case study sites develop practical guidelines as a basis for professional development, but in the course of our work we came to regard guidelines as having an overall negative effect rather than making a positive contribution. Guidelines came to be seen as symptoms of the fears felt by professionals and agencies rather than a characteristic of a confident profession or workforce. Where guidelines were in place, they were often either ignored or became unworkable, and teachers and care workers felt guilt at their non-compliance. Or they would be followed slavishly, though almost always with a sense of regret that 'things had come to this'. Overall, we found respondents fearful of being seen as physically or sexually abusive. Many behaved as though they did not trust themselves and had to prove to others (and vice versa) that they were innocent of any malevolent intent. In addition they did not trust others (adults and children) to judge their actions as innocent and appropriate, and did not trust children (and sometimes adults) to refrain from false or malicious allegations. These fears were evident and sustained in spite of the fact that most interviewees accepted that touch was essential to very young children and other young people, especially those who were described as kinaesthetic learners.

Even though the research deliberately involved staff who had claimed to be 'touchy feely' in their approach, in the event most proved to be similarly cautious, with the exception of Summerhill School. Access to and observation in this school helped direct our thinking towards wider issues such as trust, and to consider a much broader range of 'touching' behaviours, including 'distance' and what we began to call 'relational touching'. We came to the view that to talk about 'touching' in isolation and to regard it metonymically (as a part which represents a whole) was less helpful (and implicitly pornographic and/or fetishistic) as opposed to discussing the whole context of the relationships in which it takes place. 'Touching' elided so easily into 'touching up', however bizarre and remote that possibility in real life as opposed to risk culture. Such conversations are revisited and developed in Chapter 5 and in the concluding chapter where we finish with a paradox: attempts to police 'touch' make sexual and physical abuse an ever-present in professional minds. The morality of suspicion and fear create a kind of presbyterian pornography of surveillance, suspicion and insane precaution. Such an ethos is the abusive meeting place of moral panic and policy hysteria where presumptions of guilt and risk drive out professional values of trust, concern and care – and where innocence itself has to be regarded as an admission of guilt through lack of due precaution.

In brief, Chapter 1 sets the scene for the rest of the book and outlines some of the broader debates around touching and draws on available international literature. It considers the contradictions between what is considered 'good' and 'bad' touch; discusses touching as risky for both adults and children; addresses notions of desire in the pedagogical relationship; and situates such discussion within the frame of a moral panic.

In Chapter 2, Catherine Scott addresses the cultural changes and altered social models of relationships between people. She argues that as trust has declined suspicion has increased to the point that everyone now is potentially either a victim or an abuser. Suspicion is therefore aimed at anyone in a position of power or authority, including teachers, researchers and scholars. More specifically, Catherine discusses some of the prohibitive effects of ethics committees on research into sensitive topics such as this, and outlines how she was prevented from replicating the ESRC research in an Australian context, as had originally been envisaged. An ethics of ignorance was preferred to the risk of knowledge. These prohibitive effects are not only pertinent to Australia, but come as a warning to others, as the potency and sclerotic effects of ethics committees are increasingly apparent in academic life in the UK and elsewhere.

Chapter 3 addresses legislation that impacts on this issue, and argues that while we found no specific legislation inhibiting the touching of children, legislation is nevertheless contributing to the overall panic which does affect touching practices. The example selected to illustrate this process is the recently implemented Safeguarding Vulnerable Groups Act (2006) which has led to an increase in the number of adults who are now vetted so as to check their suitability to be near children. This not only leads to a category of adults considered 'not fit', but has also helped to further increase the number of guidelines which include 'no touching' as good (or at least safe) child-care practice.

Chapter 4 develops these ideas specifically in relation to the questionnaire returns from our research, and is one of six chapters which address the research data more directly.

Chapter 5 is theoretical and some readers may choose not to engage with it. It assumes some prior reading and/or knowledge on the part of the reader as it engages with the writing of Jean-Luc Nancy and Jacques Derrida (among others). In our theoretical excursion we consider a theory of 'touch', or of 'feeling', as we have come to prefer. The chapter includes illustrations of 'instances' or 'tangents' (selected from outside the research project) where issues of body/touch/senses are prominent in relation to parts of our argument, so as to put 'flesh' on the 'body' of touch, as it were.

Chapters 6 to 10 each focus on a case study site, i.e. preschool (the authors), primary and junior school (Helen Lawson), secondary school (Helen Bowen), school for those experiencing severe physical and emotional difficulties (John Powell), and Summerhill School (the authors – a much fuller version of this chapter can be found in Stronach and Piper 2008), and draw directly on the voices of many of the research participants. Even though the research in all of our case study sites included the whole range of research methods, and followed a similar pattern, these chapters are not written to a formula.

Finally, Chapter 11 revisits some of the themes we refer to throughout, and concludes with an appeal for the abandoning of 'no-touch' professional practices.

There are many people we wish to acknowledge as contributing to the ideas and subsequent writing of this book, including all members of the Touchlines project research team: Helen Bowen, Helen Lawson, Maggie MacLure and John Powell; also Tom Barfield for some initial analysis in relation to the survey returns; and all the research participants, whom unfortunately we cannot name. However, we are able to thank all those who comprised the Summerhill community in 2004/5, who welcomed us as visitors into their school, and allowed us the freedom to find our own research sample. In addition we would like to thank Hannah Smith for early conversations and for sharing her own research, all of which had a direct impact in encouraging us to carry out the pilot studies, which led to the subsequent ESRC funded research. Catherine Scott maintained an interest in the research throughout and sent many thoughtful emails which contributed to our thinking. A further significant contribution came from Josie Appleton who made her own research data on the effects of the Safeguarding Vulnerable Groups Act (2006) available to us, and which provide much of the substance for Chapter 3. Thanks also to John Piper for assisting with the proof-reading of numerous earlier drafts. Finally we wish to thank the many professionals (practitioners and academics) who responded to media commentaries on the research and published material, and who trusted us with their own experiences, all of which had a direct impact on our work.

Heather Piper and Ian Stronach, Summer 2007

Chapter 1

Problematics of touching

This chapter offers an introduction to key issues around touching behaviours that are encountered by professionals working with young people. The research initiative began with small-scale pilot research projects in 2000–2 that helped to identify the nature of the problem. Typically a primary school teacher had remarked: 'Physical contact could be misconstrued by a child, parent/carer, or observer . . . it is unwise to attribute touching to the style of work or way of relating to pupils' (Piper 2002). In practice, getting it right involved guesswork: 'I was afraid to ask for guidance and was trying to gauge "correct" touch behaviour from observation' (Smith 2000). Repeated injunctions in education and other settings included always having a second adult to witness intimate care routines, minimising the cuddling of young children, and even requiring particular ways of doing this, such as a sideways cuddle so as to avoid any full-frontal contact. These concerns were not confined to the UK and had also been discussed in the US, Canada, Australia and New Zealand in terms of a moral panic (Tobin 1997), a product of risk society (McWilliam and Jones 2005), and as a consequence of a litigious culture (Furedi 2002a). As a result, many child-orientated arenas were rapidly becoming 'no touch' zones (see Johnson 2000, for example).[1]

Good and bad touch

The tendency to consider touch as essentially good can be evidenced by numerous sources and is clearly not a new idea. Many child-care workers, teachers and psychologists (Katz 1989; Slunt 1994; Caulfield 2000) regard touch as essential for 'proper' child development: 'The child experiences his or her world meaningfully through sight, sound, smell, taste, touch and action' (Tobin 1997: 41). Others have suggested this is not only applicable to children as we are always 'bodily' in the world (Sartre 1943/56; Tobin 1997). It has generally been assumed that it would be more damaging for a young child to be touched too little than too much, as touching provides sensory information to the child that is an essential part of healthy development. Literature concerned with the caring of young children promotes cuddles, holding and stroking as good child-care practice. However, child development manuals (especially those relating to young children) are often written with the parent or parent substitute in mind, on the assumption that they (parents, grandparents and siblings) will be the main touch givers. Relatively recently the professionalisation of child care, the tendency to send children to 'school' at younger ages, and the introduction of the extended hours scheme in the UK has expanded the child-care workforce, which now includes more men. This has resulted in, or at least coincided with, an increased emphasis on the inappropriateness of touch: 'Teach, don't touch' (Colt 1977), even in very early years settings. Attempts to comply with this 'regime of the normal' have resulted in an apparent mind–body split, with the inherent danger of forgetting the capacity for feeling (Tobin 1997). Some have commented that 'teachers use their minds to manage children's bodies until children can do so for themselves' (Phelan 1997: 89). Consequently 'children's identities are connected to their failure or success in managing their bodies in accord with their teacher's demands' (Leavitt and Power 1997).

A contemporary common attitude towards touch is one of helplessness, where workers sometimes feel they must 'break away' from what they assume to be policy in order to best meet the needs of the child. Smith (2000) was advised to 'always keep an obstacle such as a desk between you and the child'. This was regarded as the 'safest' option for the adult, whose precautionary interests were implicitly prioritised over any needs of the child. Such 'no touch' discourses permeate our lives in numerous seemingly incidental ways, and in some instances 'no touch' develops into 'don't speak' or even 'don't be'. Adults admit to being nervous of speaking to children in informal settings like shops, supermarkets or in the street, as they are well aware of the 'don't speak to strangers' discourse:

> If I was to see a child in distress I would dial 999 [emergency number] before approaching them. I have come across too many examples of hysterical over reaction from both parents and people in positions of authority to risk my career.
>
> (see Radio 4 Message Board 2006)

Johnson (2000) has drawn attention to the continuous repetition of these 'like stories' and 'like discourses' that both disturbs and compels further consideration of the popularity of 'no touch' policies and practices.

Implicit in much of the writing that promotes touch as essential and good is the assumption that adults have a monopoly on the decision-making, which may result in the dismissal of children's wishes and desires. Yet many argue that touch should be initiated by the child: 'it's all in the body language isn't it . . . a child will let you know' (Smith 2000). A contradictory discourse states that a child not wanting to be touched may well be 'deprived' and in need of our intervention. It is hard to see how the voice of the child can ever be heard (let alone valued) given this confusion. In one of our earlier studies we found that different infant teachers reported contradictory ways of responding to the need of children to be touched. One teacher stated: 'We are an infant school and this practice (touching) is appropriate for the age of the children we teach', whereas another responded 'under no circumstances must you hug a child or put them on your knee . . . we do not believe that we should act towards children in our care as their mums or dads do'.

Paradoxically, alongside these concerns there has been a recent increase in massage at schools and other child-related settings. Books and videos promoting the positive nature of this touching practice proliferate (Field 2002), and the UK government has encouraged such massage as 'safe and therapeutic' touch (New Opportunities Fund 2002). Baby massage classes for parents are held in an increasing number of clinics (now freely available in Sure Start areas) and many schools have introduced massage classes aimed at reducing stress especially for 'difficult' pupils. In some schools peer-massage is encouraged, this involves children massaging each other for seven minutes each day (*Massage in Schools Programme*) also aimed at reducing stress. In some examples teachers are aware they should not touch a child (as it may be misunderstood) but are encouraged to send very young children off into rooms with adults who are relative strangers ('touch professionals') for a 'massage' (e.g. *The Quiet Place*). Arguably touching children is becoming a 'therapeutic', 'organised' and 'sanitised' practice. The professionalisation of touch appears to have removed it from the world of the 'natural' and inserted it into the world of the 'technical'. We question whether massage should be a first choice option for children, when less organised practices should arguably prevail. It is also interesting to note that Her Majesty's Inspectorate when inspecting Summerhill in 1999 (HMI/Ofsted 1999) had observed a male teacher massaging the shoulders of a girl sitting in front of him at a meeting of the school. He immediately reported the incident to the Social Services (Stronach *et al.* 2000, and see also Chapter 10).

Touch as risky for adults

We agree that fears surrounding touch satisfy all the prerequisites of a moral panic, and with Johnson (2000) who observed that such panic helps to create and support mechanisms of social control: 'We have in fact let the moral panic irrationally define us and (mis)guide our understandings of children and how we interact with and relate to them' (ibid.: 22). Others consider that such moral panics are out of all proportion to the actual threat (Hall *et al.* 1978). Professionals 'appear to talk "with one voice", of rates, diagnoses, prognoses and solutions . . . media representations universally stress "sudden and dramatic" increases . . . beyond that which a sober, realistic appraisal could sustain' (ibid.: 16). A consideration of the fears around the risk of sexual allegation against adults in caring situations led Silin to suggest that the panic serves to 'rewrite sexuality in a way that distances adults from children and alienates us all from questions of sexual desire' (Silin 1997: 223, and see Chapter 2).

In areas relating to the touching of children some now behave as though permanently under the scrutiny of the panopticon. Many, for example nannies, work under the constant lens of the video camera; and others feel the same pressure: 'Never cover up the window of the classroom door. It prohibits administrators and other teachers from looking in' (Johnson 2000: 102); 'Ensure the door to your classroom is open' (Smith 2000). Those working without the apparent security of having their actions observed often try to ensure they only touch children in public, and in effect construct their own imagined cameras to oversee and regulate their behaviour (Watney 1987; Rose 1990). They appear to regard both themselves and their students as potentially dangerous. This defensive behaviour may have resulted from the moral panic, but could now be interpreted as evidence that people do not trust themselves or the children in such apparently 'tempting' circumstances. The Catch-22 nature of such situations and responses means that it is always possible someone could claim abuse or harassment on the grounds that they were only ever spoken to in public places and were treated as a threat, which made them suspect the other person as some kind of repressed 'pervert'. We now inhabit a climate where affectionate or supportive touch is interpreted as extraordinary and potentially abusive, which seemingly constructs aggressive touch as a 'normal' threat that has to be kept under permanent scrutiny.

In many contexts, fear has led to the suspicion that adults are likely to have ulterior, negative motives: 'At the same time that we celebrate the triumph of every new piece of child protection legislation, every nursery observation camera installed, every paedophile convicted and placed behind bars, we are being forced to acknowledge some very troubling implications for anyone in close proximity to a child' (McWilliam 2000: x). Men especially are assumed to be 'perverts' (if not 'wimps') if they seek to work with young children. Various explanations have been offered for this. One suggests that to define 'caring' as essentially female renders it unskilled work. Men are therefore deemed only able to 'care' by being sexual, which paradoxically ensures that women remain entrapped in the 'caring' sweatshop (King 1997). However:

> At first it was gay men who were under suspicion. Then, suddenly, it was all men working in the field. Now women are discouraged – even prevented – from holding children on their laps or helping them in the bathroom. The point is not that we should be more upset by the demonization of straight women than of gay men. The point is that the moral panic in early childhood education, which focused first on gay men, is spreading. One bad experience retold many times in the press is generalized to an account that allows suspicion and fear to rule.
>
> (Tobin 1997: 7)

Accounts of men's defensive behaviours are increasingly common. Parents 'insisted that we re-think our hiring of a male. We have had a couple of parents who have pulled their children out. It's too bad, but there is a bias towards men in the field' (Johnson 2000: 42). Schools in our own pilot studies offered similar comments. An infant school head teacher remarked 'we have no male members of staff, so no guidelines relating to entering girls' toilets or attending to females by a male teacher' (Piper 2002). Such comments excluded similar observations about female members of staff, often frequent visitors in boys' toilets. A male teacher in a secondary school described how he had responded to a girl crying because of the death of her grandfather by putting his arm round her shoulder when accompanying her to the next lesson. While his actions were spontaneous he found himself panicking, and immediately went to 'report himself' to a female member of staff regarding what he had done and why. He added he was not worried so much by what the girl might do or say, as he was fairly confident in her ability to understand the situation for what it was, but was more worried by the interpretation others might put on the situation, especially pupils who might choose to be malicious. 'Some things one can see for oneself. Other things depend on the telling of the tale' (Thompson 1998, in Johnson 2000: 35).

Touch as risky for children

These debates have developed alongside a professional practice that promotes notions of 'good touch' and 'bad touch', and a child's right to decide for themselves who touches them, where and when:

> Good-Touch/Bad-Touch is a child abuse prevention curriculum designed for children in preschool through the sixth grade. It works as a tool to teach children the skills they need, to play a significant role in prevention or interruption of child abuse/sexual abuse in their own lives.
>
> (Atlanta Project 2002)

Such initiatives are concerned to ensure that powerful adults do not take advantage of vulnerable children. Particular accounts of 'power' are central here – a young child can only possess power by stealing it from the adult. It tends to be assumed that power can only be obtained by resorting to lies or accusations or trickery, as the powerful are unlikely to relinquish their power voluntarily. This is a medicine-wo/man understanding of relationships (Andrews 1981), and although there may be instances where such games are played, this is not an understanding that should permeate all our behaviours and go unchallenged. It has been noted that hierarchies are not just represented by spaces between jobs, but *also* by spaces between bodies (Witz *et al.* 1996). Interpretations need to depend on much wider experiences than those under scrutiny, which suggests that understanding is necessarily complex, and context- and person-specific.

Considering ideas around sexual harassment Diprose (1998: 14) comments:

> What you find erotic . . . is stamped with the social history of your existence [and explains] why a person can feel violated to the core of her being in situations that an outside observer may not consider sexual or serious.

Within some child-orientated situations a category and level of 'attraction' between adults and children is acknowledged. For example, some adoption societies allow adoptees to reject one or two babies before accepting one for adoption, as it is understood that smell and sight, and instincts hard to put into words, are important in how people get on. Similarly some nurseries allow 'attraction' to dictate who will be the key worker for a particular child, resources permitting, as a child will gravitate towards one adult in preference to another and this is often reciprocal. However, once children attend school and adults are in shorter supply such 'attraction' is (re)interpreted as favouritism, at best, and to be avoided. A rather odd situation emerges where 'best practice', often unspoken, but understood, dictates that it is best not to touch those we want to touch, but that it may be good to touch others, in the spirit of inclusion. Such behaviour makes the risks for children potentially greater than normally acknowledged. The relatively small risk of abuse by the professionals (Tobin 1997) is surpassed by a much greater risk of emotional and physical sterility. It is normally safe to assume that those who do not want to touch each other probably will not do so. In situations where one person wants to touch and the other does not, then usually most children and adults will read the cues appropriately, and the odd mistake can soon be rectified. However, it is possibly in this category where there is a capacity for misunderstanding and abuse of power from above or below, providing the relatively few examples that fuel the moral panic. On the other hand, as a result of these pressures, those who want to touch each other will feel unable to do so, and thus the touching needs of many children cannot be met. It is perhaps unsurprising that a muddled and confused practice has emerged in such a situation.

Pleasure and desire

'Denial of desire is the very production of it' remarks King (1997: 240). The identification and consideration of pleasures and desires is the area of this debate most open to misinterpretation, and therefore remains the most avoided and obscured. Professionals often attempt to hide personal pleasures and adult desires whilst 'forgetting' childhood desires (especially sexual). In doing so, children's relatively straightforward desires are rendered unimportant or inappropriate and virtually taboo. 'Many of our colleagues . . . have warned us that writing about the pleasures and desires of young children and their teachers is foolhardy . . . We know that an interest in children's sexuality may be mistaken for sexual interest in children' (Tobin 1997: 7). More recently, a related hypocrisy has been noted in the UK – between registers of purity and prurience: 'In particular, that neo-Victorianism is caught in the tensions between a largely pornographic media and its "economy of titillation" and a prudish if hypocritical official morality to which media and politicians also subscribe' (Stronach *et al.* 2006: 18). Thus, children playing doctors and nurses or kissing games is not exceptional, and it is not unusual for a teacher to enjoy hugging a child who is distressed but 'it is the teacher's acknowledgment of pleasure in the feel of a child's body and in giving pleasure to a child that is odd and disturbing . . . the topic (is) so awkward not because it is a rare event but because it is rarely discussed' (ibid.: 12). There is no available discourse that would permit or support acknowledgement or discussion. Field *et al.*, (1994) noted that adults who did not resort to describing touch as 'hitting, pushing and pulling hair' would instead describe it as some sort of sexual activity. They also argued that desire and all aspects of the eros appear conflated with sex, with little space left now for other considerations. Phelan (1997) suggested that work with children is defined more in opposition to the erotic than in tension with it. Yet Tobin (1997) remembers a not far distant time when professionals easily discussed drive theories and penis envy in relation to children, and points out that it is not long since children's sexuality was considered unremarkable.

Now we regard ourselves as a society of potential paedophiles, however, any such discourse is taboo. Foucault wrote of a similar situation in the Victorian age when 'Everyone knew . . . that children had no sex, which was why they were forbidden to talk about it . . . repression operated as a sentence to disappear, but also as an injunction to silence . . .' (Foucault 1980: 4). Mindful also of Foucault's (1977) discussion of the medicalisation of the body, and of sexuality as a form of social control, Tobin (1997) conducted a comparative study between Irish and American early years workers and found differences in interpretations of children's behaviour. Kissing games were regarded as 'normal' in Ireland – 'kiss chase is our big game. The girls think it is brilliant' (ibid.: 30) – whereas in America the same scenario developed into a discussion of infection between children. Similarly, when considering a young girl masturbating, the US professionals again interpreted and transformed the scenario into one about vaginal itch and infection. Felman (1997: 25) notes how 'ignorance is linked to what is not remembered [and] what will not be memorised'.

Against the trend, not all professionals allow their behaviour to be dictated by suppression and the fear of the (often) imagined thoughts of others:

> I refuse to let the ugly spectre of fingerpointing to be a chokechain. I smile and I wink at my children. I hug and tickle my children . . . Being

confident and secure that my actions and intentions are rooted in caring and nurturing I shall continue to be this way'.

(female early years teacher quoted in Johnson 2000: 52)

Also, 'I have been known to carry someone back to the nurse's office, even if they could have walked. I believe this gives the child much more comfort and relief' (male early years teacher quoted in Johnson 2000: 52). Hooks (1994), after describing a scene when a university male student arrived late to a class and came to the front of the lecture whirled her round, resulting in much giggling, commented that:

we danced our way into the future as comrades and friends bound by all we had learned in class together . . . [adding, that we must] . . . find again the place of eros within ourselves, and together allow the mind and body to feel and know desire.

(ibid.: 198–9).

Perhaps a society that makes certain words taboo or 'naughty' (and touch appears now to be one such word) ensures that adults will have inappropriate responses. 'Misnaming of the need and the deed gives rise to that distortion which results in pornography and obscenity – the abuse of feeling' (Lorde 1984). It is interesting to consider this against instructions often given to children, for example, 'Use your words' (Smith 2000). Oken-Wright (1992: 15) claims that children soon 'learn to use language rather than their bodies to get what they want'. Given the restrictions on the language we are allowed to use, 'using our words' is no simple task. Phelan (1997: 77) has observed that in an attempt to avoid difficulties arising in the first place, many demonstrate 'a concern with order [that] belies a fear of the erotic'. Self control is taught by prohibitive behaviours – 'thou shalt not go near; thou shalt not touch; thou shalt not experience pleasure; thou shalt not speak; thou shalt not show thyself, except, as Foucault reminds us, in darkness and secrecy' (Phelan 1987: 82; and see throughout). She interprets this as an attempt to erase any pleasure that adults and children experience through body touch and bonding. 'Exercising self control means follow(ing) certain patterns of behaviour' (Arendt in Warner 1990: 41). But we are reminded that 'teachers are not the villains here . . . the logic of order and classroom management regulate[s] teachers as much as children' (Phelan 1997: 86).

In contrast to the state of 'order' is a state of 'disorder', where bodies touch, and 'During erotic moments, boundaries are blurred, and established patterns of relations are disturbed; these are moments of exuberance and excess for teachers and students, moments that are unreserved, lavish, and joyful' (Phelan 1997: 78). But fear has led to objectifying the body as a distancing strategy. Crossley (1995: 43) adds: 'the child's body is more than an object; it is a body-subject, an active body always/already engaged with its environment in the process of sense-making'. In accepting this mind–body split children learn to live and 'conform to a structure not based on human need' (Lorde 1984: 58). However, we are reminded that 'the erotic is not a question *only* of what we do; it is a question of how acutely and fully we can feel in the doing' (ibid.: 54).

In an attempt to break out of the current stalemate, Grace and Tobin (1997) describe their 'boundary-crossing' and 'pleasure-getting' activities with young children in their classes. They draw on Bakhtin's (1968/84) discussion of the idea of the carnival, and his (1975/81) concept of pleasure, entailing both *plaisir* and *jouissance* (*plaisir* being more conformist than *jouissance* and can be expressed in language, whereas *jouissance* is more intense and heightened, and generally involves a temporary loss of subjectivity). They invited the children to produce videos about anything they liked, and noted these tended be quite rude, featuring 'bottoms' and 'poo', etc. The films were often parodic, grotesque and frequently featured the forbidden. Bakhtin regarded the classroom 'as a site of conflicting agendas where the high [teachers and the curriculum] and the low [children and their interests and desires] meet' (in Grace and Tobin 1997: 168–9). Grace and Tobin found that parody served to break down barriers and allowed space for critique that challenged assumptions. The forbidden as expressed in the videos similarly created a space where it was possible to discuss violence, sex and pleasure. It was also possible to explore alternative understandings of power, and to discuss the interactions between the 'high' and the 'low', using dissent, satire and laughter. The process was not only beneficial to the children, but allowed adults to challenge their own practices. They claim that any attempt at rationalising and regulating these carnivalesque pleasures makes them lose their essence and vanish, as 'they . . . live briefly in the interstice between freedom and structure until their moment is spent, and pleasure can be enjoyed in and of the moment, for itself and nothing more' (ibid.: 186). Such moments are enjoyable, creative and beneficial for everyone unless we adopt an instrumental approach to education, and a 'Victorian' approach to child development.

It has been suggested that some other societies and cultures are less frightened by touch, and are less prone to regard all physical contact as sexual or violent. Anecdotally we are aware that in some societies where affectionate touch is not even on the agenda as something requiring consideration, let alone regulation, similarly touch as a form of punishment is considered unremarkable (we take this to mean a spontaneous clip to the back of the legs if a child runs out into the road say, not beating a child until it is bruised). Such observations and differences are interesting, and perhaps warrant a more comprehensive research project. In any case, it appears that some cultures are less concerned with the 'ordering' of young bodies, and with children 'using words rather than bodies'. In this context Field (1999) has commented that French people touch more than Americans; Douglas (1978) noted that Japanese parents stroke their children, whereas American parents tend to touch their children with jerky movements. The cultural differences *are* remarkable and long standing; in 1966 Jourard observed combinations of couples in coffee bars in cities across the world and noted the number of touches that took place between two people in a given time; in London no touching, in Florida two touches, in Paris 110, and Puerto Rico more than 180.

We could speculate that in situations where young bodies tumble around, bump into each other and the professionals who look after them, there may perhaps be a more hazy definition of self and other, in which identity is not always confined to the skin and its contents. 'The desire for the heightened sense of self is the central meaning of getting pleasure with the other. Here the desire to lose the self in the other and really be known for oneself can coalesce' (Benjamin 1986: 92–3). But when 'pleasure occupies a smaller and smaller public space and a more guilty private space, individuals do not become empowered; they are merely cut off from the source of their own strength and energy' (Vance 1984 in Johnson 2000: 71). Just as there was no nudity before clothes, so too might we note a parallel inversion. There was no morality before pornography. As A.S. Neill puts it: 'pornography is simply sex plus guilt' (Neill in Vaughan 2006: 147).

Conclusion

Living our lives defensively, in response to the moral panic, as though rare events are likely to happen at any moment, makes little sense. Goldacre (2006) has agued this point statistically by taking the example of HIV tests. He points out that:

> the predicative value of a positive or negative test that an individual gets is changed in different situations, depending on the background rarity of the event that the test is trying to detect. The rarer the event in your population, the worse the very same test becomes.

Goldacre shows how if the risk of HIV in a particular area is 1.5 per cent then by testing 10,000 people one could predict 150 cases accurately out of 150 cases, which on the face of it seems quite good. However if the infection rate were one in 10,000 this would result in two positive results, one which *is* positive, and the other false positive. In other words the chances of a correct prediction on whether someone is really HIV positive are 50:50. Goldacre then speculates the likely accuracy for predicting events in human behaviour which as he states, is clearly much more problematic. 'Let's say 5% of patients seen by a community mental health team will be involved in a violent event in a year. Using the same maths . . . [the] predictive tool would be inaccurate

97 times out of a hundred'. He asks 'will you preventatively detain 97 people to prevent three events'? Given the statistics for the number of professionals who abuse those in their care nationally in any one year are not readily available, it is difficult even to make even this level of prediction. It would seem safe to assume that the figure is nowhere near 5 per cent, or else there would be a (inter)national outcry, yet, most professionals are behaving defensively assuming they and/or those they know are likely abusers. The odds against this likelihood would suggest a radical rethinking of the (non)sense dictating current practice.

Observing how the media joins in and plays both ends of the moral panic off against each other in the desire and need for sensation is also worthy of note here. The dreadful dangers are pointed out, and preferably illustrated with some real but rare incident that can be represented as an imminent threat (quote from unvetted journalist, 'I could have been anyone'). Then the excessive response is condemned as a bloody nonsense (nursery workers not putting on sun cream as 'PC gone mad!' for example). The media when reporting 'stranger' abuse also manages to adopt this same condemnatory tone whilst simultaneously elaborating a pornographic account. It promotes a titillation of the self-same story which serves as a pornographic refuelling that both cancels out and yet makes possible the moral condemnatory tone. Each feeds off the other and both 'sell'. This is not balance, or sensible professionalism, but arguably the need for a declining industry to sell newspapers through 'sex and sensationalism'. It could also be argued that the defensive behaviour of professionals along with this pornographic refuelling by the media (and of course ourselves in conducting this research) help to reproduce the very situation we would all claim to decry. It is our proposition, therefore, that the defensive claims and practices evident in the majority of our case studies help towards the production of this synergy, i.e. what they most feared – the fear of accusation of some form of abuse. More worryingly, if we accept that 'denial of desire is the very production of it' (King 1997: 240), it is also possible that these same defensive practices are contributing towards the creation of a nation of abusers (see subsequent chapters).

Chapter 2

Relationships

Ethics committees and research

Catherine Scott

This chapter focuses on the growth of the ethics phenomenon in the context of a culture of increasing distrust and suspicion. Throughout it is argued that the characteristics of the relationship between the 'abused' child and the abuser now shape contemporary cultural models of relationships between all persons, especially where some power differential exists. These cultural models endow ethics committees with a potent brief to protect research participants from the potential harm believed to lurk in their dealings with the 'powerful' and 'unscrupulous', who may violate their rights. Researchers who wish to explore sensitive issues such as the problematics of touch are increasingly regarded with a similar level of suspicion to the professionals who work with children and young people on a daily basis, and are frequently required to have their proposals vetted by their university and/or other external ethics committees. The last few decades have seen a considerable growth in the power and influence of these committees, especially within an academic context. The rationale for their establishment and continuing development is the prevention of harm. However, this intent to protect has arguably become a licence to harm via its ability to prevent research, silence debate, and stymie the acquisition of knowledge about difficult issues, such as those discussed throughout. This argument is illustrated by reference to practical examples, including recent experiences with ethics committees in an Australian context, and is offered as a warning to others in societies who are following a similar trajectory. Arguably this regulatory practice both reflects and simultaneously feeds the fears and mistrust including those manifest in the touch moral panic.[1]

The age of the victim

The growth in the number of ethics committees, their power and influence, and the fears surrounding touching have not occurred in isolation but need to be considered alongside trends evident in wider society. The contemporary era has been labelled by some as the 'Age of the Victim' because increasing numbers of people put themselves forward as victims with a claim to recognition, acknowledgement, recompense, and care. Browsing any newspaper or magazine or tuning in to television or radio programmes reveals any number of persons or groups who are described as 'victims' – of other people, natural forces, disasters, diseases or accidents – or as 'survivors' of the same. This phenomenon is something to be considered and better understood, rather than taken on face value (Furedi 2002a, 2002b; Steadman Rice 1998). One particular victim, the abused child, has become a potent icon for the times. The image of the abused child, now almost universally understood to be the sexually abused child, is such a ubiquitous icon in Anglophone culture that it seems that few recent novels, plays or film scripts lack an act of abuse (Baxter 1997). These fictional acts serve as explanatory devices in the narratives in which they occur: characters act as they do because they were 'abused'. If fiction holds a mirror to the society from which it emerges, this epidemic in fiction tells us something important about how people now understand and explain themselves and their acts, both to self and to others.

Estimates of the actual occurrence of child abuse vary considerably, but are often proposed to be shockingly high – one in four, for instance. If this figure is correct, then the worrying corollary is that there are a very large number of adults who prey on children, but when pushed on this issue, few professionals or lay people agree with this supposition. Yet an industry exists to detect and prevent abuse by this apparent army of paedophiles, and consequently in many Anglophone countries anyone who works with children is required to obtain a police clearance – as if all paedophiles come with a criminal record handily attached (see Chapter 3). Various measures are additionally proposed to track and identify sex offenders, so that the communities in which they live know that they have a monster among them. Children are also 'taught' at school and elsewhere to defend themselves against abuse via various programmes with messages such as 'if it doesn't feel right, say no' (Scott 2006).

There appear to be no comparable similar proposals to track murderers or to notify communities that perpetrators of other sorts of crimes have taken residence in their midst. Child sexual abuse has become the worst of all crimes (see *Observer* 7/1/2007). Why this may be the case is worthy of consideration as understanding the meaning of icons is a powerful way to comprehend the psychology of a culture or era. Indeed, the obsession with potential sexual harm to children should be taken as something akin to a cultural psychiatric symptom, rather than a reflection of reality; a 'moral panic', in other words (Cohen 1972; Fitzgerald 2005; van den Hoonaard 2001). Nonetheless, the belief in the existence of numerous sexual predators has shaped legislation (e.g. Safeguarding Vulnerable Groups Act in the UK 2006) and social attitudes to all adults, even attitudes of adults to their own motivation and probity.

It is worth considering the nature and characteristics of the icon. The sexually abused child is, above all else, the ultimate innocent victim. Currently, children are understood to be without sexual desire and by law cannot be taken to consent to sexual activities. Any improper contact between an adult and a child must be an act of exploitation. The children in these cultural stories are always very young: little more than infants. Recent events in Australia evidence these presuppositions about the nature of the abused child. A former Governor General lost his position, not because he was suspected of child abuse, but because of accusations that, as a senior member of the Anglican Church, he covered up or failed to act on child abuse perpetrated by a junior cleric. While this controversy was raging I interviewed people informally as to what acts they thought the junior cleric to have been guilty of. They mostly replied that he must have 'done terrible things to tiny children'. The 'victim' of 'abuse' in this case was actually a young woman who, being just below the age of 16, cannot legally be said to have consented to the affair, but who as an adult, has indicated that what she desired – and desires – was for the cleric to leave his wife and family and to marry her. There is no doubt that the cleric's behaviour was unwise in the extreme, but his offence did not match the image conjured by reports of the events and which had led to the subsequent disgrace of the Governor General.

Fables of child abuse are thus tales of exploitation of the innocent and powerless, of blameless individuals forced to engage in activities against their will and best interests. They are ultimately about relationships between people, and in these uncertain times the abused child and her abuser have become models of how persons are now considered to relate to each other. Everyone, it seems, is either an abuser or a victim of the same. The cultural history of the 'abused child' appears to provide a useful template for understanding why abuse and exploitation have become the feared but accepted cultural models of relations between people.

Sexualising childhood

The identification of archetypal 'abuse' as 'sexual abuse' requires some further investigation. Sexual liberation was touted as a necessary freeing of people from the chains of tradition, inflicted on their minds and persons by the Church and other discredited institutions. All were to become self-actualising individuals, unafflicted by old-fashioned hang-ups. Indeed, in the last few decades, Anglophone public culture has become hypersexualised and clothing styles, images, language and story lines that only a few years ago would have been considered grossly indecent are now commonplace. There is a possibility that the perceived identity of the abused child as a victim of sexual predation may have its origins in the unsettling 'in your face' sexual openness of public culture. Many may feel 'victimised' by the inescapable sexualisation of public life.

The paradox of the obsession with children as actual or potential victims of sexual predation is that they have become sexualised in a way they previously were not. Endless public iterations of anxiety over the sexual harm supposedly inflicted on large numbers of minors and the florid reporting of 'international rings' trading in child sexual pornography have turned children into objects of forbidden sexual desire. The repeated pairing of the image of the child with the image of the sexual victim has made many people anxious about their own feelings and impulses, how others will perceive their actions, and even whether their own children or those in their care will 'turn them in' for fictional offences. This anxiety is reminiscent of the injunction 'Don't think about the bear!' in that, once embraced, it is hard to think of anything else. Repeated stories about children as objects of lust create mental associations and set in train a whole range of fears and unease that would not have existed otherwise. This generalised distrust of motives towards children has meant that even the utterly blameless accept that they should submit to police investigation before they can be allowed near young people.

The ubiquitous cacophony over child abuse and child pornography has made conducting research with young people especially difficult. 'Violation' of children's privacy has become an extreme concern. It seems that every contact with a child is a potential occasion for abuse, and that every image now has a potential pornographic use or overtone. Whereas parents could photograph their children and their team-mates at sports or similar events, and schools could freely use images of their pupils to publicise their activities, special permission to do so is now often required. It is ever more difficult for researchers to conduct research that requires them to photograph or film children, and in some ethics proposal forms photographing or filming children are listed under 'high risk activities'. My own research on classroom communication is seriously compromised by these injunctions, which has no explanation other than that every image of a child is now considered a form of pornography likely to fall into the hands of sexual predators, even a fuzzy and anonymous photograph of a classroom full of bored kids. Alternatively it could be based on some sort of superstitious belief that a photograph is a form of identity theft and its viewing by the 'unauthorised' a form of violation.

Cultural change

Concern about 'widespread' sexual exploitation of children appears to have its origins in the 1970s. By the early 1980s, detecting the signs and symptoms of abuse among school children was becoming a key issue for both teachers and school counsellors. At the same time, articles about child abuse began to appear in the popular press, and members of the public and of the professions were urged to increase their efforts to detect and report abuse. Legislation was passed which defined teachers and school counsellors as mandatory notifiers of suspected child abuse. Mandated reporting of suspected abuse is also common in other Anglophone cultures and the requirement to report suspected abuse extends to other professionals who could be exposed to situations where real or potential abuse might be uncovered: for example, there is now considerable concern about 'elder abuse' and there is a proposal that police checks be introduced for anyone who works with older people (see subsequent chapter).

Exploring other social and cultural changes occurring around the same time provides a powerful explanatory device for the discovery of the supposed army of victims of sexual predation. The era saw a concerted and deliberate attack on traditional morality, codes of conduct, and social structures of all sorts, in the name of 'liberation', or more correctly, individuation. Hierarchical ways of relating were challenged – husbands were not to have authority over wives or the old over the young. Restraints and restrictions of many kinds were cast aside as pathology-inducing anomalies left over from less enlightened eras. I have written elsewhere (Scott 2003) about how this dismantling of traditional value systems has led not just to greater personal freedom but also to greater insecurity and mistrust of other people, both as private individuals and as professionals. Put another way, freedom has become the ultimate virtue, but freedom is a complex construct, and its operations in the real world are more messy and uncertain than on paper. In reality people come with differing levels of personal and social resources and a 'level playing field' leads just as easily to exploitation of the weak by the strong, as it does to the 'Age of Aquarius'. Freedom, then, has its discontents (Bauman 1995, 1997), and these are manifested in relations among people.

Historically, hierarchical systems managed uncertainty and risk via placing responsibility in the hands of those with more power and access to resources. Persons in positions of authority protected those further down the 'natural' order. Monarchs cared for their subjects, husbands for wives, parents for children, teachers for pupils, priests for parishioners, and so it went on. This is not to say, however, that in 'the old days' duties were never neglected or power abused, but expectations existed that most would do their duty, wrongs be avoided, or punished where they occurred, and that the responsibility for managing the intractable uncertainty of human life would be communally shared. More recently however, those who in a previous era held positions of power, responsibility and authority – parents, teachers, doctors, priests, day care workers, nurses, scout leaders, etc. – have been 'unmasked' as unworthy of the trust placed in them via the 'revelation' that many have been found guilty of child abuse. Anyone, it would seem, who has any power is potentially an abuser of innocents. 'Trust no one' is the potent between-the-lines message of the age. Moral codes exist in order to decide 'who's to blame' (Douglas 1994, 1996). The dismantling of the old value systems, and the related discovery that anyone in a position of authority was 'to blame' (which in a real sense they were – as authority equals responsibility) has left a moral vacuum at the heart of our culture. Without a ready system for apportioning responsibility and blame we are now all under suspicion, and in addition, suspicious of everyone else. The cultural obsession with child abuse can be seen, to use the psychiatric terminology, as a massive example of 'displacement', the discharge of energy and anxiety onto an object or activity that substitutes for the true source of pain or distress.

Certain aspects of human cognition lead to the adoption of an apparently universal model of the moral cosmos, one characterised by the conflict between ultimate good and pure evil (Baumeister 2001). Baumeister discusses what he calls the 'myth of pure evil', in which evil persons are characterised by various attributes. They: inflict deliberate harm; inflict harm for its own sake; harm good and entirely innocent victims; belong to an out-group – the enemies or the outsiders; have always been evil; represent the antithesis of peace, order and stability; are egotistical; and have difficulty maintaining control over their feelings. Examining these categories, it is easy to see how they map onto religious models of the cosmos, with their saints and demons, and how the righteous are beset by the forces of evil. It is also possible to see how the cultural icon of the abused child and the selfish, lustful, irredeemable abuser also fit this model. It is but a short step to propose that the abused and the abuser have taken over the role formerly played by saints and demons as cultural definitions of pure innocence and pure evil. It is no wonder, then, that this template is applied to the interaction between many groups and individuals, such that each now plays the role of either the victim or the abuser. Just as historically there was little incentive to identify as one of Satan's minions, now the pressure is to side with the victims by being a victim (and thus one of the virtuous), or join the righteous who crusade against abuse, rather than risk being lumped with those who perpetrate it.

Research ethics committees: intent to protect or licence to harm?[2]

In our contemporary 'privatised' individualist culture the structures have been levelled and it's every man and woman for him or herself. Of course these changes have been dressed up in the more palatable language of 'choice'. 'Choice' is understood to be good, and who, after all, lobbies for more restrictions on his or her own activities.[3] The notion of 'informed consent' owes much to, among other things, the sovereignty of personal choice. No one must be forced or coerced into consenting to any process or activity that he or she does not fully understand, in order, it is believed, to avoid the possibility of exploitation and victimisation. Of course the essence of the abused child, unable to consent, is that he or she has been forced to engage in harmful activities with a more powerful and predatory adult.

Consent is a major issue addressed by ethics committees. Much time and effort are expended to make sure that participants are freely consenting to involvement in research, that they comprehend exactly what that involvement requires of them, that they know their rights and understand that they

can withdraw their consent at any time. The lengths to which ethics committees go to ensure that these conditions hold have become nothing short of
extraordinary, and requirements to 'fix' the consent process are often the
means by which approval of research proposals is delayed or denied. It is
almost as if all research participants are identified with vulnerable children
who cannot truly consent to involvement with researchers. Certainly the
model participant depicted by ethics procedural requirements is an infan-
tilised individual who cannot know his or her best interests but must have
these protected for him/her by the ethics committee. The situation is most
extreme for those potential participants who are deemed especially 'at risk':
the disabled; children; indigenous peoples. Particularly in the latter case the
obsession with making consent truly informed has led to the norm that
consent forms must be several pages in length. It seems possible that such a
blizzard of words is likely to obscure more that it reveals, especially for those
whose literacy may be poor.

There is an element of bad faith in these endeavours. With the introduction
of the concept of consent comes a subtle – or not so subtle – shift in responsibility. If one has consented to something then any ill-effects become one's
own fault: it's not rape if you said 'yes'. This attempt to shift or pin the blame
has further eroded trust. Conversations with those involved with the ethics
process at Australian universities have revealed the extent of the effort to
extract iron-clad 'consent' from research participants and how they have been
affected by the way that participants are currently regarded. Participants are
considered as potential litigants who may sue the university for harm eventu-
ating from involvement in any research process. The 'innocent' are thus
revealed to be as self-serving as the rest of us and this ambiguous image of
research participants as simultaneously vulnerable and risky (as evidenced
specifically in relation to the touch panic) undoubtedly further complicates
the response of ethics committees to the tasks they face.

Tussles for power among different influential groups – governments,
political parties, industry, unions, the professions – have also emerged into
this shifting cultural landscape with its obsession with harm to innocents,
and such developments further complicate the picture. There has been a
tendency to centralise power (Charlton 2002). Scholars, researchers and
teachers have not escaped these attempts to wrest power away from 'rival'
groups and to place it in the hands of those at the centre (Scott 2003). It is a
venerable political ploy to use preventing harm as an excuse to extend
control (Mueller 2006). Ethics committees were instituted to 'prevent harm'
to the human participants in medical and behavioural research. While there
is sometimes considerable potential harm to participants in medical
research, there is much less evidence that participants in social scientific
research face similar perils (Mueller 2006; O'Brien 2006). Nonetheless a few
bad examples have provided the necessary evidence so that Australian, UK,
North American and other communities have responded and their ethical

committees have become increasingly powerful, intrusive, demanding and insatiable, such that research is now restricted and stymied in ways scarcely credible a few decades ago (Scott 2003).

University managers and administrators have found ethics committees to be a useful way to control faculty, who traditionally enjoy considerable autonomy in their work (Mueller 2006; O'Brien 2006). Similarly, conservative political forces seeking to bring to heel the professions, including academics and researchers, have found a powerful implement in the 'oversight' provided by auditing tools, including ethics committees (Charlton 2002; Power 1994, 1997; Scott 2003). What better excuse for increasing surveillance and control than the desire to protect innocents from 'abuse' of power by 'mad scientists' and unscrupulous, self-serving researchers. Ethics committees thus function against this backdrop of anxiety over the supposed dark army of predators preying on the innocent. In North America training films have been produced to assist members of ethics committees to perform their duties. In a cultural context of intense distrust of those in authority, and a powerful model of human interaction as characterised by 'abuse', these films commence with a montage of images, some of which feature the Nazi doctors who performed unspeakably cruel research on prisoners – as fine an example of pure evil as can be located in the modern era. From the start, then, ethics committee members are invited to see themselves as crusaders against exploitation and abuse, and the researchers, whose work they assess, as being on the 'other side'.[4]

Not researching 'touch'

It is against this background of reading and relevant experience that led me to make contact with others with similar interests from around the world, and following correspondence was offered the opportunity to become involved in the research that forms the basis of this book. It was hoped that I might be able to provide comparative data from an Australian context. In previous research projects I and other colleagues have encountered considerable difficulty gaining approval from university ethics committees to do even very innocuous research with children in schools. Even when it has proved possible to satisfy the committee, further obstacles can still arise. In Australia it is no longer satisfactory for parents to consent to their children's involvement in research: now the children themselves must consent and indeed sign consent forms – even five-year-olds – thus entering into contracts that are strictly illegal. Yet children may not be permitted to engage in research about educational issues when they have perspectives that differ in important ways from their parents and/or teachers. Thus, 'protecting' children can mean removing their voices from such debates.

As described earlier, the ESRC funded research consisted of different phases: to begin with a short questionnaire was to be sent to schools and early years settings asking if policies were in place about physical contact between staff and children, and to whom we could speak about the policies, and for a copy of any that existed. In addition the questionnaire invited respondents to indicate whether they would like to be involved in the subsequent research activity, as a sub-sample of schools and settings were to be visited in order to interview staff, children and parents about touching practices, and about current policies and their perceived effects on relationships within the school setting. In order for me to conduct this research it was necessary to jump two hurdles: the ethics committee at my host institution and the ethics apparatus at the state Department of Education. Given the anxiety-provoking subject I now wished to investigate, I approached the task of gaining 'ethics approval' with considerable trepidation.

The whole thrust of the research made the university ethics committee members very uneasy. The proposal unleashed a storm of criticism over minor matters like the positions of page breaks, and trivial aspects of the wording on consent forms. There was also the 'issue' of what to do about those children whom we would encounter in schools who had 'been abused'. Making the requested changes did not satisfy the committee as more and more amendments were sought. With the prospect of a never-ending series of nit-picking demands stretching before me, delaying the start of the project, I decided to ask for permission to distribute the questionnaires and to later seek permission to do the following face-to-face work. I was given consent to send out the questionnaires.

Subsequently I approached the state Department of Education and met with a similar series of problems, including instructions to reverse changes that I had already made so as to satisfy the university ethics committee. However, some demands were considerably more stringent than those previously encountered. As an example, the working title I had given the project was deemed unacceptable: I could not call it *The Touch Project*. This was apparently 'too suggestive', a claim that is diagnostic in itself, revealing as it does the extreme sexualisation of everything. However, the demand most difficult to satisfy was that I was to interview not only teachers, students and parents, but that I must include a large number of education bureaucrats and policy makers. I pointed out that I was not receiving any funding to do the research and that this would greatly increase the cost quite apart from the purpose of the research being to discover the views of those more directly affected. I succeeded in keeping the project name, but could not persuade the Departmental ethics committee to budge from their position of demanding that I interview administrators and legislators. I can only speculate why the Department wished me to extend the research beyond its intended scope, as this was never explained adequately.

In the meantime, quibbles over page breaks and wording continued. It was now many months since I had attempted to start the project and so, exhausted and demoralised, I gave up. From these and similar experiences it would appear that researchers are assumed to be at best ignorant and at worst selfish, manipulative and unscrupulous. The first view leads to offers to 'help' the researcher understand her faults and failings, the latter closes down communication completely, which is more or less what happened in this instance.

Conclusion and suggestions for future action

The contemporary era is an anxious one and concern about the safety of children is rampant, distorting relationships and fashioning a model of human interaction in which everyone is a victim or an abuser. Attempts to curtail the possibility of exploitation of the weak by the strong have caught university scholars in their nets. Ethics committees police research to prevent harm, which can also prevent research. This process not only hinders research, but also increases the general climate of fear and suspicion. Yet evidence suggests much of the current anxiety is overblown and unnecessary, leading to more harm than it prevents. However, attempting to question and research the prevailing climate of fear, including asking the vital question of how children are affected by living in a society where any contact with them is regarded as potentially abusive, is considered difficult and professionally dangerous. Silencing those most affected by the moral panic over child abuse prevents us from better understanding the state in which we now find ourselves and makes more remote the possibility of injecting a little sense into the debate.

A problem as large and pervasive as the one discussed here seems to defy easy solutions. However, one useful recommendation is that the benefit of programmes designed to reduce harm, including that to research participants, be checked against the facts. Evaluation of the outcomes, intended and unintended, of regimes of research reviewed by ethics committees is a necessity. This should include the consequences for researchers of being subject to the review process. How many are unable to begin their projects? Which sorts of projects are most likely to be refused? What potential knowledge is being lost? How many give up on research as career? Also of interest is how potential research participants experience the informed consent process. Does it make them more or less likely to become involved? Does it tell them what they need to know; or is it, rather, 'too much information'? Such evaluation would hopefully provide information that could inform policy decisions and help pull us, as a culture, back from the brink of total distrust of all against all. A sharing of views on the points raised would be of interest and value, as would any observations about the different models of relations between researchers and participants that occur in communities where ethics committees are absent or less powerful. A potential source of useful data could be the statistics on actual harm to participants from countries where ethics committees are not such a dominant part of academic life. If it could be demonstrated that the stringent requirements to which many Anglophone researchers are subject make no difference to outcomes for participants, there would be a powerful case for reviewing processes and policies. The main implication from this chapter perhaps, is the necessity to make explicit models of persons currently implicit in thinking about the relationship between researchers and research participants, teachers and pupils, and educators and their colleagues. These relationships affect professional practice, including touching, and the concerns of many expressed throughout this book are well founded.

Chapter 3

The Criminal Records Bureau

Policing access to children

It became apparent early in the research that there was considerable confusion over the relevant UK policy and legislation. For example, many claimed that their no touching practices were 'because of the Children Act' when attempting to justify their risk behaviour (see also Lindon 2004, and Chapter 4). Yet an examination of such legislation clearly showed that it was the welfare of the child that must be of paramount concern. Nowhere could we locate any formal limitation placed on physical contact between children and non-family carers. In spite of this, once the legislation and the assumed principles on which it is based are translated into standards and guidelines, problems arise which are further exacerbated by interpretation during inspection processes. Ofsted inspectors, quality assurance officers and child protection inspectors all interpret policy in a variety of ways, and tend to impress upon those responsible for managing child-oriented settings of their responsibility and the need for internal policies and procedures (see Chapter 4). In each of these 'translations' the precautionary ethic ensures that the 'risk' is added to by being 'at risk of being at risk'. 'Playing safe' strategies lead to an accretion of precautions, resulting in the 'ratchet effect' that we note elsewhere. In England, where all our case studies were situated, the key justification for the wariness about touch appears to have come from the Child Protection section of the National Care Standards. This states: 'it is important that staff avoid putting themselves in a situation that may lead to allegations being made against them'. This 'Standard' is clearly and arguably culpably oriented to the protection of the staff rather than the child. It also illustrates well the 'at risk of being at risk' logic. But even if it 'merely' reflects the current mainstream view and dominant approach and practice, it has clearly impacted on adult/child behaviours in professional and child care settings in a range of ways that our research found to be more negative than positive.

Criminal Records Bureau checks

Even though we found no specific legislation which banned touching, nevertheless there is legislation which arguably now feeds the general panic around child abuse, and which contributes towards inhibiting certain behaviours, including touching. Much of the discussion in this chapter relates to recent and contemporary developments and consequently events which have occurred since the completion of our case study research, but which impact on related practice. An example is the recently implemented Safeguarding Vulnerable Groups Act (2006), which followed in the wake of the murder of Holly Wells and Jessica Chapman in the UK in August 2002. Their murder by a school caretaker led to a rapid rise in the number of 'adults' (some of whom are only 17 years old) who require vetting for offences against children, via the Criminal Records Bureau (CRB) procedure.[1] The Bureau, established in 2002, was intended to coordinate the checking of teachers and other professionals. Previously, in spite of long-term concerns in relation to child protection, a number of 'lists' existed: List 99 (for those barred from working in schools); the Sex Offenders' Register; and the Protection of Children Act list. Information was generally held on the Police National Computer and/or on local police files. A CRB check comprises a search through these relevant lists and records. One of the aims of the Safeguarding Vulnerable Groups Act (2006) is to enable the formation of a centralised list from the many separate lists and the means by which each individual working with children can be entered into an online register which is continually updated and available to prospective employers, including parents of young children seeking nannies.

The UK government's poor record in keeping centralised and computerised systems of information on our behalf, most recently evidenced by the Home Office, and Her Majesty's Revenue and Customs' loss of the child benefit database in transit, suggests that confidence in such systems would be foolhardy, but we would not wish to be understood as advocating abandoning all vetting. Clearly one list is better than many, but for it to balance equity and efficiency it should be limited and proportionate. So while this coordination of lists might appear to make sense, it is worth noting that since 2002 the number of people vetted each year has risen from one-and-a-half to 10 million adults, in other words a quarter of the adult population in the UK now needs to go through this costly (£76.2 million in 2005/6, a fraction of the costs anticipated for 2007/8) and time-consuming procedure.

Once it was essentially professionals with a statutory responsibility (e.g. social workers and teachers) who were subject to this level of vetting, with the start of each new job. However, 'Father Christmas', nannies, music teachers, hospital workers, bell ringers, volunteers, sports coaches, internet chat-site moderators, friends of foster carers, in fact anyone who might be expected to have any kind of contact with a child, must now be checked, and the list of categories is continuously increasing. A satisfactory check applicable to one job is not transferable, and there are many who claim to have been checked numerous times in a very short period of time:

I have been CRB checked six times since I began working with kids in around 2002, because I've moved around, doing summer play schemes for kids in different places and doing different jobs, while training to become a speech therapist.

(Manifesto Club 2006a)

While a number of children's charities claim such 'anomalies' will shortly be sorted out, checking is an expensive business (either £31 or £44 per time – depending on the level of check, and which of the 3000 'umbrella bodies' is providing the service). Those organisations tasked with carrying out the procedure have experienced a rapid increase in income as the vetting industry has taken off.

Beyond the initial vetting procedure at the time of entering employment, many organisations choose to repeat checks with existing staff every few years even though this is not strictly required. Organisations are encouraged not to trust each others' checks. For example, a school will check its supply teachers even though this will already have been done by the agencies who recruit them (Ofsted 2006). Many have been checking workers who do not strictly require checking 'just in case'; in part because organisations fear the £5,000 fine each time they do not comply with the regulations. For example, a number of hospitals have checked laundry maintenance staff and administrative staff, even though they rarely, if ever, meet patients. Representatives for the NHS have pointed out that such actions contradict the Rehabilitation of Offenders Act (*Personnel Today* 23/01/06), but there is an eagerness in many employers and managers to comply with the law, as they understand it, so as to ensure they are 'covering their back'. In this vein foster agencies appear to have been breaking the law by vetting visitors to foster carers' households (i.e. non-family members and those without any relationship with the agency) which further illustrates the confusion and defensive practice evident in this area. It would appear that many individuals and agencies are more than willing to volunteer themselves and their staff for regular checking in order to 'prove' they are fit to be near children, and of the seriousness of their commitment towards child protection.

This expansion in vetting is feeding and encouraging a mistrust of all adults, as every person is considered first and foremost a potential child abuser (see Chapter 2). To be an unchecked adult near a child is now considered irresponsible, and in some instances seemingly akin to child abuse. Many search for omissions and loopholes so as to identify 'forgotten' groups who may be slipping through the net. For example, the NSPCC (National Society for Cruelty to Children) has brought attention to the 30,000 under-16-year-olds who are still school children yet who attend some courses in further education colleges, suggesting that this necessitates the vetting of adult students, including 17- or 18-year-olds who study in the same classes. This would seem to suggest that other 17- and 18-year-old students (at least in the UK context) should similarly be checked, as they share a school and its facilities with younger children. In addition it was noted in a Commons debate that 22,000 foreign exchange students visit Britain each year, and therefore host families should also be vetted (Sanders 2006). Those who educate their children at home are shortly to be subject to the same procedures as nurseries and schools, including Ofsted inspections. Given these current trends it might be expected that shortly a debate will ensue about whether all parents and prospective parents should be checked. Those eager to find loopholes in vetting practice so as to achieve even more 'robust' child protection might suggest that, as the majority of abuse takes place within the family, couples should be subjected to the same checks to see whether they will make 'suitable' parents and appropriate carers for other children who could be expected to come round to play. The proportion of adults subject to CRB checking is likely to increase even more dramatically unless a sense of proportion is applied to the current situation.

There are many concerns in relation to excessive vetting that deserve to be explored, including the way it undermines civil liberties. A number of adults have been unsuccessful in job applications because checks also revealed spent convictions for offences which had nothing to do with children – such as pub fights. Another direct result is a reported decline in the number of volunteers in organisations such as the Girl Guides, Scouts, and also in football coaching and other amateur sports. Given reports like the following, this is unsurprising:

> I had some volunteers helping me out at a sports camp – young guys in their early 20s, wanting experience so they could take their coaching qualification. Shortly after we began, a council representative arrived and asked for a quick word. This 'quick word' actually involved quizzing me on my team's credentials: 'Who's that over there? What qualifications do they have? Are their police checks available for parents to see?'

> (Travis 2006)

Such an approach is hardly encouraging to young people who are willing to give time to help even younger people enjoy the same experiences they enjoyed, and provide them with opportunities to participate in sports, another government agenda. Similarly, some parents are being dissuaded from helping out in schools. Spontaneity is inhibited so that, for example, arranging a trip at the last minute is impossible, as all involved adults would need to be vetted first. One particularly bizarre example was that of a head teacher who could not enter his school because the result of his check had not come through:

> Newly-appointed Chris Fenton took up his post 11 days ago but can only enter his classrooms when they are empty because he has not been cleared

by a criminal background check . . . Mr Fenton is turning up before the youngsters arrive in the morning, leaving the premises during the day and returning in the evening when they have gone home, to carry out administrative work.

(*Daily Express* 17/09/05)

Such defensive behaviour is hardly likely to inspire confidence in those young people who are pupils at the school. We are concerned here particularly with the way aspects of the moral panic around child abuse, via this process, creates an administrative and organisational culture which encourages children to mistrust all adults. Being near children is now something which requires state clearance at a much higher level than is required for many other arguably more sensitive and dangerous activities, for instance selling explosives (Disclosure Scotland 2005). As we argue later, this widespread mistrust of adults undercuts the interpretive procedures that people use to 'read off' morals and intentions from behaviour, and disables the sociocultural resources which children and young people (and adults) would otherwise mobilise to assist them in dealing with others on a case-by-case basis. Any judgement they could have been expected to develop will be impaired, and we suggest the over-regulation illustrated by routine mass vetting will have unintended and unwanted consequences.

Consequences for Christmas

Christmas provides a telling example of the way that excessive vetting and a lack of trust have had noticeable negative consequences for many children. Risking accusations of nostalgia, Christmas was once a time when adults and children would interact and contribute without fear and suspicion, but the vetting procedures have impacted on children's lives in ways that may come to be considered regrettable. Traditionally, Christmas included organisations, companies and clubs hosting Christmas parties, with a male member dressing up as Santa; adults attending children's nativity plays; and all ages from young to old singing together in choirs, or ringing the Christmas bells. Now however, everybody from volunteer Santas, to bell ringers, to those helping out at Christmas parties, must be CRB checked, even if they are only 17 years of age. These 'child protection' procedures have a negative and even preventative effect on everything from enclosed grottos, to sitting on Santa's knee. It is now more typical in department stores for a roaming Santa to hand out presents under the less atmospheric strip lighting, so as to keep all activity visible and free from possible suspicion.

The expectation for Santas to be CRB checked includes those volunteering at small-scale community events, such as schools, local charities and village halls. The then Shadow Minister for Children (Tim Loughton MP) volunteered

to be one of Santa's 'elves' at the grotto of an animal welfare charity of which
he is president, but this was forbidden because he did not have a CRB check
processed at the time (Sanders 2006). While it is perhaps reassuring that the
vetting culture does not bend to status or privilege, nevertheless this
approach to the involvement of a public figure who is known to the organisation, and who was very unlikely to ever be out of sight of others, makes the
process and decision making within it appear nonsensical. Santas employed
by department stores, or who are supplied by a 'Santa's' agency', are also
routinely CRB checked:

> Hire the 'real' Santa for your Christmas party or event. No false beards
> here! We have a number of real 'look alike', experienced (and CRB
> checked) Father Christmas, with excellent costumes available for
> Grottos, parties, promotions and events. Prices from £230.00 per day.
>
> (Kidsco Projects 2006)

It is worth adding that a mother who advertised that she was selling Santa
letters on eBay, stated: 'The magic of Christmas is here. Let me send you a
letter to your child from Santa . . . I am CRB checked' (Brettingham 2006).
We question of course the compatability of magic with vetting.

Churches, charities and local councils are similarly developing defensive
practice. The Churches' Child Protection Advisory Service (CCPAS) advises
the ministry to 'use one of your organisation's "approved" children's workers
as Santa . . . If using someone else, then Father Christmas should always have
a suitably dressed assistant present, who *is* an approved worker' (CCPAS
2002). Rotary Club guidelines state: 'The standard CRB check is recommended for people acting as Santa on a regular basis . . . clubs should invite
those Rotaractors who have undergone CRB checks through their employment or profession, to act as Santa and his assistants' (RGBI 2006). Similarly
a policy adviser for the Department for Education and Skills stated:

> Anybody who isn't eligible for a disclosure must be supervised. If the
> grotto is in a school, you would expect there to be a teacher close by, close
> enough to see what is happening. If a father acting as Santa happened to
> have a CRB check, that would be great. Then he could be left on his own.
>
> (Brettingham 2006)

These last examples are actually subverting the formal process by missing the
point that at the time of writing CRB checks are not transferable between
organisations. The policy adviser appears to be developing 'standards' on the
hoof, which supports our earlier claim that it is not always the legislation as
such which is responsible for much current questionable practice, but the way
this is interpreted in action by a range of stakeholders, often anxious to cover

their backs. We also ponder the phrase 'isn't eligible for a disclosure' which seems to imply that some adults are ineligible – a roaming paedophile perhaps?

In addition to the vetting procedures there are also new guidelines covering Santa's behaviour with children. Some of these guidelines are 'home-made' (see Chapter 4) while others emerge following consultation with, or directive from, the local social services and/or the NSPCC (see below). Examples include guidelines which 'suggest' that Santa's grotto should not be dark or enclosed, and that Santa should never be alone with a child. The CCPAS (2002) warns: 'Ensure that Santa is in an area which is well-lit and public'. The Lions Club International (2004) advises: 'ensure that Lions Club members (specifically those dressed as Santa) are not left alone with children. Two Lions members need to be present at all times'. The child protection adviser from the Diocese of Guildford agrees: 'we would advise that Santa isn't alone with a child', adding: 'my recommendation is lots of elves, and set it up, so it is very open' (Janet Hynde, Chichester diocese, UK). A Welsh shopping centre addressed this issue by placing CCTV cameras in Santa's grotto and noted: 'We've left the Georgian windows clear of decoration so that parents can see clearly what is going on' (Wainwright 2004). What everyone is worried might 'go on' if such surveillance were not so tight is never articulated, but the silence serves to imply that men (and it is usually men who dress as Santa) are frequently dangerous in unspeakable sexual ways. The relatively few instances where strangers do abuse children have fuelled the moral panic to such an extent that all must now be presumed guilty. Yet we are not aware of any instances over the years where Santas have been accused of abusing children (and such cases would presumably have made the headlines), and we doubt that any reduction in any such cases could be indicated, in spite of these extreme and expensive measures.

Guidelines differ on the question of whether Santa should be allowed to kiss children or have them sitting on his knee. A spokesperson for Selfridges remarked: 'Santa doesn't have children sitting on his lap. The kid is sitting next to him, and there is shaking hands, but no other contact' (Manifesto Club 2006b). The idea that children 'shake hands' with Father Christmas while 'sitting next to him' seems a little formal for something that is intended to be 'fun'. The Rotary Club pushes the boundaries by stating: 'Santa or [his] assistants should not actively invite children to "kiss" Santa. If a child wishes to kiss Santa this should be on the cheek . . . It is preferable for children to shake hands, or "blow" a kiss' (RGBI 2006). The CCPAS also adopts an only 'if the child asks for it' approach: 'There is no reason why children should not kiss Santa on the cheek providing this is initiated by the child and not Santa' (CCPAS 2002). The director of the The Ministry of Fun (!), which runs Britain's only 'Santa School', grudgingly remarks: 'We don't encourage children to sit on Santa's knee. If a child offered, then Santa will go along with it' (Manifesto Club 2006b). On the other hand, The John

Lewis Partnership prefers to place all responsibility firmly with the parents of children in their stores: 'Santa is not allowed to pick children up and put them on his knee; if a parent lifts a child on to Santa's knee, that is okay' (ibid.). But the Roman Catholic Diocese of East Anglia (2004) is more cautious: 'Father Christmas must not ask/encourage children to sit on his knee' (ibid.). The Roman Catholic Church has had to deal with a number of child abuse scandals in recent years, so is no doubt particularly keen now to be seen to be doing the 'right thing'. More generally however, it is not merely the variation in the above guidelines that is significant, but the fact that they exist at all. Trying to regulate and micromanage the smallest detail of what was once a relaxed and informal traditional event says a great deal about a society.

Some comments made by those responsible for helping organise Christmas parties in this culture of vetting serve to put in context some of the ideas raised above, and also help to illustrate the extent and sterility of the current trend:

> All of our volunteers are referenced and police checked. Those who aren't CRB checked we have in different colour t-shirts. The CRB checked are in burgundy, those who aren't are in white t-shirts. This is so . . . those in charge can ensure that there are a mix of those who are referenced and those who aren't. Or if something happens, there is a referenced volunteer present. All volunteers get child protection training – on the morning of the party, we also give them a child protection pack. This advice includes 'not to go anywhere alone with a child', 'not to pick up a child', and 'not to initiate contact'. There are volunteers on guard on the toilet door; to ensure that there is never a situation where there is one adult alone with children . . . This is necessary to ensure that you don't have a one-on-one situation between a child and an adult volunteer. These measures are necessary these days unfortunately. Part of it is to safeguard the volunteers from allegations.
>
> (H. Lisowski, child protection representative – guidelines developed by liaising with the local social services department and the NSPCC)

This Christmas party, for children from the local community, was arranged by Bristol University (2/12/06). The example is interesting in a number of ways. Those volunteers who have been fully checked are visibly distinguishable from those who apparently cannot really be trusted. Training emphasises a series of what 'not to do' instructions (don't pick up a child, etc.) rather than what to do, such as make sure every child is happy, included in the fun, and so on. Volunteers are really guards who check on each other, making sure that nobody can sneak into the children's toilet with indecent intent. It is significant that such advice is given by the local social services and the NSPCC, which carry the weight of authority so their advice is unlikely to be challenged.

This is not an isolated example: at another party arranged by Henshaw's Society for Blind People, Manchester (2/12/06), non-CRB checked friends and family were prevented from helping out, as they had done in previous years:

> The parents are always with the children, and our volunteers are all CRB checked. Before, we had a lot of friends and people to help out at our Christmas party, but we have stopped that now, because we feel that we need to be protecting ourselves. We can't encourage adults to take children dancing or face painting at the party if they aren't CRB checked. Since this summer, we stopped having people supporting children through Henshaws if they are not CRB checked. Our volunteer coordinator here is now constantly sorting out CRBs for people. Sometimes the checks take so long to come through that volunteers are losing enthusiasm and moving on before they even begin. Santa is the husband of one of the members of staff, and is CRB checked. Before the children would queue up to see Santa, but now Father Christmas goes around tables and gives out presents. At least now they don't have to sit on his knee – we are aware of these issues.
>
> (W. Thompson, team leader, children and family services)

Here it is acknowledged that the organisation feels the 'need to be protecting ourselves'; it is clear that child protection is really adult protection. The coordinator spends most of their time sorting out CRB checks, which does not seem a good use of time and money for a charity depending on public donations. The relief at the end that 'at least now they don't have to sit on his knee' is particularly sad given these young children can not even see Santa and largely rely on touch for communication (see Chapter 9 for a development of these ideas). Similar concern was expressed by a representative of the Unison branch at Carlisle City Council who had been responsible for organising Christmas parties for the past seven years, and who was planning to hold its eighth for the children of Unison members during the Christmas of 2006 (10/12/06):

> When we first organised our Christmas party seven years ago, we had it in a community centre and did everything ourselves. Now we have it at the Sands Centre, and they take care of health and safety issues . . . All our volunteers are employees, and they are all CRB checked. Parents stay with children and look after them, at the party. Volunteers can't take children to the toilet . . . Last year we put up posters saying that photographs would be taken at the party, and if parents wanted they could opt out. This year we went further and asked parents to fill in a form when they apply, to say if they don't want their kids to be photographed . . . People know us, and we have seen these kids grow up. Parents sometimes

ask why we need these forms. This is just in case, we are being proactive, to make sure that we are covered for anything.

(Paula Norris, Carlisle City Council)

In this final example such is the level of concern that even the CRB checked volunteers are not allowed to take children to the toilet. The party has been relocated to a 'safe' centre where everyone is checked, parents can opt out of their children being photographed, which presumably means other parents can only take pictures of their own children with adults. But the organisation feels this level of precaution is necessary so they are 'covered for anything'. This example is particularly telling given this is an organisation where every-one knows everyone and has done for many years – and epitomises some of the most bizarre consequences of the current situation.

Death of Father Christmas?

Christmas is not the only area where such precautionary behaviour is apparent as evidenced throughout the rest of the book. However, vetting principles and procedures, and how they have impacted upon Christmas, help illustrate the lengths to which many organisations feel it necessary to go, so as to prove innocence. It could be argued that such organisations are unwittingly simul-taneously corrupting the 'innocence' of children who would once have been more inclined to trust other people's parents, Father Christmas, young volun-teers and adults (especially those they have known all of their lives) arranging parties on their behalf. Adults and children are now expected to place their faith in a CRB certificate above trusting their own judgement, which is arguably a perverse form of child protection. It could be argued that child protection agencies and others appear to be assessing the risk to children by adopting a 'no claims' approach. The assumption that child abusers will have already abused, and will already have been prosecuted for abuse, and which necessitates the vetting of swathes of the population, displaces attention from the majority of abuse which takes place in the family. It also seems likely that adults operating within such constraints are likely to be less sensitive to the unique situations of each and every child, and each and every situation. Defensive practice which limits the amount of touch experienced by blind children at a party suggests an inappropriate sense of priority. Adults mainly concerned with watching their own backs are likely to experience serious difficulty in looking out for the interests of children. As stated, children too will be less likely to develop their own judgement which is not seen to count for much anyway. The explanations above that 'these measures are necessary these days' and that organisations must be 'covered for anything' raise more questions than they answer. Since there is no sound evidence that volunteers at large children's parties are more likely to harbour clandestine abusive intentions now than they did, say, in the 1970s or 1980s, they can only be understood to refer to the need to protect adults from a culture of mistrust and anticipated accusation. This implicit or explicit suggestion is heard regularly from agencies with special and, arguably, vested interests, and who go on to claim that even if only one occurrence of abuse is prevented by mass vetting activity and associated guidelines (which could never be demonstrated), then it is all justified. We suggest that such an argument is simply missing the point.

Our point is that each social and cultural context comes with baggage that makes it more or less easily unpacked as a site of particular danger in matters of touch, innocence and corruption. Christmas as we know it, and Father Christmas in particular, is clearly characterised by many features that make it (him) easily incorporated into panics around child abuse and touch. In terms of the discourses of 'touch', a triadic relation has now developed whereby Santa is *profane*, as well as secular and religious. He is placed under suspicion, a kind of house-arrest, where a further set of polarities develop within the earlier polarities and contradictions: benign–malign; giving–taking; amusing–abusing; friendly–exploitative; known–unknown; and family–stranger. In the audit culture Santa has become a figure of contamination (Douglas 1984), who now requires checks against his past behaviour. He has 'previous' of course, in the Bacchanalian versions and aspects of solstice celebrations; in particular the German St Nicholas was known as an 'eater of children' (Curtis 1995: 22). Such a medieval European doppelganger version of Santa was common, and is now being revived by the audit culture (via CRB checking). Santa is now 'stranger danger' (even when known to nearly everyone in the room), sequestered in his den with our vulnerable children. Has he molested children in the past? CRB checks notwithstanding, will he molest children in the future? In anticipation of this ever-present threat, his actions must be made visible. He must not sit children on his knee; the windows must not be obscured in the grotto, which are now constructed in 'Plexiglas' (Thompson and Hickey 1989: 377). 'Elf' police must accompany him at his station. Parents should be very careful to ensure that no Santa is left alone with their child. There must be no kissing. If published, photographs of children with Santa are likely to be pixellated for fear of alerting other predatory 'Santas' out there in the nightmare of intimacy that is now the Christmas season.

Such fears do not come from nowhere in relation to the Christmas ritual over which Santa presides. In its carnivalesque moments there always were and still are aspects of sexual licence for adults – flirtation, parties, secretaries on bosses' knees, mistletoe, office flings, etc. Nor is Santa as lecher a cultural impossibility: *Playboy* has from its inception in 1953 worked this theme (Hall 1984), in the belief that 'behind every jolly elf is an energetic monster' (ibid.: 68). Christmas is a ritual of deliberate deception, where the old deceive the young, and where material reward is provisional on spiritual belief, or at least a necessary pretence of it. But such unruly behaviour was always a hidden adult scenario in a ritual where the adults *know*, and the children don't. Children inhabited a Christmas world of heightened sentimentality where care, concern, innocence and the efficacy of magic were unusually their lot. Santa as Father represented a generic celebration of the family as together, united, giving, tokenising love for each other, and idealising that togetherness. That is the heart of the myth, and it is perhaps significant that when Santa and Christmas go cross-cultural, it is the 'togetherness' of a relationship that remains a central focus, when the trappings of religion and specific cultural tradition are displaced. For example, the Christmas of Japan in the 1980s is a piece of 'Eurokitsch' that constitutes 'a major celebration of romantic love' (Morean and Skor 1993: 121). In that instance Christmas is not the *pretext* for young couples to book themselves into hotels for the night, it is the text itself.

What the audit culture has done is to write suspicion and fear into the heart of the Christmas ritual. Inverting the values that Santa epitomises, and what Lévi-Strauss (1952/93) referred to as our 'small desire' to avoid 'fear, envy and bitterness', the adults are invited to simultaneously celebrate Santa in principle (as generous, the bearer of gifts, friendly, loving) yet place him in practice under intense, systematic and suspicious surveillance. Santa becomes Satan, in an abrupt anagram. In such a scenario of profane inspection, Santa is abolished as an ideal, as a generic Father, as an 'interlude' or as a sponsor of any kind of moral economy. The same audit culture invests the other half of the Christmas ritual, not just through surveillance, CRB checks and suspicion of child-abusing priests, but more universally in undermining from within notions such as trust, responsibility and even a Christmas notion of 'peace'. 'Peace' in the audit culture becomes interminable weapons inspection – in the case of Santa, largely a farcical search for Weapons of Miss Destruction. 'Innocence' is another victim of omnipresent suspicion, and so too does hope give way to fear. You cannot be suspicious and fearful of an ideal without destroying it. Audit is thus the death of Santa as complex and contradictory ritual, capable of whatever kind of uneasy synthesis. It is interesting and significant that this discourse of Santa has a contemporary home in the pornography of *Playboy*. Santa, as dirty old man, is a common motif there, and the fears that this might really be so – that the world is essentially pornographic and children must be ceaselessly defended against its encroachments – fuel precautionary behaviours that themselves rest on an underlying pornographic view of the world, as we argue elsewhere in this book. They destroy Santa's moral economy, such as it is, leaving only the exchange of commodities, still wrapped as 'gifts' it is true, but bereft of trust for the red and white stranger, and his supposed virtues of generosity, universal friendship and concern for the happiness of children. Are crackers safe, or should their contents be subject to a risk assessment? And what if these anonymous gifts contain bombs? We parody, of course, but endless and endemic distrust becomes the burden of a proper responsibility.

Conclusion

Christmas has been analysed as an example of 'terminal materialism' (Belk 1985: 96, drawing on Csikszentmihalyi and Rochberg-Halton 1981), in so far as the ritual descends into mere commodity exchange and even 'self-gifting'. One half of the equation swallows the other in a final act of consumption. But here we have a different ending, one that we might want to call 'terminal auditerialism'. The regime of audit cannot tolerate the ideals of Santa and thus invades the ritual with its profane – and insane – suspicions. The problem is made worse by the fact that Santa asks nothing in return and that is a matter for the greatest suspicion. A stranger bearing gifts to the young is the central nightmare of audit and 'touch' discourses (don't accept sweets from strange men). Santa/Satan is then expelled in two directions – privatised within the home, or safely relegated to distant spectacle as part of a parade or tableau. Perhaps this announcement of his death is premature, and we kind of hope so, but it does seem to us that the audit culture has made him terminally ill, in a number of additional senses.

Finally, we suggest that fears surrounding Santa help illustrate a dynamic between policy and practice which we refer to throughout. This dynamic is different from previous regimes that connected policy to practice. Notions of 'loose coupling' would typically regard practice as a loosening of policy prescriptions, where there is slippage as a residue of tradition and inertia; in other words, in the past professionals and others have tended to take the least restrictive interpretations of policy and guidelines. For example, professionals working with drug users would turn a blind eye to some aspects of criminal behaviour (e.g. drug taking) if they thought they could help the user in the longer run. Yet in the logics of the precautionary regimes discussed throughout, the opposite effect is created. This and subsequent chapters demonstrate how each layer *tightens* proscription, through the succession of law, standards, guidelines, regulation, procedures and practice. The determination of practice is peeled away from individual conviction or convention by considerations of audited risk. Audit thus posits and makes omnipresent the potential of the sexual monster – the 'inappropriate toucher' or the 'inappropriate Santa' – and in so doing actualises both a new inhumanity of care and a new insanity for the self. We suggest this relates directly to the moral panic around child abuse more broadly, as discussed in earlier chapters. These issues are not merely relevant for professionals but to society as a whole, as evidenced here. We agree that a 'society that treats caring for children as requiring more protection than selling explosives is in serious trouble – and indeed, may find itself unable to bring on the next generation' (Manifesto Club 2006b).

Chapter 4

Guidelines and dangerous bodies

The half-closed door

In the previous chapter, we looked at some of the ways in which the audit culture has invested everyday social practices with its precautionary ethic. The intensity of this scrutiny is nowhere greater than in the professional arena, where professionals have a responsibility *in loco parentis*, and where the policing of 'touch' is at its height. We begin with the notion of 'dangerous bodies' and the ways in which parts and wholes are policed. 'Risks' range across legal, medical and sexual discourses although it is predominantly the nexus of legal and sexual discourses that prevails in the documentation we examined, and in the survey returns. This chapter is based on 402 such returns; mainly but not exclusively from preschools (167), primary schools (113), secondary schools (45), further education/higher education colleges, and other agencies (28). These returns referred to local institution-based rules as well as to LEA guidance and national guidance emanating from Ministries. They have been anonymised; the level of institution is identified where relevant.

The 'danger'

For some, the whole body of the child or young person is identified as a risk arena, and touch is proscribed almost entirely:

> We operate a 'no touch' policy. Simply DO NOT touch.

> If in doubt, put hands in pockets.

> A no-touch policy is taken as the ground rule. Beyond that staff are expected to use common sense.

> Not wiping them when they go to the toilet.

> (preschool)

> The only circumstance in which a teacher should have physical contact with a pupil is where the teacher feels that unless some physical restraint is placed on the pupil there will be a consequence of injury to someone.

While it is recognised that, where a pupil is in extreme distress, there may be a natural desire to provide physical reassurance, it is advisable to avoid contact and seek other means of comforting if possible.

(secondary school)

Most of these prohibitions are rather easier to enforce in secondary schools than in preschools, where the exigencies of toileting result in some rather complicated risk manoeuvres:

Our policy at toileting is that we cannot assist the children when using the toilet (wiping bottoms, etc.) . . . If a child soils themselves we contact parent/carer to come and change them, although when they have an accident (wet self) we are allowed to put a change of clothes on the child.

The same active/passive reference to 'wetting' (as accident) as opposed to 'soiling' (as implicit agency) is present in the next example, where the soiling procedure is explained in still more detail, so that:

. . . if a child has *soiled* him/herself [original emphasis] then we will firstly contact the parents and the following procedure will be followed:
(a) Explain that their child needs to be changed (and if obviously ill, will need to go home)
(b) Ask if they would like to collect their child or come into school to change them. (In some circumstances if the child is considerably soiled then we may not be able to change them in school)
(c) If parents are unable to come into school then ask permission to change and wash the child
(d) If permission is given then ask if we can use a cleanser/wipes and ask if the child has any allergies to soap etc.

What is interesting and typical in this example is an extreme proceduralisation, a step-by-step round of permission-seeking, risk assessment, specification, training, response and recording (which in some cases is then followed by 'a reflection on implications for future training, policy development, and implementation'). Such practice ignores the practicalities of time and discomfort in favour of a due process where all risks and dangers have been anticipated, including the possibility that the soap may be as dangerous as the body. Such proceduralisation is not restricted to toileting: 'Acceptable physical intervention would include . . . leading a student by the hand or arm *after proper training*'. In this world of extreme circumspection, a language of multiple negatives, impersonality and emotional disengagement is common: 'if staff do not become involved in any overt form of physical affection then there will be no reason or excuse for allegations of impropriety' (LEA).

Documents describe touch as 'appropriate', 'secure', 'safe', 'acceptable' and stress that it is advisable, 'wherever possible, to depersonalise interactions', in the interests of 'managing the pupil'. In one preschool, students were advised 'to *handle* them [three- to four-year-olds] as little as possible', for fear of parental accusations of impropriety. Where 'touch' was legitimised, it received a technical expression, recommending the 'light *placement* of the hand on an arm', or a suggestion for the '*use*' of touch in order to ensure that 'care and concern for the child is *demonstrated*'. Communications with children were expressed in the same depersonalised register: 'When a member of staff *receives a disclosure* from a child' (our emphasis). A 'disclosure' is usually understood to be a child telling a professional that they have been subjected to some form of abuse.

In general, the expression of 'care and concern' is technicised and dehumanised on the basis of what seem predominantly to be legal fears – 'the touching of another person can constitute battery'. Touch may also be 'gratuitous' (a recurring term); it may be perceived as 'inappropriate' and careful professionals must realise that they are 'vulnerable' in the face of any 'malicious allegation' of physical or sexual abuse. In particular their good intentions may miss the point:

> Staff must, however, bear in mind that even perfectly innocent actions can sometimes be misconstrued and must therefore conduct themselves accordingly.

> Even when totally innocent of ulterior motives, this misconstruction [by pupils] can return in the form of malicious accusations, which even to deny, can cast a shadow over careers.

Both these examples point to an implicit nightmare of surveillance – the professional is surrounded by the possibility of misconstrual. This is a common theme. Another document indicates that abuse is 'particularly serious' if true, but if not true, it constitutes a 'serious ordeal' for the accused, and 'can result in long term damage to a person's health and career'. While this last point is clearly true, the most trivial forms of assistance are banned under such a regime, so that touching the other's body in any way has to be regulated out, and where any possible incriminating evidence of such touch has to be avoided:

> Staff don't place bobbles or clips in children's hair.

> Staff don't use force to restrain a child *in case of bruises and red marks*. (our emphasis)

This suspicion is profound, extending beyond notions of professionalism, trust and reputation. 'Innocence', as we saw, was part of the danger. Indeed it becomes a duty of professionalism that other professionals are to be distrusted, that children and others requiring care are to be regarded with suspicion, and that the professional self, itself, has a duty to place itself under permanent self-scrutiny. LEA guidelines indicate the scale of this:

> be prudent about their own conduct and vigilant about the conduct of others . . .

> Research has shown [it is not cited] that some professionals are extremely skilled in identifying vulnerable young people and forming relationships with colleagues, which often ensure that they are not challenged or distrusted and use the system to their own advantage.

The same all-encompassing caution is evident in early years settings:

> When working with young children they are bound to touch us but we must ensure that we respond appropriately *knowing we are overlooked*. (our emphasis)

> We constantly draw attention to each other so that if an issue crops up we have a witness that can protect us.

We argue that out of such an environment has developed the rage for regulation. A series of auditable, recorded procedures guard staff against the law and regulatory agencies such as Ofsted, and against their fears and fantasies of such surveillance. Training is necessary to inculcate this heuristic of 360 degree suspicion. The state inaugurates these concerns and, amplified by the media, they proliferate in a chain of translations that intensifies risk and precaution down through LEAs, care institutions, schools and individual professionals. A founding ambiguity in state regulation is the contrast between specific regulation, such as 'persistently refuses an order to leave the classroom', or 'behaving in a way that is seriously disrupting a lesson' with generalised permission to exercise reasonable force against pupils 'engaging in any behaviour prejudicial to maintaining good order'. LEA and school guidelines follow suit, specifying or prescribing precise behaviours, while simultaneously acknowledging that it would be 'inappropriate to lay down hard and fast rules'.

There is a pervasive fear that 'touch' 'opens the door to formal complaints, legal action and media attention'. This provokes the ratchet effect that is discussed in other chapters. As a result, any 'duty of care' for the wards of professionals receives only oblique expression (seldom one-sided, often contradictory) as a precautionary ethic raised up against the dangerous bodies of young people and the contamination of 'touch'. So any allegation of abuse 'must be reported to Social Services and Ofsted immediately'. Staff are warned by their managers that they 'could be liable for a claim of negligence if they fail to follow the guidance within this policy'. This is instruction rather than guidance. Nevertheless, this particular primary school document simultaneously makes a characteristic gesture to the need to exercise 'professional judgement' and 'common sense'. Uncertainty is seen to be unavoidable, since the issue of 'reasonable' behaviour will always be 'potentially challenging in criminal or civil law' (school) and dependant 'on all the circumstances of the case' (LEA)[1]. Thus the precautionary discourses tend to lead in two contradictory directions. The first is towards ever more specific and extensive regulation, even if the advice is sometimes quite contradictory:

> . . . in general hold long bones. You should *never* [original emphasis] hold a pupil face down on the ground or in any position that might increase the risk of suffocation.

> In exceptional circumstances . . . the young person may be brought to the ground, preferably face down.

The second is an acknowledgement that professional discretion is necessary, that some forms of touch may be necessary, and indeed beneficial to emotional development, good relationships and institutional ethos. Nevertheless, it was clear from the data that fear and paranoia prevailed: 'Don't touch. Don't grab, push or prod. Don't swear. Don't hug, pat or stroke. Don't get too isolated with a child'.

This is child-centredness with the child as dangerous object, full of the potential for abusive events to take place. Secondary schools were more likely to define 'no touch' in terms of disciplinary registers, rather than the sexual or the medical, often making reference to state regulation, local authority guidelines and documents approved by the governing body. Thus 'behaviour policy' translated most readily into the sorts of physical restraint that were legal, and in paradoxical attempts to define these precisely, while at the same time leave them open to professional discretion. The delivery of behaviour policy was hedged round by an administrative machinery that included the opening of an Incident Book, the undertaking of Risk Assessments, and the detailed recording of incidents, signed and witnessed, on forms suggested to the school by the LEA or the Ministry: 'If you are concerned that a situation may arise with a pupil that requires a restrictive physical intervention, you should carry out a formal risk assessment following the school's guidelines'.

Where touching was not absolutely prohibited, guidelines often cited the 'common misperception' that the 1989 Children's Act stipulated that 'any physical contact with a child is unlawful' (LEA guidelines). The legal position as revised via 550A of the 1996 Act was explained in detail in LEA guidelines, across which there was considerable uniformity. Again, there was the same contradictory emphasis in precise specification of appropriate behaviours and more general appeals to common sense and professionalism. In the same document an LEA affirms that 'these guidelines . . . do not offer simple one-step answers to cover every situation in complex areas of practice, law and accountability', but nevertheless aim at 'briefing staff to ensure they know exactly what action they should be taking'.

We have illustrated the 'no-touch' phenomenon as a preoccupation with the whole and undifferentiated body, and now turn to the ways in which such discourses address the different parts of the body, treating some as 'hot' (i.e. dangerous) and others as 'cold' (less risky but still requiring precaution).

Hot and cold body parts

Staff need to be aware of parts of the body that are more acceptable than others to be touched.

As we have seen, there are a large number of 'no-touch' practitioners, but it is true of our sample, at least, that most institutions attempt to police the touching of their clients' bodies through identifying both what can and what should not be touched. The notions of 'acceptability' and 'appropriateness' govern these decisions. It turns out that the least dangerous contact is with an 'open hand' placed 'at the centre of the back'. More liberal regimes of the body indicate that shoulders are also an appropriate site for touching:

Staff may touch a child from the shoulders up.

Staff may place a hand on a child's shoulder as a means of congratulation or reassurance, but not for any sustained period.

Access to such touch should be from the side rather than the front or back of the child, in the case of restraint, or from behind in another school's guidance, or 'between wrist and elbow' in yet another resolution of the dilemma:

Generally, holds which involve gripping the young person from the side are likely to be safer than holds which involve gripping the young person in front or behind.

Restrain them from behind, round upper body.

The child's hands are also deemed by some to be an acceptable site for congratulatory touch. In stipulating five acceptable touch scenarios, a secondary school licensed: 'Congratulating children on achievement (e.g. a handshake on being awarded a certificate or trophy)'. A primary school also licensed hand-holding, explaining to staff that 'hands are considered to be non-private areas and therefore they can be held when showing concern'. There was sometimes an expressed preference for 'holding clothes rather than skin' and for an emphasis on teaching children that their bodies were 'private' and should not be exposed to others. This precaution extended to procedures for changing young children's clothes: 'When changing a child whose clothing *all* [original stress] needs replacing it would be done in two stages – first remove and replace the top then again with the bottom half of the body'. In this way, presumably, the provocative danger of a wholly naked child is averted. Whatever privacy is retained by such a procedure, however, is undermined by the common insistence that another adult has to be present, or within sight, or must have been informed. Parental permission was also usually required – by phone, actual presence or pre-established agreement. 'In order to protect yourself, we operate an open door policy within the preschool'. And for example, parents are asked in writing whether or not they object to: a 'change of wet or soiled clothes, changing a nappy/comforting your child if distressed, injured, or for reassurance' etc. In another, more extreme version: 'It is important therefore that if you do not wish your child to have any physical contact with a team member, this is confirmed in writing to the manager'. Coldness has often been popularly associated with the English, but here coldness appears as an object auditable by the audit culture rather than the vernacular one. One school sought to balance privacy against such public exposure by advocating a 'half-closed' door: 'these [changes of clothes] should be carried out as openly as possible, taking into account the child's need for privacy e.g. door to first aid room half closed to protect privacy rather than shut fast'.

It was recognised that in subjects like PE, CDT, or in First Aid situations, a certain amount of additional touching might occur. But even here, there were meticulous attempts to avoid certain taboo parts of the body: 'It is not appropriate to touch a child's bottom during PE lessons. In negotiating some pieces of apparatus it may be necessary to hold a child's hips'. It is clear enough from such examples that these precautionary discourses construct an implicit regime of the body whereby some parts are more appropriate for touch, and some are taboo. In general, the centre of the child's back was furthest away from sexual organs whose touch was usually but not always prohibited by implication and omission rather by decree – just as 'wiping' (often in inverted commas) made redundant the expression of the word 'bottom'. There were however some explicit prohibitions:

> Adults may not rub children's tummies.
>
> Boys' testicles may not be examined under any circumstances.
>
> Staff need to be aware where they are holding the young person and if they are touching the genitals or any inappropriate part of the body then they should cease at once.
>
> Physical contact must not be in response to or be intended to arouse sexual expectations or feelings.
>
> Some [nurseries] have been given rules about sitting children on cushions on an adult lap. (Lindon 2004: iii)
>
> Staff may not apply suntan lotion to children.

Other schools allowed the application of suntan cream but only 'in view of other staff'. Or only by the same sex, with consent, and the 'utmost sensitivity'. Most of these precautions were implicitly sexual in nature and the need to avoid 'indecency' and the perception of possible sexual abuse was spelt out in many documents. Preschools had policy statements that promised to 'exclude known abusers'. But there were similar concerns at all levels of institution:

> Guiding Principals [sic]. Staff should always avoid touching or holding a pupil in a way that might be considered indecent.
>
> (college)
>
> Adults who have not been registered as 'fit' persons will not take children unaccompanied to the toilet.

Similarly, in preschool settings nappy changing was limited to those who had undergone a CRB check to make sure they had no convictions for sexual abuse. We did, however, come across one relaxed response to such matters. A preschool teacher said of the children, 'they may need some reminders or physical assistance to undo clothing, sit on a toilet, unravel their willy and point it in the right direction, wipe their bottom, wash their hands etc.'.

The question of what might be touched was (t)horny, but no more so than the where, the when, and under what circumstances. The key to location issues was that the adult must be visible to others, via 'vision panels' [windows] that made observation of private areas possible – like bathrooms, and First Aid rooms. With other rooms the principle of the 'open door' was asserted, with the knowledge and within 'visual access' of other adults. It is unwise to dismiss the conceptualisations of 'visual access' and 'vision panels' as mere technicist follies. The notion of the 'window' carries the notion of 'looking out' to a 'view' that is external to the gaze. The import of the new language is a 'looking in', an inspection, or a deliberate making visible of what might otherwise be obscured and hence suspect. It is therefore a form of confession. Touching behaviours were occasionally reported to be more relaxed in unavoidably public spaces, like corridors:

> In corridors there is a fair bit of hands on shoulders in a friendly way but this is always with several other people around.
>
> ... there would be no problem with a male colleague giving a female student a hug – e.g. a brilliant exam result – in a group situation.

The greatest emphasis in all settings was on not being alone with a child at any time. This may require the presence of another adult, trained and officially cleared of criminal offences (see previous chapter). Sometimes, training was not thought to be sufficient protection and the supervision of another adult was still required, and then again there were attempts to minimise the 'danger' of one-to-one encounters (tuition, counselling) by arranging the furniture in a sexually defensive kind of way. And there were gender issues to be considered – male supervision was more suspect than female. Such a precautionary ethic also gave birth to the concept of 'lone working', for which guidelines had also to be produced, as well as the obligatory 'Lone Worker Risk Assessment Form':

> Applications of suncream or any medical attention will be carried out in view of other staff. Only adults who have been registered as 'fit' persons will accompany children to the toilet.[2]

> Try not to be in a closed area with a single child, if you are working in a room ensure that the door is left open and is near to other staff.

> If child comes for comfort, other adult to observe.

> In the case where the meeting is for extra tuition, it is advisable to sit in a position which is visible from outside the classroom and, if possible, to work across a desk rather than alongside the pupil.

The panic for visibility (and naturally, the photographic darkroom was considered a place of special danger) was sometimes accompanied by a suspicion against any form of repeated affectionate gesture. Repetition could be a 'harbinger of abuse', or 'prelude to abusive behaviour'. The counter against this 'minefield' involved a mixture of brevity (in relation to the affectionate gesture), an absence of recurrence so that the gesture would not be open to misinterpretation, a rotation of staff engaged in such supervision, a discouragement of such an ethos as dangerous – promoting 'unnecessary and unjustified contact', and in one case a fear that instances of such affection might spiral out of control. It seemed rotation should replace relationship, and any repetition of affect avoided. In each of these moves professional mistrust is normalised in the practices of protection:

> Such contact can include informal and formal gestures, such as putting a hand on the shoulder or arm, which if continuously repeated with a particular pupil, could easily be misconstrued.

> Staff should not make gratuitous physical contact with their pupils and should not attribute touching to their particular teaching style or as a way of relating to pupils.

> A member of staff hugging a resident may lead to residents hugging each other – initially this may well be a positive act until residents or staff who may be perpetrators of abuse use such physical contact as a means of intimidation and the 'harbinger of abuse' to the more vulnerable children . . . So ask yourself how healthy it is to create such a precedent in the first place.

Again, it is significant that the above fears are accompanied by the usual disclaimer; once again the discourse points in two different directions: 'Nothing in this document should come as a shock, nor should it serve to frighten staff into placing "barriers" between themselves and the young people'. There was nothing wrong, after all, with 'an affectionate bear hug'. In most documents, that kind of statement was followed by, 'However . . .'.

Hot, cold and warm

Thus far we have indicated the extent to which moral panics about child abuse have been translated into the microregulation of professional behaviours. There is, in our view, much madness in these translations. A world in which the least likely events are the most anticipated, discussed and legislated against is a world of Borges-like insanity in which crucial and life-affirming elements of humanity have been abandoned. It is a kind of moral inversion of any notion of education constituted in and through relationships between teacher and taught. But at least there was opposition from a minority to this inversion. Not everyone was prepared to acknowledge the 'anorexic thin line between affection and abuse'. Some continued to believe that affection was 'essential to human relationships' and to any definition of a 'caring profession'. Not surprisingly, it was especially preschools that resisted the 'no-touch' culture:

> We are still a 'touching' type of establishment.

> We are a nursery school. As such it is vitally necessary to establish warm, supportive relationships with young children – so staff are encouraged to touch and cuddle our children.

> I feel that many children do not get enough love and appropriate physical contact with their parents/carers.

> They are welcomed by name and maybe a tickle under the chin. If you don't show affection – they can't learn to be affectionate.

There were also those who were saddened or angered – 'quite distressed and incensed' by the new culture of suspicion and surveillance. They felt that the foregrounding of touch and abuse as a predominant 'care' issue converted the discourse into something that smacked of 'dirty old men'. The discourse was 'ridiculous'. This anger, in one case, extended to the focus of our research. One respondent took the research to imply that such policing was a good and necessary thing, and wrote feelingly: 'Oh yes, just keep stoking up the paranoia and fear that all those who work with children suffer from!! You sad people'. So there were those who resisted both the 'hot' and the 'cold', preferring to rest things on 'warm relationships'. They felt it was 'very sad that some very young children were being denied cuddles from people who are caring for them six hours a day or more'. There were also some institutions who responded to our enquiry in 2004 that refused to have written guidelines on the grounds that they were 'unnecessary and impractical'.

Conclusion

This review of documentation and guidelines justifies the view that we are discussing a moral panic. But whose panic is this? Is it state-led? The documentation makes it clear that 'policy' since the 1990s has increasingly emphasised the need to police 'touching' practices. As we see later in the Summerhill chapter (10), in 2002 Her Majesty's Inspectorate (HMI) was adamant – 'no touching'. But there is an interesting phenomenon whereby the panic is also fed from the bottom up – by LEAs and schools that strengthen precautions in what we have called the ratchet effect. Our analysis showed that a great deal of copying went on but that some elements of exaggeration were also manifest. Thus in copying an admonition against physical abuse, a school would add its own aside, 'even in jest'. It is not surprising to us that the Children's Act was misconstrued as a no-touching prohibition. Such forms of 'policy inflation' are common. The problem is that the ethic of precaution is stronger, more precise, and easier to audit than any notion of 'professional judgement'. It is also an auditable object in that paper policies, guidelines, risk assessments, incident forms, etc. are accessible to audit, and their absence can be taken to imply a negligence that appeals to 'common sense' will not redress. If the policy is 'in the air' rather than 'in black and white' it may be more real, but not in terms of audit. This can be seen in the attempts to promote a blanket 'no-touch' policy, while at the same time allocating the remainder of professional action to the adjudications of 'common sense'. This is to treat common sense as a remainder or what is left after pervasive nonsense has had its way.

Another interesting feature is that the no-touch panic has permeated an education and social care system that has some strong formal elements of devolution. Schools have governors, who consider these matters. They are supposed to 'govern'. Headteachers have more powers in relation to LEAs than they used to have. They have 'autonomy'. The state offers mainly 'guidelines', and invokes the need for professional judgements to be made. Yet it was vivid in the data that all these subnational systems acted overall in a kind of ventriloquist daze. Despite the many invocations of 'widespread local consultation', the same sentences appeared almost everywhere. For example: 'non-abusive with no appearance of indecency or intention to cause pain or injury'; and 'This policy on Physical Intervention has been agreed by the Governing Body in the context of their Policy and Behaviour Management'. There was in effect a national script. Voluntaristic guidelines were transformed into coercive instruction by the expectation of accountability centred on guidelines. Indeed, in several LEAs it was expected that schools would simply enter their names into the blanks left in the LEA scripts, themselves mainly derivatives of national guidelines, and adopt the 'model' policy and specimen 'forms' that accompanied it:

> The staff at [name of school to be entered here] school believe that physical touch is an essential part of human relationships.

> [name of school to be entered here] acknowledges that physical techniques are only part of a whole setting approach to behaviour management.

While the motives behind such compliance may be discussed, in general the uniformity of most policies and practices suggests that schools were happy to have their beliefs and philosophy anticipated.

So what occasions this panic? We have sympathy with the view expressed by one angry headteacher who wrote:

> Bear in mind the lesson of history – eccentric grumpy old ladies were burnt to death as witches by jumpers on a hysterical bandwagon . . . Not everyone who comforts a hurt child should be at risk of being labelled as a paedophile.

There are elements of a deeply irrational and disproportional response to a perceived yet widely exaggerated risk. There are elements of scapegoating, and a lack of concern for evidence and balance. There is a 'better safe than sorry' mentality that licenses a disproportionate response. There is an odd sexualisation engendered by the very discourse that tries to suppress sexual risk. If we talk about the dangers all the time, we reconstruct educational and social care discourses as sexualised risk, and insist on suspicion, mistrust and surveillance as the fundamental precautions of teaching and caring. There is the same epistemology at work in these 'risk' calculations as can be found in witchcraft discourses (Marwick 1964, for example) of an earlier era.

Chapter 5

Saving touch
Private parts and public wholes

> Never hug or kiss them, never let them sit on your lap. If you must, kiss them once on the forehead when they say good night. Shake hands with them in the morning.
>
> (Watson 1928; cited by Synnot in Classen 2005: 41)

> The body enjoys being touched. It enjoys being squeezed, weighed, thought by other bodies, and being what squeezes, weighs, and thinks other bodies . . . Nothing ever becomes the sum or the system of the corpus. A lip, a finger, a breast, a strand of hair are the temporary and agitated whole of a joy that is each time temporary, agitated, in a hurry to enjoy again and elsewhere. This elsewhere is all over the body, in the body of all the parts, which each can be a part of another, in an indefinitely ectopic corpus.
>
> (Nancy 1993a: 203)

It's not difficult to guess which quotation we favour. Nasty US behaviourist and his deadening psychology of family 'touch'? Or voluptuous 'jouissance' from the French philosopher that Derrida extols as the 'greatest thinker about touching of all time' (Derrida 2005: 4)? No contest. But the contrast softens when we look in the first paragraph at the universalisms of 'never' and 'they', 'them' and 'you': they exist just as much in the universal personification of 'the body' and what 'it' enjoys as a 'corpus'. And: 'Says him'. One wants to say to the second author, 'Speak for yourself'. Both indulge in the kind of universalist prescription by now familiar to readers of this book. It is true that the advice (explicit or implicit) is contradictory, but the epistemology is not. These are opposites on the circumference of a circle, collusive antagonisms within the same circuit, and a rather masculinist one at that. In plural senses, they *face* each other, actively as well as passively. In both, father knows best. This chapter will have as its major theme the nature of such linked oppositions and their conspiratorial moments. This chapter provides a more theoretical backdrop to the rest of the book which we consider to be important as we identify inadequacies in related theory. It also offers three cases, or 'tangents' as we have called them: we feel they are helpful in spelling out theory and its application to specific events.

The excess of touch

We start with a brief excursion into 'touch' as a historical and Western cultural form. It will help us understand a curative, therapeutic strand in the thinking of 'touch', a sacred moment that interacts with and against an opposing profanity. There are many 'touches' in such histories. We recall the 'saving' touch of the Christian God, filtered down through a surrogate divinity to the 'royal touch' of European divine monarchs: 'And he laid His hands on them one by one' (Luke 4: 40); 'Salvation saves by touching, and the Saviour, namely the Toucher, is also touched: he is saved, safe, unscathed, and free of damage. Touched by grace' (Derrida 2005: 100).

Hem of robe, sacred royal touch, mediator of divine intercession, cure of scrofula. This is the 'grace' of touch to which Derrida refers. This is 'touch' from on high – where touch touches rather than is touched. No mutuality here. Rather typically, Derrida sees such 'touch' – a 'Christian thinking of flesh' (ibid.: 243) – as always beyond itself as a sensibility. And he identifies, as usual, an *aporia*: 'What this says is that the sense of touching may not come from the senses; the proper sense of touch is foreign to sensibility' (ibid.: 247). We translate that into a more general conundrum: what is the gap between 'sensing' and 'making sense'? In that kind of accounting of 'touch', the tactile is always metonymic – something more is going on, unsaid, unsayable, a tactile that is tacit, in-tangible yet in-tact. The language itself conspires in paradoxical deceit.[1] Perversely, the embodied is the ghost of the disembodied, touch's weird doppelgänger, present in a ghostly absence more potent than any mere physical presence. A body-without-organs, in the language of Deleuze and Guattari (1988), but still a body, we want to insist.[2] This is one aspect, at least, of Nancy's 'ectopic corpus' – the body as a 'dark reserve of sense, and the dark sign of this reserve' (Nancy 1993a: 193), or in another version, 'a place of passage' (Probyn 1995: 6).

That all the senses have significations that exceed their materiality and borrow from each other in order to express their essence is, of course, a commonplace and a cliché in everyday talk and popular culture – 'more than meets the eye'; 'a word speaks volumes'; 'grasping a meaning', 'handling feelings', 'scathing criticism', 'you'd be like heaven to touch'[3] – but we will argue that the nature of that excess is not a mere addition or a completion of sense, nor even a subsumption of the material, physical, embodied nature of 'touch' in itself, or rather in the self that it both lacks and exceeds.[4] I can only say what I mean when I fail to say what I mean and have recourse to metaphor in order to repair the damage of non-sense. There is something about the 'interaction' of touch that we need to explore, and that includes the ways in which the everyday metaphors of the senses – 'seeing' meaning, 'holding' discussions, 'feeling' truths, 'making' an argument – cross over from one sense to another. They 'dis-tract' each other in order to make sense, and in an apparent attempt to evade an all-too-obvious tautology. How do we, in this sense, 'come to our senses' (Stoller 1996: 181)?

The access of touch

Thus far, we have addressed a transcendent, metonymic sense of touch, curative of bodies and meanings. But there is a more immediate kind of touch. We agree with Nancy and Hutchens – there is a peculiar reflexivity to touch, lacking in the other senses: 'The sense of touch feels itself feeling itself' (Hutchens 2005: 55, citing Nancy); 'It is by touching the other that the body is a body, absolutely separated and shared' (Nancy 1993a: 205). That has to have some truth in it, yet must 'face' an apparent opposition – that touch in touching cannot touch itself. That kind of reflexivity moves through the other senses, in semantic cross-overs that we shortly illustrate, and lead Derrida to address 'what touching might have to do with seeing and the other senses' (Derrida 2005: 18). He concludes, 'All the senses are included in this *tactile corpus* (his emphasis), not only touching, but also seeing, hearing, smelling, and tasting' (Derrida 2005: 75). There's a kind of multi-sensory onomatopoeia going on here. Just as words may sound like their meaning, so too do the other faculties make sense *with* each other, perhaps in the sense that Nancy deploys the 'with' relationship in *Being Singular Plural* (2000) (see later).

Some of that convoluted immediacy is caught in the peculiarity of the grammar of the various senses. In terms of 'touch' verb and noun coincide, as with 'taste'. In the other senses verb and noun diverge: see/sight and hear/hearing are semantically kept apart, though we will also have to return to 'touch' in relation to its suppression of its alter ego, to 'feel' – which appears nowhere significant in the literature on touch. We will argue that to 'feel' has emotion written into it, or very closely alongside it, carried by the double meaning of 'feel' as touching and emotionally responding, whether in pleasure or not. The sound of the words even differ onomatopoeically – a percussive 'touch' against a drawn-out caressing 'feel'. In addition, touch seems a more technical expression, whose emoting stands outside of its act, in some context of intention or reception. Is there a hidden technicism here that an expression like touchy-feely might address if it were less a term of mockery?

If senses borrow from each other in order to mean, a more hierarchic economy is apparent in the case of 'seeing'. Conventionally, in the West, it is said that 'seeing' came to triumph over the other senses (Desjarlais 1996; Foucault 1975, 1977). The 'gaze', the 'Enlightenment', the religious icon, the Christian 'Light of God' all testify to the cultural power of 'seeing' as the unveiling of revelation. In a Christian world, we are enjoined to see the Light, religiously, and even medically in the reformulated medical 'gaze' (Foucault

1975: 115). That, at least, is the usual story. Such a 'perspective' (in a double sense) is of course not beyond challenge.

So we have the senses in an unexplicated relationship of 'borrowing' from each other, thinking with the other, and then again, in a subordination to various versions of the Light or Gaze. How else can the senses relate? In particular, what can 'proper' touch be, in itself (the one it doesn't have), and in relation to the other senses involved in making sense. These are all issues that stem somewhat at least from a Christian sense of touch as fundamentally ambivalent and yet transcendent. Touch, in such contexts, has always a meaning outside of itself, a reference that washes back into its content as a kind of 'grace', as Derrida pointed out, or as we would like to add, a form of disgrace, an impropriety that has its own transcendent history, in error and sin.

The historic nature of some of those proprieties/improprieties is at least clear. Religious, royal and medicinal touch travels from high to low. The one touches, the other is touched: there is no contamination of reciprocity in the exchange, no reflexivity at the level of the physical or spiritual exchanges. A message is sent, a spiritual communication from above to below. The act may be curative, but it would be improper if the toucher was also in the same sense touched by the other. There can be no magic in mutuality, and the one who is touched is submissive to the 'laying on of hands', 'sent under' by that act of 'skinship'. And, of course, yet another plane of touch is involved; 'tact' mediates between these two states: 'A certain tact, a "Thou shalt not touch too much"' (Derrida 2005: 47). At the same time, such dislocations of meaning precipitate a conflict between the intangible (cannot touch) and the untouchable (must not touch) that Derrida refers to as the 'différance of tact' (ibid.: 298). Like all conflicts it takes place, or makes place, at a border, a limit: 'To touch is to touch a border, however deeply one may penetrate, and it is thus to touch by approaching indefinitely the inaccessible of whatever remains beyond the border, on the other side' (ibid.: 297).

Thus far, in starting with a religious dimension of touch, we made some trace of the curative, noting also that the senses were transcendent in another way, in that there was always a synecdochic relation of part to whole. In addition, 'seeing' was typically a privileged sense, in a metaphor at first redolent of religious insights, then with more 'Enlightenment' secularities of sense. Instead, we preferred a constellation of the senses that centred on (though no centre, that) on the tactile or haptic.[5] In this kind of labyrinthine thinking the part has no whole, the whole no part – in a rather ghostly, double metonymic gesture that we will continue to unpack in this chapter.

The taboo of the body and transgressive touch

A further Christian 'thinking of the flesh', of the ethics of touch, is from below rather than on high. The body as sinful, base, beneath us, is not a leitmotif in Christian thinking. It was philosophised into a body/mind dualism by Descartes as part of that tradition of body suspicion. That separation is marked in language by the way that we say: 'I have a body', not: 'I am a body' or: 'My body has me'; in such thinking the body is our nearest and dearest commodity, maybe a bit like Winnicott's (1953) 'teddy' as a transitional object. Just as 'teddy' was supposed to help our transition from infancy to childhood, a relational bridge from self to other, isn't the Western body a mnemonic and barometer of a similar journey from life to death, the medium through which 'mind' becomes 'soul'? Thus the body manages to combine, in the same space, the most literal of physicality with the most metaphysical of significances. So sin, error, purity, life and death are all part of the profound cultural ambivalence about the body, and about its touching practices, that has its own ghosts as well: 'Can such a rule, understood as a prohibition, actually operate, however effectively, without producing and maintaining the spectre of its transgression' (Boholm 2003: 163)?

That question echoes through this book. We think here about the taboo that thought us into our thinking in the first place, as touched and touching selves, through a certain version of a body and its touching and becoming relationships: 'a body is what cannot be read in writing' (Nancy 1993a: 193). Nor can we forgive Christian/Western thinking this kind of combined prohibition, inhibition, exhibition. A ferocious pre-hibition is in play, in foreplay that is oddly, simultaneously, the unfolding of display. Each of these '-hibitions' masks the touch of the Latin verb *habere*, to hold, once again to touch and so to possess. Nancy: 'But the skin is always exhibition, exposition, and the minutest look is a touching that brushes against it, and exposes it once more' (ibid.: 205).

In contemporary Western culture, such pre-ventions translate the tangible into the visible: it is the 'gaze' that has characterised pornography for so long – the *voyeur* witnesses rather than participates; the orgy is one of visibility, although even there the pornographic 'gaze' carries with it a kind of vicarious touching, where seeing is always a form of onanistic doing. And there may be a cultural shift underway. Perhaps the age of the 'toucheur' is upon us, where touch rather than gaze becomes the new 'thinking of flesh', as new metaphors of touch begin to proliferate, like 'grooming'. Can there be a satiation of the pornographic gaze (especially via the web) that spills over into more physically active senses? That is certainly the contemporary nightmare that the media promotes, disseminates and condemns via spectacle and scapegoating: exhibition and prohibition collide in a pornographic display. And sometimes, we show one by hiding or displaying it 'cropped' (Nochin 1994: 31), in a tease of meaning, and a fetishistic one at that. Nevertheless, we should be cautious about claiming special novelty for this 'Western' crisis – 80 years ago Mead was already writing about 'the present problem of the sex experimentation of young people' and drawing utopian conclusions from 'native' attitudes to sexuality (Mead 1928/43: 193).[6] Perhaps we should regard such crises as recursively endemic to our culture, a rite of passage stuck in its cultural liminality. But it need not be a Christianised religion that attends to 'touch' – India's 'untouchables' are testament to other cultures and religions where 'touch' and 'defilement' are associated in ways that Douglas addressed in her seminal *Purity and Danger* (1984). Such taboo is an anthropological commonplace. Touch can save, or it can damn (Burton and Heller 1967, cited in Autton 1989). 'It can heal or it can wound (Laderman and Roseman 1996). And it can curse. They who devour usury shall not rise from the dead, but as he ariseth whom Satan hath infected by a touch' (Koran, Sale translation, nd: 30).

If religious and secular worlds are often split in their response to touching, it seems that such a dichotomy is sometimes less prominent elsewhere.[7] And if the Earth is a body, often a female one, a Mother Earth – like the Inca *Pachamama* (Howes 2005, in Classen 2005: 30) – then the scope of the metonymy is limitless. Desjarlais emphasises how the body in its materiality is central to shamanistic rituals that seek to return the lost soul to the body by 'hooking the spirit' (Desjarlais 1996: 148). He sees such invocations as 'an imagistic poem, evoking an array of tactile images' (ibid.: 151). Taylor suggests that an important way of addressing touch issues is to ask: how are bodies 'given surface'? (Taylor 2005: 747). Others have punned the need to study 'skinship', 'skinscapes', or 'skin knowledge' (see Merleau-Ponty 1990 and Weiss 2000 for examples), giving them very different meanings. In a Japanese context, Zur and Nordmarken point to the intense physical relationship of the mother to the children, and dub the relation 'skinship'; in another context, Howes reports how the Peruvian Cashinahua deny that the brain is the seat of knowledge. There is 'skin knowledge', *ichi una*, whereby the skin thinks touch. We return to that interesting 'skinship' contrast between the ways in which Derrida and Nancy think the body and touch, and the intense materiality of that latter kind of skin-thinking.

Tangent 1: touching on Slovenia

Anita (Slovenian colleague) and I (IS) were talking about cultural differences. She was laughing about once watching me in Slovenia working in the café adjacent to the Šola za Ravnatelje offices. First, Polona had come up and said, 'Ian' and I had looked up, disturbed, but returning the greeting. Then Andreja had done the same, saying my name and then passing on. Again, I had looked slightly hunted. Finally, Anita had done the same herself, but had then worked out what the difference was. In Slovenian culture the calling of the name is a form of 'touch' – it just says hello, I recognise you are there and greet you in friendly acknowledgement with your first name. The first name thus had a kind of double implicit 'thou' status in that kind of greeting ritual. In British cultures, on the other hand, the saying of the name is much more likely to be read as a kind of claim for attention. And that's how Anita saw me respond in Slovenia – preparing for a claim for attention that mysteriously never appeared, and seemed instead to leave me a little uncertain as to what exactly was going on. All naming and no claiming!

On sabbatical in England, Anita tried unsuccessfully to suppress her 'first name' calling behaviour. She could feel that it was read as a kind of insistence for attention that was not intended, not always perceived as such, but at least open to that kind of misinterpretation. She felt that some people stiffened a little . . . Anita also liked the fact that in Manchester when I entered the big open office where her desk was, I would behave like a Slovenian and call out her name, 'Anita, kako si?' But in that instance my use of the 'Anita' betokened the distance from where I stood at one end of the big office and where she sat at the other end, about ten metres away. I was claiming attention, I was not 'touch-ing', at least not until the use of the familiar 'si' rather than 'ste' (are thou/are you). 'Ah', we both thought at this point, now we're getting somewhere. We're beginning to dig up some of that tacit cultural enframing that separates with a subtlety that no language grammar can unearth. It is, as Mazzei (2007) would surely confirm, the silent language between the spoken language, the cultural interstices and slippages between 'translations' and the more sophisticated but seldom explicit or explicable communions of a shared culture. It turned out that the expressions 'Anita' and 'Ian' – despite being personal names bereft of any possibility of ambiguity – still had to be translated in the various contexts of their deployment. They worked in a certain uncer-tainty, with a hidden ambivalence. On the surface, they were only names called up in representative meaning, of course, but in use they were cultural performances that differed greatly (Spradley 1980). There was no dictionary for it. But in all their self-evidence, they were hermeneutic traps.

And more than that as well. Because in that mutual digging into understand-ings and misunderstandings and, even more, half-understandings that failed to be aware of their 'other half' in those imperfect marriages of communica-tion, speakers of each language unearth meanings that tell them more about their own culture as well as more about the other's. Each reflexively constructs an 'Erving Goffman' (1990) to sit on their shoulders and offer commentary. These 'Ervings' talk to each other, as we do here. Each excavates itself as well as the other in an estranging discovery that always also contains an excess of invention and creation. Because in the end everything transla-tional is a relative and singular weave of the literal, the cultural and the personal, and of the failures of each of these to realise itself. Oddly, failures in understanding are the necessary condition for understanding. What is the precise correspondence of the literal, the cultural, the personal? These are not easy questions to weigh up, and their necessary remainders are hard to divine and certainly impossible to define: 'One thus touches on either upon the intangible or on the untouchable, depending on whether one accentuates the cannot-touch or the must-not-touch' (Derrida 2005: 298). Similarly 'Bodies are in touch on this page, whether we want it or not; or else, the page itself is the touching or toying' (Nancy, 'Corpus': 46–7, cited in Derrida 2005: 225). That is at least a gesture towards the 'endless aporia' (Derrida 2005: 6), the 'différance of tact' (ibid.: 298).

A final point: it is the personal relationship – in the above instance Anita/Ian – that determines the quality and degree of cultural exploration and which ontologises and epistemologises the spaces for their mutual articulation and explication. In that process, 'touch' and 'tact' are close together (Derrida 2005), interactionally as well as etymologically. In Nancy's terms it is the freedom 'with' the other that precedes the surprise of a misunderstanding at last identified and understood.

How do we characterise this generative gap/space/aporia/chora? It returns us to the old problem of 'Mr In-between'. We like Derrida's thinking about touch where he derives from Nancy and Levinas an argument that touch always exceeds itself, as the 'trace of the metonymy' (2005: 35). A 'caress', to use Levinas's example, has to be more than a touch, a mere physical gesture, in order to be itself. It must say much more. Perhaps only the 'brush against' kind of touch contains most of itself in itself, all other touches being overwritten with an excess, a 'figure of touch' that is untouchable. And if the regime of touch can include a 'tactile corpus, not only touching, but also seeing, hearing, smelling and tasting' (ibid.: 75), then we can extend 'touch' to the cross-cultural 'touching' and 'missing' that seems so generative of the untangled misunderstandings out of which understanding arrives, taking 'understanding' to mean the partial understanding of misunderstandings. We can pass from 'sight to touch' (ibid.: 105) in ways central to one of the theses of this book via deconstruction. And one of the oddities of deconstruction, as it isn't rather than as it is, is that it is only when we depart from ourselves that we arrive at ourselves. Still, this should be a comfortable thought for educational and social researchers: learning ought to become us.

In its secular form, the absence of touch in the West (or North West, more accurately) has also been a matter of concern – especially in more 'progressive' moments of the zeitgeist. For example, Montagu's best-selling book on touch makes this claim:

> in the Western world it is highly probable that sexual activity, indeed the frenetic preoccupation with sex that characterises Western culture, is in many cases not the expression of a sexual interest at all, but rather the search for the satisfaction of the need for contact.

(Montagu 1971/86: 213)

Once in play, such a reduction is unstoppable: 'In baring their bodies, strippers may be merely asking for the attention and affection denied them by their fathers' (ibid.: 232). And what about the ogling daddies in the audience? Is this a ludicrous father–daughter incest fantasy as well? It is significant, though, that even a touch-therapy enthusiast like Montagu can't help sounding some odd notes. It's as if the licensing of touch is always a vulnerable inversion of a prohibition, an inversion that keeps breaking down. It is not an act of free speech so much as its parole. Touching is not 'natural' and has to be woven round with precautions. The advice to parents is bizarre, but, as we have seen, has many contemporary parallels: 'Erogenous zones, however, should be avoided; these include the lips, nipples, external genitalia, and buttocks – the lips because, in addition to their erogeneity, they are frequently transmitters of infection by kissing' (Montagu 1971/86: 232).

This is 'purity and danger' as anthropological farce. Scarcely less parodic is the sociological reification of such 'risks' in terms such as the 'RPS (Risk Perception Shadow)' (Mairal 2003: 185)[8] or, as we have seen, the ritual animations of 'Risk Assessment Exercises'. Predominantly, however, Montagu offers a licensing of touch as remedy, over-inflated though it is, rather than the current obsession with managing touch through the censorship of accountability discourses. In contrast with the past, 'touch' is not policed directly through taboo, which expresses the certainty of danger, but through the uncertainties of 'risk' as they apply to the 'primal risk object' of the contemporary Western child (Boholm 2003: 163; Strong 2002).

A final dimension of touch to touch upon: all knowledge in the Western tradition is to be valued, expanded, savoured, cherished, transmitted as 'education'. Except carnal knowledge. We argued elsewhere that sex education, that least carnal of carnal knowledges, is the only educational objective on the school curriculum that rehearses its own postponement (Stronach et al. 2006). Somehow, it is contagious knowledge, again a form of metaphorical touching. They teach us how to read, write and count, but they certainly don't teach us how to fuck. That would be 'dirty'. Nancy's quote, with which this chapter starts, is hard to read without a certain lascivious acknowledgement, as an invitation to know in that much mocked yet potent Biblical usage.

Taken insistently, such a cultural tendency culminates in de Sade's Juliette (1797/1968 – see later in this chapter), who is purged of religion and returned to Nature's 'fold and doctrine' (ibid.: 8). Yet such an ending can be argued to be more in keeping with the 'Enlightenment' tradition than a perversion of it – a 'pornographic extension of the new clinical gaze' (Morris 2001: 148). We suggest that only de Sade had the revolutionary nerve to treat carnal knowledge as a total subversion of religion and superstition, to marry off Juliette to Émile, and to anticipate and even outdo Foucault's sceptical rendering of the manufacture of the 'soul' in Discipline and Punish (1977).

Tangent 2: the case of the 'erect penis'

In conducting research for the Department of Health on sex education for ten-year-old children in primary schools, we observed a lesson in which pupils saw a video, discussed issues, and completed a worksheet that tested their curriculum knowledge. The aim of the programme was long-term – to reduce teenage pregnancy. The questions were direct, the diagrams explicit. The teacher and the nurses involved circulated around the small groups, helping them complete and correct answers. One of the diagrams contained a sketch of an erect penis, in the process of ejaculating.

It was the sort of drawing that, anywhere else in the school, would have been condemned as an obscene graffito. And here it was, to the whispered amusement of a few of the kids. The observer had been sitting beside two of the boys, having kind of been adopted by them. Jason said to him, pointing at the diagram, 'What do you think of that?' and immediately added, 'Mine's ten inches'. The observer made a non-committal noise, and moved away. He clearly felt unable to do anything except back away from the unwelcome turn the conversation had taken.

Later in the research, the lesson was written up as part of a case study that was submitted to the project committee at the Department of Health. The email attachment of the draft case study was blocked: the Department of Health 'firewall' would not let the words 'erect penis' enter the building. Later, shorter versions of the cases were to be posted on the website of the Teenage Pregnancy Unit. Again, we tried to include the words 'erect penis' and the diagram. They refused to put words or diagram in the case. They too would have nothing to do with the words 'erect penis' appearing on their website – 'what would the media say?'

There are a number of relevant themes here. First, there is the powerfully performative nature of the words – they were admissible in the classroom as description, a factual representation that was also drawn in order to educate, or at least to acknowledge that a full and frank dialogue was being opened up. But elsewhere (in the school, in the Ministry) these representations were taboo. They were taboo because they were performative – to name, draw, or see, was also in some sense, to act. Once again, we see how the senses switch over, those semantic crossings we earlier noted. We also see the part–whole relation of event and context. The Ministry fears the moralising outrage of the media, presumably fearing headlines along the lines of 'Erect Penis Found in Teenage Pregnancy Unit'. The teachers see the possibility of such frankness as being traumatic for some of the 'younger' kids: the usual formula of 'too late for some, too early for others' is invoked. The nurses have a medical model for the object, scientific facts that comprise sexual knowledge. But they knew that it was a delicate business, having reported their anxieties about a school governor attending the sex education classes – he had been a Church minister.

And the observer is unable to maintain conversation with Jason because a 'paedophilic' border has been crossed. Strange men, any men, do not talk to young boys about penis size. So that was also the 'observer' bounced right out of his role! Each 'sighting', then, is also metonymic – standing for various overlapping and contradictory 'wholes'. At the same time, we can read this sex education lesson – defining it broadly – as an explanation for the development of a mutually engendering morality/pornographic discourse. The children are learning the taboo, both to want what is forbidden, and to forbid themselves what is then wanted, and in different ways the adults are teaching it. In the classroom we can call it an 'education', but in the broader culture is it more of a tease, a strip-tease? Perhaps behind all that, the hidden curriculum is teaching that Saying is Seeing is Doing, is Doing Wrong (in a variety of versions of that wrong). The 'erect penis' touches everyone, one way or another, even in its essential immateriality.

So there are a whole range of secular as well as religious 'soft touches', emotional 'touchings' – either moving or prickly ('touchy') in their emotional content. They weave dangerously through different registers – violence, affection, lust, care, cruelty, education, abuse – and also institutions; the Church, monarchy, school, prostitution, sport. We intend here no taxonomy of touch, only to note, as others have done before, that 'touch' is not a self-evident thing, however 'tangible', 'tactful', 'phys-ical' we insist that it is. If touch *is,* and is not in and of itself, yet cannot be reduced to its discursive penumbra, then what is it? That is our riddle. Let's start with the body. Taylor suggests that we 'consider the body neither as an object nor as a text, nor only as a locus of subjectivity, but rather as a contingent configuration, as surface that is made but never in a static or permanent form' (Taylor 2005: 747).

We need, he argues, to think in terms of 'labile and refractory framing devices' (ibid.: 742). Hutchens takes a similar tack in his analysis of Nancy's work. We must respect 'the truth of fragmentation' and think in 'trajectories and intersections' (Hutchens 2005: 10, 5; see also Nochin 1994). Theoretical gestures such as these have much in common with our recent work on methodology and reflexivity (Stronach *et al.* 2007), where we proposed such labile and kinetic epistemologies. Drawing on the work of Deleuze and Derrida, we argued for a kind of thinking that executed the 'signature' of identity in singular, unrepeatable yet iterative acts of appropriation. We intend here to take our own advice, but also to concede the body and its experience of touch as a *material* moment finally irreducible to text, yet unthinkable outside its immateriality: 'Bodies are impenetrable: only their impenetrability is penetrable. Words brought back to the mouth, or to the ink and the page: there is nothing here to discourse about, nothing to communicate' (Nancy 1993a: 190).

There's a hole in the aporia, dear Derrida, dear Derrida

Body, object, text, self: think of them as trajectory, fragmentation, circulation, refraction. Now iterate these objects and movements in a *survol*, a signing of and off the body that is mediated by a sense of touch, that is always also a self-touching, a tripled rather than doubled 'feeling' that desires from itself as it desires for or from some other. Such touch is always a reminder of the body, a remainder of its multiple sensing, and so always in front of *and* behind itself. 'It is by touching the other that the body is a body, absolutely separated and shared' (Nancy 1993a: 204). This is reminiscent of Kamuf's 'I/we apart together' argument (Kamuf 1997: 122; Stronach *et al.* 2007: 14). Touch, then, is a survol of the senses, a multiple articulation implied by all those semantic cross-overs of the senses that we noted earlier.

To be the thing it is, touch has to be many things, even the mediation of tattoo (Schildkrout 2004), an unforgettable mnemonics, as Kafka (1919/61), Foucault (1977) and Clastres (1974/87) have all discussed this kind of touch as an unforgettable pedagogy, an inscription of meaning upon the body itself. But the tattoo of touch, as opposed to the inscriptive tattoo, is invisible, impermanent, though still there, in a kaleidoscope of sensory circulations. It has no visibility, only tangibility in the instant and the trace of memory; secret rather than visible writing. It is an 'excription' rather than an 'inscription'. We begin to realise that touch comes before the body, as writing before speech. The self, in the moment, in the ipseity of the physical, is not there, with or in the touch. That self is the bridge that links the reminder, which is also a remainder – over all possibilities of the present, here and now – to a certain promise. Reminder, promise and premonition construct the fantasy of the presence from which they nevertheless spring. And it is a 'spring', not a consequence or a logic or a causality that determines touch as ethical in the sense that it is 'free', if we follow Nancy's thinking. Thus, we want to argue, there is 'free touch' just as there is 'free speech'. Consequently, we need a theory and practice of touch – 'free touch' – analogous to theories of 'free speech'.

Such inflationary spirals, conjoining and disjoining the physical and the metaphysical, politics and ethics, bodies and feelings, have had no end, no matter how hard de Sade tried to press the flesh.[9] They contain, hold and so touch on a body (a 'cut into discourse': Nancy 1993a: 197) while simultaneously creating a void that touches the body as a 'nothing'. This is the same 'nothing' as in Derrida's famous aphorism: 'There is nothing outside the text' but not as we understand his intentions for that saying. It *is*, and is nothing. It is nothing in the same way as a hole in a bucket is a nothing, an empty space in a universe of plenty of other empty spaces. But the hole in the bucket, like the *aporia* that Derrida finds in everything, is a *performative* nothing. It 'spaces', beyond discourse: 'writing's own existence – is outside the text, takes place outside writing' (ibid.: 338). 'Thinking, undoubtedly, is for us what is most free. But freedom is this fact which less than any other can be reduced to thinking' (Nancy 1993b: 172). Such a hole/whole – in its holiness – is consequential; it drains, changes, blesses, sacrifices, performs an emptying that also fills a space differently and without paradox. It makes something happen, 'unbucketing' as it empties. It nothings something as it somethings nothing.[10] So we can say, after Nancy, 'There is no such thing as the body' (Nancy, cited in Hutchens 2005: 54), noting that this time he wishes to quarrel not with the 'body' but with the definite article in 'the body' (an injunction he does not always follow, as we have seen), and add without qualms: 'There can be no discourse of the body, yet every discourse is from the body that cannot speak about itself' (Hutchens 2005: 54). Hence the 'ectopic' place that Nancy writes about (1993a: 204), and also perhaps the notion of 'excription' as 'a corpus, an ectopic topography, serial somatography, local geography' (ibid. 207).

It also seems that the very place of physical touching, its corporeal moment, is simultaneously the precise location of its aporia, its spacing, its incorporeality. Such an 'absolute' has a temporal, biographical dimension. Touch is primary, a first sense of orality, even before orality in the infant for Nancy (Derrida 2005: 24), and the 'most basic sense' for Aristotle (Vasseleu 1998: 17). Derrida argues that Kant found it the most important if clumsiest of the senses. We touch first, and the other senses follow. Never mind self-realisation as a fantasy of the senses full of themselves, what about self-hapticisation, isn't that de Sade's equivalent achievement, as an ecstasy of touching and being touched?

Tangent 3: the body and soul of de Sade

> Madame Delbène: Before going further, let us here observe that nothing is commoner than to make the grave mistake of identifying the real existence of bodies that are external to us with the objective existence of perceptions that are inside our minds. Our very perceptions themselves are distinct from ourselves, and are also distinct from one another, if it be upon present objects that they bear and upon their relations and the relations of these relations. They are thoughts when it is of absent things they afford us images: when they afford us images of objects which are within us, they are ideas. However, all these things are but our being's modalities and ways of existing; and all these things are no more distinct from one another, or from ourselves, than the extension, mass, shape, color, and motion of a body are from that body. Subsequently, they necessarily bestirred themselves to cover in general all particular but similar ideas: cause was the name given to all beings that bring about some change in another being distinct from themselves, and effect the word for any change by whatever cause in whatever being. As this terminology gives rise in us, at best, to a very muddled idea of being, of action, of reaction, of change, the habit of

employing it in time led people to believe they had clear-cut and precise perceptions of these things, and they finally reached the stage of fancying there could exist a cause which was not a being nor a body either, a cause which was really distinct from all embodiment and which, without movement, without action, could produce every imaginable effect . . . Behold it Juliette: such is the God men have got themselves. (de Sade 1797/1968: 35–6) [Not just a God, we want to add, but the basis for a Methodology, Causes for Effects, and Souls for Bodies.]

Let us say forthrightly and repeatedly: there is nothing marvellous in the phenomenon of thought, or at least nothing which proves this phenomenon distinct from matter, nothing which indicates that matter, subtilized or modified in some or another manner, cannot produce thought: the which is infinitely easier to comprehend than the existence of God. If this sublime soul were indeed the work of God, why should it have to share in all of the changes and accidents the body is subject to? . . . If this soul were a god's production, it would not have to sense, reflect, or be the victim of the body's gradations; were the soul a thing of divine perfection, it wouldn't, or shouldn't, be able to; rather, fully formed from the outset, it would conjoin itself to the embryo, and Cicero would have been able to pen his Tusculanae Disputationes, Voltaire his Alzire, each in the cradle. If that is not so, and cannot be so, it is because the soul ripens step by step with the body's development, then with it descends the farthest slope; the soul therefore is constituent of parts, since it rises, sinks, augments, diminishes: well, whatever is composed of parts is material; hence, the soul is material, since it is composed of parts. Am I clear? We have now to acknowledge the utter impossibility of the soul existing without the body, and the latter without the former. (ibid.: 50)

There, Juliette, I have, so I think, supplied you with more than is needed that you be convinced of the nullity of this God they say to exist and of this dogma which ascribes immortality to the soul. Oh, but they were shrewd beggars who invented this pair of conceptual monstrosities! . . . Depending absolutely upon the degree of latitude in which a country chances to be located in, manners and morals are an arbitrary affair, and can be nothing else. Nature prohibits nothing; but laws are dreamt up by men, and these petty regulations pretend to impose certain restraints upon people; it's all a question of the air's temperature, of the richness or poverty of the soil in the district, of the climate, of the sort of men involved, these are the unconstant factors that go into making your manners and morals. And these limitative laws, these curbs and injunctions, aren't in any sense sacred, in any way legitimate from the point of view of philosophy, whose clairvoyance penetrates error, dissipates myth, and to the wise man leaves nothing standing but the fundamental inspirations of Nature. (ibid.: 51) [And so the capital letters deflate, leaving god, methodology and soul diminished. But what of Nature?]

The body that touches, that has contact, is for Nancy the 'absolute of existence' but in the 'surprise', 'blink', 'clinamen', 'burst' (Nancy 1993a: 159; Hutchens 2005: 79) – he has many words for gesturing at this movement – and then, in that instant, this 'untransgressible limit collapses into sense at the instant of contact, such that there are no longer merely a relation of singularities constitutive of sense' (ibid.: 55). Nancy's concern is for a certain 'freedom' that in some anarchic way always comes before itself. We can't think this freedom in terms of any signification without first anticipating it. Any such anticipatory signification contradicts the requirement of 'surprise', in Nancy's terms. That impasse is the requisite 'surprise' of freedom, which includes as much possibility of evil as of good. First freedom, then decision about good or evil – that is Nancy's ordering of ethics. This is evil, then, not as the corruption of the good, but as the possible decision of the free – a more unforgiving formula, even if one of 'open immanence' (Hutchens 2005: 64): 'To write freely is to share singularly in community's sense, to shatter its substantial and conceptually accessible linkages and scatter them beyond the confines of discourses that promise only closed immanence' (ibid.: 15). In such a formulation, freedom is no guarantee of justice, although it is a condition for it.

Words, then, are always tidying up behind the 'surprise' that made them possible in the first place. They begin in that rupture of sense that exceeds discourse. We want to posit the same 'freedom' in relation to sexual freedom and more generally to 'touch freedom'. It *is*, rather than is good or bad. Its sense *is*, and precedes signification. Thus its rationalisation is never its 'cause', which is a desire that precedes its expression as 'desired', yet will always seek to deny that prevarication.

Finally, in this chapter, we want to consider a number of issues that have arisen. First, if Derrida is right about Kant's view of 'touch' as the clumsiest of the senses, we want to disagree. It seems true that touch is the least studied of the senses in our culture – 'least research attention' (Autton 1989: 4), and it is probably also the case that touch has been the least 'theorised' of the senses, as well as subject to the greatest moral and religious suspicion. But that makes it the most neglected of our senses, rather than the clumsiest. Perhaps it seems clumsy because our thinking about it has been rudimentary. Perhaps 'skin deep' should be praise rather than criticism, invoking the all surface of all depth.

In theorising touch, we have thus far claimed both a corporeal and an incorporeal moment in touch as an 'event'. The incorporeal, the intangible, we might say, carries the excess – as promise, threat, punishment, hatred, pleasure, reward, even indifference – and it defines the touch, in its nature, in its reception, in its very being as 'touch' or even 'not-touch'. It redefines touch as feeling, through the singular thinking of plural context, self and other. It is a penumbra of signification, wherein touching is separated by thinking from feeling, and so in a certain sense, feeling happens twice, at either 'end' of the event of touch which thereby experiences a recursive erasure. This is the touch that cannot be itself, can only come after itself, yet whose presence can hardly be doubted as a transaction between bodies. As one kind of metonymy, it expresses what we want to call, after Nancy, the 'freedom' of touch: 'the fold in which thinking articulates freedom and freedom articulates thought' (Hutchens 2005: 65). But part of the relation is also one of reflexivity – touch touching itself, the 'auto-heterology of touch', as Nancy puts it (ibid.: 55). To touch in any context is to give, to make an offering of some kind, but it is also contradictory at another level, because the reflexive nature of the act means that that which gives also takes, in an impossible offering.[11] Most often, touching touches, and is touched in return (royalty, god and the doctor excepted). Again, in Nancy's terms it is an act between singularities who can only be singular through a plurality of being, in a 'with' relation that he defines as follows: 'It is neither "me" or "you"; it is what is distinguished in the distinction, what is discreet in the discretion' (Nancy 2000: 33) and '"Self" defines the element in which "me" and "you", and "we", and "they", can take place' (ibid.: 95), as Nancy focuses on the 'plural singularity of "us"' (Nancy 1993b: 147). Such constellations recall earlier, unrelated work on contemporary research identities, 'A Meyouthemus: occult pronouncement of the proscribed "I"' (Stronach 2002a: 294). At any rate, it is in this manner that Nancy conjures up the 'plural singularity of "us"' (Nancy 2000: 147).

Thus far, we can say that the 'survol' of touch mobilises all the senses – that 'tactile corpus' of sense that Derrida writes about – that it does so through several interacting metonymies, one transformative (touch/meaning/feeling), another reflexive (self-touching, touched), and each acting on the other and on itself. Both extensive and intensive, in their co-mingling they roll into each other what used to be a 'psychology' and a 'sociology', though certainly not in the unity of a new discipline. There is a vital *aporia* in the economy of touch, where the physical body appears 'intact' and where precisely it starts what we want to call, drawing once more on Nancy's more general thinking on thinking, the 'surprise' of its self. Touch touches precisely what it touches and cannot touch: that is its central paradox. It faces itself, which is no self at all, in the kind of relation of linked opposition with which we introduced this chapter.

Touching on Nancy on touching

This chapter works on Nancy's notion of 'freedom' as well as his ideas on 'touch'. We need to say a little about how Nancy sees 'free' relations between the 'singular' and the 'plural' – terms he uses to get away from conventional thinking about 'individuals', 'autonomy', 'society' and the 'collective'. In particular he is interested in 'being-in-common' and how the relation 'with' might apply to human conviviality.

Nancy argues for a 'Copernican revolution', whereby 'Social Being' is rethought in terms of itself and the possibility of its freedom (Nancy 2000:

57): 'to be human is to be incessantly surprised by the events of the world and of thinking itself' (Hutchens 2005: 62). Nancy is looking for a new way of understanding the social, avoiding the teleologies and genealogies of Enlightenment or Romanticism, and the various nostalgias or utopias of 'community', or conventional moves made on the individual/collective axis.[12] In looking to define the 'with-ness' of the individual; and its relation with the plural, he looks for a more anarchic sense of relation, yet one which is fully connected to the individual as inevitably related to, as well as differing from, the singular person. In particular he is interested in 'surprise', the unpredictable, and its stubborn refusal to give way to sciences of the social, or other forms of prediction: 'History is perhaps not so much that which unwinds and links itself, like the time of causality, as that which surprises itself' (Nancy 2000: 15).[13] In that quotation, we hear the echo of de Sade's scepticism about cause and effect. Such surprise (which always must surprise itself as such and so is irreducible to any form of prediction or anticipation) is 'a mark of freedom' (ibid.). Basically, he is arguing for a notion of freedom that is always the necessity of its own thinking that precedes itself, hence the 'surprise' of the 'freedom of thinking'. He attaches that notion to a different sense of the relation of individuals as 'singular plural': 'Philosophy needs to recommence, to restart itself from itself against itself, against political philosophy and philosophical parties' (ibid.: 25).

This kind of call is not uncommon in philosophies of difference (rather than some transcendent Same). 'Surprise' is expressed differently by Deleuze in *The Logic of Sense* but the family resemblance is striking:

> For personal uncertainty is not a doubt foreign to what is happening, but rather an objective structure of the event itself, insofar as it moves in two directions at once, and insofar as it fragments the subject following this double direction.

> (1969/90: 3)

Nancy extends Heidegger's thinking on *Dasein* and especially *Mitsein*, developing notions of 'co-originarity' (Nancy 2000: 27). We are not concerned here with a full exposition of those ideas – which are in any case a sketch rather than a full philosophy, or rather anti-philosophy. As we've seen, Nancy places the 'surprise' of thinking as a freedom that comes before discourse. Noting the contradictory ambition, he tries to posit in the self-contradictory 'address' of philosophy an account that goes beyond discourse, putting into words what words as yet are unable to say, as such. His notion of the decision, as freedom, seems close to Derrida's:

> Decision, or freedom, is the *ethos* at the groundless ground of every ethics. We have to decide on contents and norms. We have to decide on laws,

exceptions, cases, negotiations: but there is neither law nor exception for decision.

(Nancy 1993b: 163)

This sounds like the Derrida of 'Force of Law' (1992). Invoking the same 'incalculable' criterion, he then goes on to elaborate a notion of good and evil. Not only does freedom come before either, it presents them as the possibilities of freedom itself, acknowledging 'the possibility of evil's positive presence in the very affirmation of freedom itself' (Hutchens 2005: 84). Circling around a number of familiar markers of contemporary evil, he returns to Auschwitz as an evil whose aftermath is a kind of cultural defining of the occidental, adding an illuminating comment:

'Wickedness does not hate this or that singularity: it hates singularity as such and the singular relation of singularities' (Hutchens 2005: 128). Such an account has striking relevance for audit discourses on 'touch', and provides us with an account of singularity, experience and freedom that we draw on in developing a notion of 'free touch'.

The disgrace of touch

First, we have argued, after Nancy, that 'freedom' comes before any decision for good or evil. There is no 'freedom for the good', only a 'knowledge that cannot avoid the inscription of evil, in one way or another, in freedom' (Nancy 1993b: 123). It follows that any system of audit that pre-empts such a freedom by deciding in advance a regime of proscription and precaution is a form of unfreedom. A proper touch, then, is an improper freedom. It is a restriction founded on precaution and (usually falsely) perceived risk. There is a further consequence. The discourse of precautionary 'touch' sexualises the very relations it attempts to police, by inserting possible accusations/ error/evil as part of the everyday. The unfreedom multiplies its own pollution further since 'abuse' can lie in precaution as well as neglect. We extended Nancy's argument to a notion of 'free touch' as analogous to 'free speech'. Licence, of course, is unacceptable, conflating as it does the certain risk of chaos with the virtue of an uncertain anarchy. We will return later to the notion of 'free touch', relating it to the chapter on Summerhill. Here, we claim that it is a necessary idea, in relation to all the senses and not just to the privileged political space of a so-called 'free speech'. If we are to end in freedom, then we must begin with it, and any and all qualification must be subordinate.

Nancy refers to 'the modern knowledge of evil' (in Hutchens 2005: 123). He indicates a modern fascination with 'evil' – 'the diabolic or satanic' (ibid.) – that runs from de Sade to contemporary horror movies. He notes philosophy's complicity in recent genocides; his mentor Heidegger offered a 'silent justification' (ibid.: 132) for Nazi atrocities. 'Auschwitz' is the master metaphor of our times, and it continues to have and to generate many synonyms.[14] Our argument is that such 'horror', including its more Gothic elements, is deeply embedded in audit discourses on 'touch'. It is well known in psychological literature that touch is necessary and nurturing, as well as more simply comforting and pleasurable, but a kind of ruthless 'puritanism' prevails. Touch has been made unclean in the anthropology of audit, even if its absence so obviously constitutes another kind of abuse: the ectopic forced back into the womb of accountability. The abuse of omission is much preferred to the suspicion, however false and remote, of commission. Better all the sins of omission than one sin of commission – that is audit's watchword. Better safe than sane. This is a more postmodern 'knowledge' of evil. It may be that such false alarms are a helpful distraction from other, more real, horrors enacted in our name. It is also the case that the 'singularity' of touch is subordinated to a more collective assumption of guilt, in ways that Nancy might recognise. The whole universalism of 'touch' regimes is undermined by Nancy's notion of 'being singular plural' because his invocations of separation and sharing are condemned equally in a regime where universal pre- and pro-scription is based on presumptions of collective culpability that tolerate no exception in the claimed interests of 'equality', 'transparency' and 'accountability'.

Equally postmodern may be the odd relation between pornography and moral audit in our society. We started this chapter with an examination of the ways in which 'exhibition and prohibition collide in pornographic display'. We saw that collision in the chapter on Summerhill and elsewhere. That collusion/collision is highly functional in media terms (it 'sells') and it enables media to face in two different directions at the same time. The first direction appeals to a false nostalgia – for moral times, decency, modesty, obedience to due authority. The second direction points towards pornography, sexual abuse, paedophilia and child molestation, as a growing cancer in an increasingly sick society. A falsified past and an illusory present (statistically speaking) are deployed in order to generate the need for a more authoritarian and restrictive future. It is becoming familiar that 'freedom' can only be saved if we willingly (freely, democratically, urgently) undermine it for the greater virtue of security. This postmodern notion of 'sacrificial freedom' – an insane *pharmakon* if ever there was one – is developed in the 'linked opposition', the 'collusive antagonisms within the same circuit' which we earlier noted. It stands in obvious contrast to the nature of an 'open immanence, on the contrary, [which] is *monistic,* the single sense that is the world of material bodies and the singular events of their relation' (Hutchens 2005: 35).

The list of *pharmakon* grows by the day, as panics proliferate. The dangers are always there, but it is the way in which they are so similarly expressed, weighed, and disseminated that are of interest here. There seem to be new ways of fearing the Other, as terrors proliferate. In the past the Other was most often expressed in threatening collectivities, Communism, Capitalism, Godlessness. They confronted us from outside the gate. Now the enemy is within, unseen, un-uniformed. He attacks with a singular fury, in exemplary violence rather than catastrophic mass attack. Within 'touch' discourse, the paedophile is the terrorist, abductor, seducer, contaminator of 'the primal risk object' of the child. He (or occasionally she) undertakes acts of individual befriending, entering the community from within. So too with the perception of Islamic terror – from within, indistinguishable, also 'grooming', also 'preying on' and 'targeting' unsuspecting and naïve youth, removing them from their families and their common allegiances. The DfES argues that 'extremist individuals have been known to "groom" likely recruits, to "befriend vulnerable students" who of course are thereby "targeted"' (DfES 2007).[15] Here, for us, the 'primal risk object' is democracy, freedom, 'our way of life'. There is a new generic figure of infiltration, rooted in the individual, the micro-network, the cell, the subterfuge, morphing over time, but always in wait for us with an absolutely unfettered desire to deliver a deadly touch.[16]

We conclude that incorporating freedom within a frame of restrictions (or licences) is to rest freedom on a founding unfreedom. Free speech is our analogy: it must have its equivalents in the other senses, including 'free touch'. Otherwise, a means of communication is blocked off, and also, as we have seen, corrupted. The auditing of touch as national, prescriptive, prior to any considerations of context, is just such an unfreedom. For those who say such freedom is a licence for corruption, we say reread the Summerhill chapter and burn your copy of *Lord of the Flies*. We have tried in this chapter to consider a theory of 'touch', or of feeling, as we have preferred it. We have given illustrations of 'tangents' where issues of body/touch/senses are prominent in relation to parts of our argument – to put 'flesh' on the 'body' of touch, as it were. In so doing, we argued against both the surfaces and the depths of the body, arguing for a circulation and co-mingling – a copulation of the senses in sense-making might be better. It is in these ways that we have tried to make sense of the senses, of the possibilities of their freedom, and the relation of 'sense' among them. The following five chapters relate directly to our research and our attempt to make sense of our case studies.

Chapter 6

Case study
Early years settings

We have clearly established that many aspects of contemporary life are governed by fears and anxieties in relation to childhood abuse. In addition to concerns regarding abuse, many also fear disasters, diseases, medicines, environmental catastrophes, stray asteroids, wars, food, the internet, children walking to school, unsupervised children's activity (once known as play) and childhood obesity: 'you don't know if you dare do *anything* any more, and I'm just not sure where it's all leading to be honest' (playgroup worker). As we've already seen in the case of Father Christmas, it isn't only professionals who are fearful; Furedi (2001) tracked changes in parental attitudes through advice columns in *Nursery World* over an 80-year period and identified what he termed 'paranoid parenting'. Whereas parents may previously have worried about a particular aspect of their child's behaviour, they now seemed overwhelmed by the sheer weight of issues which contribute to the public panic about child safety. He cited examples: how the remote possibility that a child might choke to death on a small toy in a packet of cereals has led to demands to ban them; and how baby walkers on sale for many years have been withdrawn, in case children topple down the stairs. It has been noted that Dr Spock's (author of the post-war Bible of parenting guides) widow has recently remarked that Dr Spock would have been 'horrified by today's avalanche of advice' to parents (McDermott 2007). Fears are about nothing and everything and are underpinned by a sense of powerlessness; they appear from somewhere 'out there' and never 'in here': 'I think it evolved from that case from Newcastle, up North, that massive Child Protection thing. [Cleveland?] Yes'! The fears of paranoid parents of very young children conjoin with those of practitioners in early years settings, and as a result: 'We don't trust each other . . . more and more of us are feeling less trustworthy [sic] towards other people' (playgroup manager).

Early research stories

Such ideas were not new to us as a research team; we were already aware from the pilot studies, the survey returns and from personal experience that the early years context was just as affected by the no touch panic (see earlier chapters), as with settings dealing with older children and young people. We knew that many child-care workers felt concern about aspects of their role, including some which on the face of it could appear to be quite straightforward, such as picking up a fallen and injured child. Similarly, we were aware that it is common for staff, rather than intervening directly, to show an injured child how to open the medical box, take out a plaster, and instruct them in how to attend to their injury themselves, without ever touching the child at any time. Inconsistencies were common; for example, we had been informed by a playgroup worker that a particular child was 'always saying his "willy" was sore, but I wouldn't look at it. I just gave him a hug and let his mum know so that she can deal with it'. Yet such an account was completely at odds with another response: 'Once, a child I minded said something about being in mum and dad's bed and it made me a bit worried. I listened out for any more information from the child'. The first comment appeared to suggest that the playgroup leader was worried she will be accused of sexual abuse if she checks the little boy's 'willy', yet the governmental imperative of child protection is to the contrary, since one symptom of sexual abuse in young boys could be a sore 'willy'. The second response indicates a worker 'panicked' by incest as an issue, to such an extent that any young child having a hug in their parent's bed could be considered as offering evidence of abuse.

Such concerns and confusions would similarly be expressed by parents. A mother had informed a member of staff at her child's playgroup that she was not happy with them wiping her three-year-old son's bottom (Powell *et al.* 2004). The staff member explained that help is offered only if the child requested it, which he had done. His mother insisted that if her son needed his bottom wiped the playgroup should ring her, insisting that staff were not to wipe it ever again, and only after a lengthy exchange on the practicalities of the situation was it agreed that staff would inform her of any toileting that had taken place when she picked him up. Choices and motives are hard to interpret here, but this mother appeared on the face of it to prefer her child to be dirty, smelly and sore, rather than allow him to be touched by a trained member of staff. Again this response can be contrasted with another: 'I would not be leaving my children at nursery if I did not trust all the members of staff not to touch them inappropriately'. The first mother is apparently motivated to 'protect' her child from risky professionals while the second mother seems less bothered about both her own motives and those of staff members (which would once have suggested innocence, but in the current climate of panic is unfortunately just as likely to suggest neglect). Children are not immune to or ignorant of the prevailing confusions and contradictions and can turn this to their own advantage:

> We had a little boy and he pooed in his pants every session . . . He wasn't daft though, cos he'd say: 'Well now you will have to phone my mummy, and my mummy will come and get me', and he was right!

Such examples provided the backdrop to this case study.

Research setting

For the purpose of the ESRC funded research the early years case study comprised two playgroups, both of which adjoin primary schools in the North West of England. Given the young age of the children the data collection with them included extensive periods of observation. One of the playgroups is situated next to a Church of England school in a semi-rural location where the immediate catchment area includes a predominantly white but otherwise broad social mix of parents and children, and includes some children who travel a greater distance because of the school's religious affiliation. The second playgroup is situated in an urban and socially mixed area and includes a few children of mixed-race parentage. Again, as appears typical for nursery settings, a few children travel some distance in order to attend as a result of parents' previous positive experiences and/or the group's reputation. The playgroups have been operational for approximately 14 and 17 years and the managers in post 4 and 17 years. There are presently 32 and 65 children on roll. In one playgroup the staff includes one man who has worked there for four years, having been appointed after completing successful NVQ placements. Both playgroups meet in modern purpose-built single-storey brick buildings in their own plots fenced off from the neighbouring primary schools. One has a gate which is kept locked, and both are surrounded by small garden areas. Both playgroups are bright with many windows (although in one, the windows are too high for children to see out – or maybe this prevents others from seeing in) and are full of children's toys including board games, dolls, pushchairs, cooking corners, medical corners, jigsaws, building blocks and so on. The walls are decorated with pictures and notices and the atmosphere in both playgroups is warm, colourful and welcoming.

Touch and meaning

Initially as a research team we had tended to the view that touching was a binary which related to touching or not-touching. We had considered whether to use the word 'touch' or whether to use euphemisms such as 'inter-action', 'communication', since the power of the word, as we had noted in the survey returns, seemed so loaded. However, we soon discovered it wasn't just the word 'touch' which created a problem, but almost any word used to describe any form of touching behaviour:

> I wouldn't like to think that somebody has gone home and said: 'Claire was cuddling me for ages today' and I'd be thinking: 'Oh God it wasn't like that', because you can't explain that can you? It's the words and the way they sound.

> (playgroup leader)

Then seeing/not-seeing came into it. Children are dressed in public (privacy and modesty being sacrificed for 'safety'). In order to be protected from sexual abuse, children are publicly displayed in acts of toileting, or being changed, either through being in the view of the entire nursery, or being looked at by more than one adult. Safety was only assured by a doubling of the intrusion (two adults needing to be present for all intimate care routines, not one). One researcher watched a toileting scene from afar, turned away, and self-incriminated herself in the process as she felt like a Peeping Tom. There appeared to be a number of progressively expanding circles in this scenario, in which the researcher observes and therefore adds to the concern, the manager addresses the larger context of media scares via guidelines, their interactions confirm the significance of the concern, while the parents mainly claimed that the playgroup is brilliant while still acknowledging the effects of scares 'out there' that they generally defined as realistic in 'the current climate', and a 'sad indication of the times we live in'. Each feeds off the other, although it might be better to think of it as simultaneously self-feeding and self-limiting, since the 'ecologies of practice' as evidenced throughout limit both the possibility of adherence to the letter of any laws, and also the possibility of belief in the dark realities behind any such law.

Care and education

Our observations in the two playgroups demonstrate the tensions arising from the unique position of early years settings, which provide a bridge between the home and the school. Yet governments, parents, and others have different expectations as to what this bridge should entail. These expectations and differences change according to whatever is current policy, or the current trend, yet practice often lags behind 'policy', and professionals in any case have their own views and will have trained at different times, when different practices were the norm. Balancing care and education in these settings is never straightforward:

> I just think they're so young and you know they're away from their mums aren't they for the first time . . . it's a big thing if they fall over, obviously they're going to be upset, and then they're going to miss their mum you know they need that bit of intimacy.

> (playgroup worker)

Yet a preference for less 'care' and more 'education' is what seems to be required currently as this serves to address the audit agenda, with its need for children to read, write, and do sums at earlier and earlier ages (for example, children as young as two having mandatory portfolios that identify their learning needs and how these will be met and by whom). A by-product (intentional or not) for child-care workers focusing more on education is that this provides them with one way of 'professionalising' their role, and arguably helps them rationalise the 'no touching' practices as expressed in earlier chapters, which otherwise seem unworkable:

> I think the education side of it has almost overtaken the care side of it. They need that. At one time, maybe it was an extension of home, and a transition point between the home and the school, so there was lots of care and cuddles, and only some education. When I was at college I sensed there was a swing from the care side to the education side.

> (playgroup manager)

But as one playgroup worker observed, not all early years settings are the same, and there are distinctions and differences within and between childminders, nannies, playgroups, state-run day nurseries, and privately run nurseries, and typically confusion in understandings of these differences:

> I'm wondering if when your child's in a day nursery . . . the staff are more inclined to see your child in 'babe' terms, but if a nursery is attached to a school, there is probably more of a 'schooly' kind of atmosphere, say as a class. It's not such a common thing to have children sitting on laps etc. . . . Yet I've seen a day nursery where the staff are more, you know . . . [More formal?] Yes, that would fit with the whole ethos in a way, where with a playgroup, you might go in with a child who is crying and unsettled and that child might be sitting on that member of staff's lap while they're saying 'Mummy will be back soon, don't cry', let's distract them kind of thing, whereas in a situation like a formal state nursery which I've worked in . . . let's get on with it as though this is a school.

In spite of the differences that emerged in interviews with both parents and staff who had personal and professional experience across the whole range of provision, most adults accepted that small children had particular and specific needs that necessitated their touching, but that touching practices needed to be age-appropriate. Yet worrying about every aspect of touching behaviour has meant that many now find difficulty in judging what exactly is age-appropriate, as this could vary for each and every child:

> With little children if you didn't have any physical contact at all, even it can be something like when you hold them by the shoulders to turn them

round to face you, otherwise they'd be ambling round aimlessly, and they need more physical guidance. But if you did that with an older child, grab them by the shoulders and turn them to face the door say, it would be very intrusive and not the right thing to do, and the difficulty is when do they stop being young enough to do that?

Such judgements continue in primary/junior schools (see Chapter 7) and even parents share this confusion, and worry about interpreting their own children's needs correctly. The following quote was from a parent of a young child who was attempting to decide at what age touching becomes less appropriate, but she had difficulty with this:

> They don't always want cuddles from their parents as they get a bit older do they, so I don't know what age you'd cut it off really. I mean, it would be different for everyone wouldn't it? I mean some older kids probably still go to their Mum and Dads for cuddles.

Only in part, then, can tensions and uncertainties about touching behaviour be considered a reflection of tensions between the imperatives of care and education.

Child protection and adult protection

Identifying research themes in the research data was not straightforward. The ever-expanding circles of concern appeared more layered than stratified. Concerns were all interrelated in ways that make any selection of categories too clumsy. However, it soon became apparent that practice in early years settings is most accurately understood as being dominated by imperatives of adult protection rather than child protection. Professionals in these settings (as in others) are primarily concerned with 'covering their backs':

> Occasionally you get parents coming back and saying my child says so and so has hit them (another child maybe) but again, you can't do anything about it, if you don't know at the time. But you've always got to be careful; you've got to be beyond reproach.

Any worker who chose not to follow defensive and staff protective procedures would be perceived as a risk. The organisation would be keen to place the risk firmly with the worker so as to distance themselves from any future hypothetical allegation:

> If somebody in my setting said: 'I completely and utterly refuse to wear rubber gloves for changing children, cleaning up or anything else', I think I'd be very inclined to say: 'Well there's a statement, you sign it,

and date it'. It's a sick society I know, but you've just got to cover yourself all the way . . . I'm the world's worst . . . but in the end you've only
yourself to blame.

The rhetoric of risk and protection, and the discontinuity between the imperative (looking after children) and the nature of everyday action (ensuring the
protection of workers) is an issue for subsequent and wider discussion.

Child-led practice

In spite of much confusion most parents were clear that their children's needs
came first:

> I'd be mortified if my daughter had fallen over and didn't receive a hug,
> even if it means sitting them on the knee and patting the top of their leg,
> or rubbing their back, because that is reassurance. A plaster – I'd be
> mortified again if I went to pick her up and she'd gashed her leg open
> and they hadn't put a plaster on. I'd be angrier they'd not addressed the
> cut than with any touching. I think the touching bit when a child falls
> over completely goes out the window because you want to see that they're
> all right, and see to the gash on the knee or elbow.

But just when it appears that some kind of 'common sense' practice prevails,
the belief that touching children should be child-led is introduced:

> When they're little it's easy to give a hug . . . but when they're older . . .
> I don't know now, it varies, sometimes you hug them, but I'm always a
> bit cautious, perhaps I respond, but don't always initiate.
>
> (playgroup leader)

'Child-led touching' was additionally confusing because adults would need to
decide what was appropriate asking, but even this wasn't straightforward as
children might need their nappy changing for example, but be unable to ask:
'It's about the difference between the child coming to you and you going to
the child, but then you wouldn't leave a distressed child anyway, wherever
they were, would you?' So the difference between unasked-for and asked-for
touch can be blurred. Crying, for instance, can be read as 'asking' for a cuddle,
so can being 'upset'. But when 'asking' seemed not to be working some children would be persistent:

> But she came back three times to ask if she could sit on my knee. Now to
> me that's giving me a message, she wants to sit on my knee, but not for
> any reason, maybe she just wants that contact.

The legitimating of unasked-for touch is one of the distinct features of touch with *young* children. Young children are eligible for unrequested touch often within the legitimating structure of *loco parentis* and the corollary is the entitlement to *ask* for touch, such as a hug, or help with dressing. Yet failing to ask for touch is sometimes represented as not 'natural' for young children:

> What happens is, we have children who have experiences that make it very difficult for them to accept touch and give touch and that impacts on them from a very early age. These children become touch defensive and they may be the ones who then, as they're getting older, they become aggressive and quite brusque and they push people away, they have lots of barriers around them, they're emotionally defensive.
>
> (adviser on behavioural difficulties)

Even with these young children there appears to be a preference for portraying the child as 'asking for it' so as to avoid being (mis)interpreted as following one's own desires rather than responding to the child's, or ignoring the child who does not know what's good for them. But 'asking for it' is also central to paedophilic discourse so any protection it offers to the adult will be fragile. As researchers we soon adopted the generalised confusion as the modus operandi:

> I became aware that I'm getting an overwhelming urge to touch some of these children on their cheeks, heads, but stop myself – not sure why. Stopping touching is taking much more concentrated effort than touching would. I don't think it would be inappropriate, but am mindful that most practice seems to claim an adherence to the 'if the child seeks it first' rule, arguably these children are, they're leaning on my pad, against my knees, and so on, but – I become a recipient of touch rather than a giver.
>
> (field work notes)

In such situations the issue of adult protection frequently dominated the nature of the workers' response. Given that most adults choosing to work in nursery settings claim to love their work, and to love the children in their care, this conflicting concern with actually 'caring' appears to be almost schizophrenic.

Civilising controls

From the research data produced by the project as a whole, it was perhaps the two playgroup settings which best illustrate the idea that children's bodies are subjected from birth to the civilising controls of adults (see Chapter 1;

Elias 1939/2000; Tobin 1997). Adults were frequently observed controlling all aspects of children's bodily processes: 'Go to the toilet Ben, and *be* careful'; 'Kyle did you wash your hands?'; 'Dean did you wash your hands when you went to the toilet?' and so on. Such comment made an incessant backdrop to all group activity, but the data suggested an even larger 'touching' context still. The children go through the nursery experience with a whole series of broader touching instructions. For example, a child far from the site of a loud crashing noise exclaimed: 'I didn't do it'. An adult reassured her with: 'Of course not, you weren't there', but in the child's head, she had 'touched' something without permission, and felt the need to get her disclaimer in early. This was a disciplinary kind of touching, a tic-like anticipatory working of self-regulation, surprisingly similar to that expressed by the self-reporting teacher in Chapter 1, who placed his arm around a pupil who was upset and then promptly reported himself to a deputy head!

There were other incidents of 'touching', for example, an imperative for the 'bottom' to be firmly on the floor during story-time, for the feet not to be kicking. There was also licit touching that was carefully and comprehensively policed, including many hand-washing instructions and checking, and inconsistent attempts to control the hygiene of baking sessions, while the hygiene threats from running noses and snotty hands were disregarded. The cleansing therefore appears more or less ritualistic and perhaps performs a civilising role rather than an actual cleansing role. 'Touching' could be variously interpreted and regulation extended to include the touch/grip of possessing, taking away, giving, claiming, stalking, staring, stealing. The contexts were multi-layered; were practical and experiential, and surfaced as 'issues' with competing registers of appropriateness. These included health and safety, child protection, covering your back both literally, by not picking up children to wave goodbye to mum on one occasion, and metaphorically, by taking risk precautions (see below).

Workers' confusion and guilt

Confusion over what is legislation, what is the status of guidelines whether internally or externally imposed, and what is good practice was further compounded by the guilt expressed by many, and which generally resulted in over-defensive behaviour:

> Plasters. Now here's a good one, Quality Assurance officer again, she said: 'I notice in your First Aid box (we've got some pink plasters in there – I'd forgotten about that – they shouldn't really be there) you've got plasters in your First Aid box, you're not allowed to put plasters on children'. So I said: 'Oh, well, when I was at College, the first-aid tutor said to me: "Blood spillages must be covered, and plasters are quite effective if it's just a small spillage"' . . . So she said 'You have to use melolin and

micropore tape'. And I said: 'Well I'm only going on the guidelines I was given at college'. I said: 'Obviously there are different ideas and thoughts on it' and she did get back to me, and they'd had a big debate about it, and she said as long as we get parental permission we can use plasters, but she'd added: 'Of course Mum could provide the plasters and the child could put their own plaster on' . . . So of course we got out our own consent forms . . . so I've added on to that now: 'Maybe if necessary, may we put a non-allergenic plaster on your child?'

(playgroup manager)

Those playgroup workers not caught up in such confusing situations and who are seemingly still able to react more appropriately would nevertheless feel guilt if they did in fact touch a child:

Another little girl . . . came running back one day, quite bizarrely, threw her arms around me and said: 'I love you, Mrs Smith' and she'd never done it before, and I thought should I have pushed her away? I mean you don't go cuddling the children, you don't go and pick them up and start cuddling them, but you don't reject them either.

Generally guidelines were regarded as an imposition:

To attempt to introduce guidelines . . . would be counter-productive and a step away from the high quality of care offered by the professional carers, far better they use judgement and trust.

(manager of nursery)

I know there are horrible people out there but I do find it sad when I hear school staff tell me that there is no physical contact with the children . . . What kind of adults are we bringing up?

(manager of 'Out of School Club' for young children)

In spite of the general confusion children somehow managed to find their own way through:

Children learn which are the adults they're physical with and which they're not, it's quite interesting, isn't it?

(playgroup manager)

Such differences relate both to distinct mechanisms for dealing with (internalising or rejecting) the potential for guilt and self-policing, and also different degrees of willingness to adhere to guidelines and to accept 'risk'.

Gender tails

Gender and sexuality are of particular concern in early years settings. Men have tended to be regarded with suspicion (see earlier chapters). However, the playgroup that employed a man claimed it had not experienced too much difficulty:

> Dave doesn't feel that he's experienced any difficulties by being a man. Occasionally a parent may look a bit surprised when they first bring a child and see him, but this surprise very quickly disappears and there hasn't been any incident of parents not using the playgroup because of Dave, as has been reported elsewhere.
>
> (playgroup manager)

But the claim that Dave and his manager agreed on him performing in the same way as everyone else was later contradicted:

> I must admit, it's not very often that Dave does toilets. [And is that because he's been told not to or he chooses not to?] No, neither, it's just circumstances, we work as a team and it depends on who's doing what and who's available to supervise the toilets. [And it's not been an issue with parents . . .?] We've had one or two parents who've said the children are a bit scared of Mr Bunbury. You need to meet him, he's about six foot something, six foot three maybe and he's not a skinny little bloke either, he's quite stocky and he's very Mr Bunburyish! He's lovely with the children and they all warm to him in the end but I think, the parents initial reaction is: 'Oh, does he work here?', and they are a bit taken aback, but they soon become very reassured.

Later observation suggested Dave was actually quite reluctant to 'do toilets'. Meanwhile the playgroup without a man on the staff team hypothesised:

> Researcher: Incidentally, has it ever arisen that a man has applied for a job, and would you consider it, and would it make any difference?
>
> Playgroup manager: For *these* staff he'd have to be good looking! We'd all be on the interview panel!!! (*lots of laughter and joking – then*)
>
> Playgroup worker: We hope that we'd be as fair with a male applying as we would with a female applying.

Some female parents were also supportive of male workers in child care and related settings:

> Some people . . . can't see why a man would like to work with little children. I think this is why we haven't got so many male nurses. If you think about it we are seen to by female nurses when it comes to the bits and

bobs, having a catheter fitted, it's always a female but wouldn't it be nice for once if it was a male, but they're so few and far between. My health visitor was a man, he'd got no kids and he said he wasn't in it for the wrong reasons: 'I'm in it because I love babies and kids'. He was brilliant, far better than some of these health visitors we have now, that are mums.

Another example:

The men workers weren't allowed to shower the women [parent discussing their own work as a care assistant], but the female workers were showering the men, so I don't really see what's the difference then?

Notwithstanding that no doubt a paedophile would also claim: 'I'm not in it for the wrong reasons, I'm in it because I love babies and kids', these comments are interesting. As we have learned in earlier chapters, men are attributed with over-developed appetites for sexual wrong-doing in comparison to women and as such are considered sexually dangerous. Our case study examples seem untypical of society as a whole where there is generally more concern with men working in early years settings and in caring roles more widely. Perhaps though it is not surprising that only boys' genitals were mentioned in the research process:

The only other thing is the toileting, if you've got to wash a child down or wipe then, we do encourage them to do themselves, but then you've got to go through this amazing procedure of working out what the boys call their little tail and the most amazing names some of them come out with. [So how do you do that, do you ask them?] What do you call this? Sometimes they'll just look at you blank as if it's nothing and sometimes we try and encourage them by saying well could you hold it and point it down the toilet – it's really funny. [So would any of your staff hold it and point it down the toilet, or do you always get them to?] No. What I tend to do is get hold of their hand and use their hand to try and direct them.

and:

We think it's worse with little boys really . . . Because little boys sit on the toilet, some of the boys like to stand up and if they're not aiming in the right direction or are sitting down, it's like we need to 'tuck them in properly' and it's like touching them in their privates . . .

Gender issues are further compounded by a confused notion about some individuals' sexuality:

When I was at College there was a girl who was in a lesbian relationship, and she was a primary school teacher and somebody said . . . He didn't understand that her preferences were nothing to do with the children . . .

While gay men have been subject to these types of assumptions, the inclusion of lesbians is perhaps telling. However, young girls apparently still have no sexuality, as in Victorian times:

> The nurse places the stethoscope on the other boys' chest after he has lifted his jumper over his head, who then starts to giggle, then 'tweaks' his nipples a few times in the direction of the other two boys in what is best interpreted as a sexually suggestive way – all three giggle quite loudly. The stethoscope ritual is repeated and the rather provocative 'patient' makes a throaty [dirty?] sounding laugh – the three boys sound like a trio of leery old men propping up a bar. The playgroup leader hears this and swoops over with a 'What's going on over here? Pull your jumper down, we don't want to see tummies'.
>
> (observation notes)

It is unsurprising that touching behaviours with a potential for a sexualised interpretation should provoke a high degree of confusion and inconsistency within and between workers. Tummies here clearly signify much more than tummies. There is a displacement from nipples to tummies as presumably tummies are considered benign, unlike nipples and genitals. Nipples are silenced perhaps because they are normally associated with women. Similarly little girls' genitals generally have no name in professional contexts (beyond front bottoms!), and such silencing provides both a lack of language and therefore a lack of any response when it comes to dealing with little girls:

> After about a minute Leah brings the spatula and lies on top of Caitlin which involves some shuffling around until they are lying on top of each other, front to front, (an even more explicit sexual pose if one is inclined to think in these terms) Leah then places the spatula in Caitlin's mouth. This continues for a while without anyone seemingly noticing (or maybe not considering it significant as it's two girls).

Observing the uninterrupted 'gendered' play of young children was surprisingly mixed and typical stereotypical play was not always apparent:

> Meanwhile two boys (Ollie and Daniel) are hugging each other with great affection. Daniel in the spirit of fair play then starts to hug the boy on his other side who is sitting next to me.

and:

> The dolls' table is to my left, and for the next 45 minutes three or four girls and one boy play at dressing the dolls (mainly the Cindy type,

although there is a Cabbage Patch doll which the boy attends to). Initially the boy watches attentively, but starts to join in enthusiastically after about ten minutes or so.

If these children are typical then there seems some hope that as men they will be likely to consider 'caring' as an appropriate career choice. However, it seems just as likely that they will learn the ever-present dominant script and soon come to regard themselves as sexually dangerous.

Hygiene facts and phalluses

One of the main explanations offered in support of a no touch policy in these settings (apart from covering one's back and being seen to do the right thing) was a concern with disease (reminiscent of the young children playing kiss-chase and masturbating as discussed in the research in Ireland and the US – see Chapter 1). We had also noted this in previous research. Smith (2000) had observed a worker on the occasion of her birthday asking the children to give her a kiss, but she was quickly warned off by another worker referring to 'cold sores going around' (which was fictional). In that example most children gave kisses on the cheek and 'it was as though everyone had "clocked off" for the moment and enjoyed it for what it was, a celebration' (ibid.). Infection and an apparent concern with germs and bodily fluids was also evident in our research sample:

> I've got a feeling that it's something to do with all bodily fluids/spillages, you should wear gloves. But quite frankly, you don't always remember to put on gloves. When you're doing mass toileting, the last thing you think of is putting gloves on and it can be more of a mither [bother] than it's worth sometimes, but strictly speaking you should wear gloves . . . I mean if they were dirty I'd put gloves on straight away, but for the ordinary, everyday toileting, I wouldn't, like for pulling pants up. [So if a child cuts themselves, you just deal with it as if it was your own child?] Yes, with gloves on. [With gloves on! and is that because you think they've probably got some infection, or is because that's what everyone's doing?] No, it's just standard first aid procedure. [But it must be about some kind of infection then, mustn't it?] Yes, it's about HIV and AIDS, and like changing children who are dirty; you can actually contract Polio from that. I didn't know that, somebody told me that a few years ago, it was on a course or something, so it's another reason you should wear gloves, but a lot of it, is common sense. But to be honest, trying to put a plaster on a child's finger when you've got them stupid gloves on, if it hasn't stuck to you! On the odd occasion where we've had to change nappies, you've got them plastic gloves on and that sticky thing from the nappy sticks on your gloves, and you peel it off and you've got a big hole

in your glove, sometimes it's just not practical but at the end of the day, if you stick to standard hygiene then you should never be at risk yourself, and unfortunately, at the end of the day, you've got to think of yourself first. But everyone who works in a caring setting doesn't.

Yet further proof of the concern with staff protection rather than child protection in relation to 'hygiene' is also evident:

> At some point they both dress up in nurses' dresses . . . other children drift over (some pushing their children [dolls] in push chairs, rocking them so they won't be a nuisance) with various ailments, and are subsequently taken into the treatment room. The first patients include three police officers . . . Then the 'patients' are subjected to a battery of medical interventions. This always includes a spatula in the mouth (interesting double standards on the bodily fluids infection debate), 'open your mouth', various injections are applied orally and on other body parts, mainly arms and legs. The stethoscope (or other plastic contraption) is placed somewhere on the stomach which involves the nurse or the patient raising the jumper of the patient a few inches.

and on another occasion:

> Sarah is lying immediately to my right with her head next to my foot, a boy walks past and treads on Sarah's face, she cries and leaps up. A playgroup leader is there in a flash, 'Was it an accident?' It appears to have been so, leads her to the sink, takes a tissue and wipes her tears and her bleeding lip, this involves pressing Sarah's head against her front (again interesting slant on the bodily fluids debate – no plasters or nappies – but close attention to bleeding lip).

In these examples, the gloves are interesting. If the worker cares, they have to touch; they have to treat children like their own, but with gloves on. The many references to 'bodily fluids' and 'spillages' made the rubber gloves seem like moral contraceptives, avoiding any contamination of intimacy, ditto holding the hand that holds the willy. On reflection it was hard to avoid a satirical laugh at the role of the gloves in making it difficult to put on the plaster without tearing away some of the glove. The two prophylactics cancelled each other out instead of fortifying the hygiene. Other germ scenarios noted included HIV/AIDS and also polio (carried in faeces apparently). Yet there was also a different kind of licensed touch, via children's stethoscopes so that the nature of the game licensed access to the body/touch of another. However, concern with infections is not evident in children's dealing with each other and even with adults and children when attending to the bleeding lip, and such examples perhaps suggest that claims about infection are somewhat disingenuous.

Guidelines and professionalism

The playgroup managers and workers had mixed and sometimes contradictory feelings about the use of guidelines in respect of touching behaviours. One playgroup had interpreted our sending out the questionnaire asking about any guidelines they may have, as a suggestion that they *should* have them. They had subsequently written to all parents asking for advice and had prepared guidelines prior to the first visit. Yet they had discovered:

> it isn't possible to put anything into writing that will help [and therefore] any written guidelines won't help – most of what happens is human nature and you can't do anything effective to alter that . . .

> It doesn't matter how much you put in your documentation, there'll always be something missing. I think the other thing as well is, if you're putting everything in, dotting the Is and crossing every T, it makes it very difficult because all the while you're on your mettle – ooh, I can't do that, can't say that, can't touch that, and before you've finished, you're in a sterile situation when you don't know if you dare do anything any more and I'm just not sure where it's all leading to be honest . . .

The playgroup manager speaks here of a 'sterile situation' as the culmination of no-touch possibilities where everything ends in a 'knot' of proscriptions. The child becomes hyper-visible in these sorts of regimes. A spectacle for remedy where every move is demarcated, enacted in full visibility, previously licensed or proscribed. 'Sterile' is apt given its double sense of absolute cleanliness, and complete barrenness. But in these situations it could be argued that everyone (except the audit self) loses out. The following extract from an interview with one of the playgroup managers is included in full as it encompasses many of the difficulties encountered in current practice and was particularly influential in our decision making in finally considering guidelines to be more negative than positive in their effects:

> . . . And one of the things he's just learned to do [a boy described as having some behavioural difficulties] in the last few weeks is say 'no', he's very assertive, he likes his own way, he knows what he wants to do, and sometimes he'll comply and if you go and get his hand and lead him over, he'll come and join you. But on this particular day when the Ofsted inspector was in, he went out to play with a parachute (this is something that we sometimes do with them), we waft it up and down, the children can sometimes stand under it, or we put a ball on and bounce the ball on it. Now all the children can't obviously play with the parachute all at one go, so I selected x number of children. No before that, we were just wafting it up and down, fast and slow, up and down and he wanted to go under it his own way, and I said he couldn't do that. Now as he was

standing next to me I had hold of him around his wrist, holding the parachute. So he was holding the parachute, and I was holding his wrist. He wanted to join in but he wanted to go underneath. And I said: 'No you can't do that yet, we're doing this first', and then I picked some children to go underneath and 'cos I didn't pick him straightaway, he pulled away and stood in a corner. But this is after I'd had a hold of him and we've done all the wafting up and down, so he was kind of sulking in the corner, so I just ignored him . . . And then when it was his turn to go underneath he came back and then he went into a frenzy . . . He had a wonderful time . . . if the ball comes off there's always a mad dive and I wouldn't let him go because there's a clash of heads and I was telling them only one person must go for the ball and he wanted to go . . . so he didn't like that. So that was the end of that and I was feeling somewhat harassed by this time 'cos that's how it is if you don't give in to him. So when the Ofsted Inspector did her feedback she picked up on this and she said: 'In your policy document you say if the a child doesn't want to join in an activity you say they are provided with an alternative activity', so I said: 'Yes'. But she said: 'You didn't do that outside with that little boy'. So I said: 'Yes but that little boy wanted to join in the activity but he wanted to do it on his terms' And I said: 'He had to do what everybody else was doing for the safety of everybody involved'. 'But you could have let him go and read a book inside with a member of staff', so I said: 'Well that might have altered the staff ratio slightly and especially with the activity like the parachute we need all the staff members available'. 'But it said in your policy document that you could have sat with him' and da, di, da etc. (and this is what I was telling her), but to do that is me giving in to him having his way. But she wasn't satisfied with my answer I don't think. But like I pointed out he's got behaviour problems and it's agreed with the parent, the parents are quite happy for us to keep this firm line.

The conversation between the quality inspector and the manager is a good illustration of the kind of contradiction referred to throughout not only in this chapter but others too. The child who is difficult is made to wait his turn. The inspector notes that the playgroup's own regulations say that an adult should have taken him elsewhere to read, but the manager wants to teach him (and he has been improving, and his parents say he is improving) that he has to learn to take turns. The child is allowed to sulk, but the inspector sticks to the letter of the law, the playgroup's own law after all, even if it was only developed because the inspectorial regime forced the manager to produce it in the first place. This kind of disagreement throws into sharp relief the nature of an 'outside-in' professionalism which is pre-specified, comprehensive and rule-bound, as opposed to a more 'inside-out' professionalism with an open, virtue-based judgement not just of context but also of 'case' in the historical sense. Someone is always watching, and must be watched in their watching by making public and visible all procedures that might occasion a sense of risk that while statistically minimal has to be legislated for in its possibility in all situations. The same logic, if applied to air travel would permanently ground all planes; a tiny number do crash, but the logic of remote possibility works in the other direction, towards licensing, not proscription. Such ideas, produced through research in the early years setting, are relevant more generally, and many can be identified in the other case study data.

Chapter 7

Case study
Primary and junior schools

Helen Lawson

The school selected for this case study was an infant and junior school set in the midst of the Forest of Dean, Gloucestershire, a rural area of England. Iron ore and coal mining were very important industries for the area and the 'Forest Freeminer' tradition still exists. Anyone born in the Forest of Dean within the Hundred of St Briavels, and who has worked in a mine for a year and a day, has the right to open up their own coal mine. Those born in the Forest of Dean also have 'Forester's Rights' which gives them the right to graze their sheep and pigs in the Forest. The population in the region has been fairly static with people living and working their whole lives in a fairly small area. This school was established over a century ago and the main part of the school is a single storey, traditional, red-brick, Victorian building which up until a couple of years ago had changed very little. However the school has recently undergone quite a large amount of construction work and refurbishment which provides a new classroom, entrance and reception area and toilet block. It is a small, relatively isolated school with 80 pupils divided into three classes with roughly four boys for every three girls, and all the staff are female. Many of the pupils at the school are from families whose parents, grandparents and, in some cases, great grandparents attended. Unsurprisingly the head describes this school as 'family oriented':

> The actual school is run on a big family basis where everybody looks after each other and we try and do a family ethos approach . . . I mean because we're so small. There are only 80 children, all children know each other. We have buddy systems set up where some of the older children buddy the younger children, look after them, and they take that role really seriously. If a child falls over they cuddle them, they bring them in. And it's done very much on the basis as you would with your nuclear family.

The junior school provides a very interesting setting for examining touch between young children and professionals and, indeed, touch between young children. Often when they start school very young children still need help with a variety of activities such as toileting and dressing as in preschool contexts, and they often want and need physical reassurance from teachers and other adults within the school setting:

> We desperately want to try and keep the culture of this school and many other local schools like this, the same. We want to keep that family approach. We want to keep that because the care is all part of it. The parents know that if their child comes here and they're upset in any way that they're going to be comforted, that they're going to be looked after . . . if a child has an accident, I mean, we've got a duty of care to look after that child and to clean it up if you can't get hold of the parent, you know, so, you're not going to leave that child desperately trying to do the best that it can. You automatically go in and clear up.
>
> (headteacher)

As children progress up the school they require this sort of help and support less. Thus teachers and other professionals are working in an environment which is complex and ever-changing as each individual child develops. There is no automatic cut-off point that is reached once a pupil is a certain age. The amount of help that a pupil needs will depend on his or her needs. This is how one teacher tries to make sense of when and how to touch her pupils:

> There are certain areas on a child's body that I wouldn't touch. No way! And a lingering touch is out of the question. No way! I feel comfortable with a touch on the arm, a flat hand on their back. I rarely cuddle children even though children in Reception come looking for it. If they're very hurt or very distressed I might do so for a short while, until that child was ready to go, ready to move away.

The above concerns about where and how to touch a child, and for how long, seems at odds with the family ethos of the school as described by the head. For the head teacher there do not seem to be any worries about when, where and how to touch a pupil. For her, a pupil's needs come first, though she is aware that touching pupils is not without complications:

> . . . if they want a cuddle and want to be sitting on somebody's lap and cuddled that's what we do. So we take it very much from the child as to what the child is needing. Here all the staff are happy to do that though they're very, very much more aware these days that there could well be an issue. And they don't want to leave themselves open to any problems. When we go swimming we make sure that we've got two adults in each changing room so that there can't be any allegations made against any member of staff.

This highlights the fact that touch is not a simple one-way process. The adult is not always the instigator of touching that occurs between pupil and teacher. Often it is the child who comes to the adult for comfort and reassurance: 'In the playground children just literally run up to you for a cuddle and any adult that is related to the school, they come up and cuddle and they want that cuddle and that contact' (headteacher). For some teachers this presents them with a number of dilemmas. How long should I hug him for? Should she sit on my lap? Do I wait for him to break away, or do I do it first? What are the other teachers thinking? Is this right? But even though these worries are ever-present, teachers and adults working in this school felt strongly that to introduce guidelines on touch would be detrimental to the emotional well-being of the child:

> You come into the profession because you care about children, you care about the education of children and you want to make life better for them, and part of all that is the general well-being of the child where you're there like a surrogate mother, surrogate parent. You are, if they're not 100% well, giving them a cuddle, supporting them, you know, if things have gone bad, trying to prop them up and that's all part of it.

This is a feeling echoed by some of the children aged nine:

> Maria: If you were sad and there was no one there for you to cuddle I would feel really upset.
>
> William: So would I.
>
> Maria: People like cuddling Miss Burton; they'd be upset if she wasn't allowed to.

The first two observations (see below) present some of the issues raised above in more detail and later the reflections of some of the teachers on different forms of touch instigated and managed by the professional are addressed. These would appear to address functional, reassuring, rewarding, non-physical and controlling forms of touching at least. Further observational analysis also reveals that some touch instigated by the child includes more reassurance, attention-seeking, and even unconscious forms of touching.

A further interesting aspect in the primary setting is touching that happens between children. There is a considerable amount of rough and tumble; girls fiddle with each other's hair; they lean on and over each other and hug each other. There is also evidence of pupils' emergent sexuality.

The observations were carried out before the teachers were aware of exactly what was being observed. They knew the research was concerned with classroom interactions but the word 'touch' was avoided until the later interviews. In the first observation there are three adults present, a teacher and two assistants as the session consisted of three year groups (reception, year one and year two) and the assistants worked with different groups of children depending on their age/ability.

Observation notes with pupils aged five to seven

As Mrs Atkins walks round the tables explaining what she wants them to do she touches children on the tops of their heads and their shoulders, often to get their attention. There is a learning support worker, Miss Smith, sitting at a table with a group of children. As all the pupils settle down to work Mrs Atkins comes up to talk to me . . . a girl approaches her to ask for a crayon and touches Mrs Atkins' arm to attract her attention. Mrs Atkins puts her arm around her shoulder and bends down to listen to what she wants. She keeps her arm there as she walks the girl back to her seat. Another boy comes up to ask her a question and again Mrs Atkins puts her arm around his shoulder to listen to him and then steers him back to his seat by his elbow. Another boy, Ryan, is misbehaving – he won't share any of his crayons – and he is made to stand in a corner of the classroom facing the wall. After a very short while Mrs Atkins goes to talk to him. She bends down so that her face is level with his and there is no touching at all while she disciplines him. After his 'talking to' as the boy walks back to his place, she gently touches his back with both hands.

Two girls are leaning against each other while they work and there is quite a high level of noise. They frequently wander over to Mrs Atkins to ask her a question or to have their pencils sharpened by Miss Brook (assistant). There is a lot of 'accidental' touch as pencils are handed back and forth. A boy comes over to Miss Brook for his pencil to be sharpened and Mrs Atkins wants him to look at something on the wall behind him, so she touches him on the head: touch-point-touch-point, to attract his attention and show him where to look. Ryan is misbehaving again, this time lying all over the table. Mrs Atkins pulls him up by the arm and holds him firmly by the forearm while she tells him off. He tries to walk away but she won't let him go. Eventually he sits down in his place.

Mrs Atkins is helping Ryan . . . he is sitting down, she is standing behind him, leaning over him with both hands either side of him and her chin touching the top of his head. There is considerable body contact (her arms against his arms, her front on his back, her chin on his head). She moves away once she's talked him through what he should be doing but within seconds he is misbehaving again. She takes him by the arm and pushes him in front of her with her hands on his shoulders out of the classroom where she talks to him. She holds him by his wrist while she speaks to him; he tries pulling away and won't look at her. She takes both his hands and crouches down to talk very quietly to him. By now he is standing still but he won't look her in the face. He starts to cry and continues to be difficult, shouting and trying to run away from her. Eventually she stands up, and in one swift movement turns him round so she is standing behind him with both her hands on his upper arms. She walks away with him like this and comes back without him a few minutes later. Meanwhile Miss Brook is talking to a pupil about his work. It seems strange that she doesn't touch him when telling him how good his work is. She touches the children noticeably less than Mrs Atkins.

Children are coming up to Mrs Atkins to show her their work – she gently touches a girl's upper arm as she asks her to sit back down, and then touches a boy on the shoulders. One girl is standing between another two seated girls leaning on both of them. A girl goes to Miss Smith who is sitting down, leans on her back and strokes Miss Smith's arms from shoulder to wrist, up and down, with her head resting on the back of Miss Smith's head. Children are then asked to tidy up. There's a lot of hustle and bustle, pushing and shoving each other out of the way. A boy goes up to Miss Smith for a hug. He stands behind her (she is still sitting down) and puts his arms round her neck. When he's finished another boy does the same and the boy sitting next to Miss Smith snuggles up to her arm. A girl who'd fallen over in the playground is upset because her leg is hurting. She's in tears and Miss Brook asks her if she would like to sit on her lap but the girl declines her offer.

Later during interview, Mrs Atkins claimed she uses touch 'in different ways to reinforce what I'm saying, like an instruction. I might give them a gentle push to tell them where to go. I might use it for reassurance or acknowledgement – to let them know, say if I'm busy, to let them know I know they're there and I'll be with them soon'. Although Mrs Atkins herself uses the words 'reinforce', 'reassurance' and 'acknowledgement' to describe her use of touch it appeared more a kind of controlling touch. In the majority of instances that she touches a pupil she does so to manage and direct what she wants that pupil to do. She touches pupils' heads to gain their attention; when talking to a pupil she always touches them, usually by putting an arm round them. This can be taken as a gesture of affection but it can also be seen as a gesture of power that says: 'I am in control. You will stand here, like this, until I decide you can go'. Particularly when in the majority of instances pupils are not seeking touch for reassurance or reward – they are usually asking a question about something. Invariably Mrs Atkins keeps her arm or hand on the pupil to 'guide' the child back to their place rather than simply releasing the child from her touch and letting them find their own way back.

Mrs Atkins says it is important that a teacher uses their common sense when it comes to cuddling or hugging a child. Generally speaking she feels touch 'should be light and brief' unless there exists the possibility of physical danger either for the child or for what they might do to others. She talks about the way she handled Ryan and feels there was nothing else she could have done. Interestingly Mrs Atkins does not touch Ryan at all the first time she disciplines him. However, when she takes him back to his place and he sits down she stands over him in such a way that he is pinned between her and the desk. The next time he misbehaves she physically restrains him. Her reasons for this are that she felt he had to be removed from the situation and the only way for her to do that was by physically pushing him in front of her by his shoulders to another room. One interpretation of Ryan's behaviour perhaps is that he upped the ante until he is in fact touched!

In a later interview Mrs Atkins says that it is important that 'adults provide the environment for children to be emotionally safe'. She says she's been thinking about issues of touch a lot since our first meeting and thinks it's 'incredibly difficult to pin down what is appropriate touch and what isn't'. She adds that 'touch can be used in so many different ways' such as touching the child's paper or book to get them to focus, or touching a chair to get them to come and sit on it, 'to get them to do what you want them to do'. She identifies many examples of non-verbal signals that 'touch' in a non-physical way such as gesture, tone of voice and the way you look at someone.

Mrs Atkins talks about the power relationship that exists between teacher and pupil and how 'touching can be misconstrued'. The example she gives is of a teacher's hand on a pupil's arm when listening to them read, and how 'for the pupil that might be intimidating. It might be a reassuring or calming touch by the teacher, but it might also be a controlling one. Or the pupil might think it's controlling not calming'. Yet she does not feel that her touch can be misconstrued. She does not see it as controlling but, as stated above, reassuring. The reason for this, she says, is because she knows the previous history of all the children, something she considers to be absolutely vital before a teacher touches a pupil in any way. She cites one little girl who used to freeze when someone touched her because of her past experiences and so touching her to calm or reassure actually had completely the opposite effect and 'was very traumatic for her'. Mrs Atkins uses affectionate language such as calling the children 'Lovely' (endearing term of address). She thinks this helps to create a calmer environment and helps children 'to enjoy the process of learning, which is what it's all about really, isn't it?'

Observation notes with pupils aged nine to ten

The pupils are doing play scripts. They have chosen their groups to work in themselves. There is one group of ten pupils all bunched round a cluster of tables, a group of six, a couple of groups of four and a group of two. The level of noise is quite high but they all seem to be working hard, either individually or in their group, apart from one boy, Josh, who just can't seem to concentrate or settle to anything . . . The pupils are working closely together but there is very little touching compared with the younger pupils. They are working side by side but none of them are leaning on each other, stroking each other, or fiddling with each other's hair like the younger ones tend to do. Interestingly the only touching is between Josh and his classmates. He tries to snatch things off the other pupils and does a fair amount of pushing and shoving. The other pupils in his group get cross with him because he won't paint the props in the way that they've agreed. The teacher says: 'Come on, you had an off day yesterday, let's try and have a better one today. Talk to your group and see what else they might want. Do you want to work on the backdrop?' He starts to fiddle around with the backdrop and the teacher moves away.

I have been in the classroom for twenty minutes and haven't yet seen the teacher touch a pupil. So far she has done everything with speech only. She doesn't touch pupils when they come up to ask her a question or to show her their work, nor does she touch them when asking them to do something. She controls the noise level in the classroom by calling out the child's name and saying: 'Volume please!' . . . She moves around the room, between the tables and amongst the pupils and there is very little incidental touching . . . One boy comes up to show her his work; she praises him but does not touch him. Josh starts to argue with one of the pupils in his group. The teacher comes over and asks Josh: 'What are you doing for your group? You need to be doing something productive and you need to be finished by ten to 12.00'. Josh argues with her, she tries to reason with him unsuccessfully and finally she tells him that she'll talk to him when he's calmed down. She walks away and goes back to the laptop. Josh goes and stands at the front of the classroom and starts to bang his head against the wall. None of the pupils take any notice of him, apart from someone from his group, Paul, who talks quietly to Josh and tries to cajole him into doing his work. The teacher eventually comes over to talk to Josh. She asks him what he should be doing and tries to get him to paint some props. She doesn't touch him at all. She tells him that he'll have to work through his lunchtime and break the next day because he's misbehaved. Josh mutters something under his breath which I don't catch but which I'm fairly sure is something rude. Aloud he says: 'But Miss, that's not fair!' Her reply: 'Tough!'

It is very noticeable that this teacher uses touch considerably less than others I have observed. She rarely touches them when they come over to ask a question and she rarely uses rewarding touch to reinforce the praise that she gives pupils for their work and she does not guide them back to their places. The pupils are also very aware of how different teachers use touch. These are the responses from pupils aged ten in answer to the question: 'Are there some teachers who touch more than other teachers?'

> Rosie: Mrs Harris, because she knows us better than the other teachers, and Mrs Lovell . . . if you're not too happy she'll just come along and

rub you on the back . . . Every night we got a cuddle off Mrs Lovell. [All of you? What sort of a cuddle?] Like that, arms round . . . [So Mrs Harris touches you, you think, more than anybody else because she knows you?] Or Mrs Atkins, I kept getting nose bleeds and Mrs Atkins came up behind me and rubbed me on the back and pat me on the shoulder every now and then and made me feel better.

Megan: One of our teachers Mrs Henson who comes in she's really nice and she touches our hands to help us with our knitting or art work and stuff like that. We don't mind that at all. [Do any of the teachers touch you when you don't like it?]

John: Yes, when you get told off they usually come up to you and sometimes they may pull on your arm a bit too hard. Mrs Jones she would grab our wrists and pull us up, move us and push us down. She's not here any more, I think she retired.

Ryan is obviously a boy with challenging behaviour but the teacher does not touch him at all either to reassure him or as a way to get him to stop banging his head against the wall. Where other teachers touch pupils' heads almost unconsciously as they move around the room, this teacher seems to make a conscious effort not to touch them. As I watch her I wonder if her lack of touch is because as the pupils are older they respond (or most of them do!) to a voice command more so than the younger children and, for example, they do not need physical guidance back to their place. When I interview her later her initial reasons for her lack of touch was 'there's no need' and also because she is new and the pupils do not know her very well. However, later on in the interview she adds her reluctance to touch also stems from her personal experience with her son who is autistic. He cannot bear to be touched and is not affectionate towards others so she has learnt to use her voice to guide, soothe and discipline, where others might use touch. The different ways in which the two teachers use touch in the classroom highlights how whether to touch or not touch depends greatly on an individual's personal experiences and feelings, and thus how complicated it would be to try and introduce generic guidelines for schools.

Among the pupils there is very little touching or fiddling, for example, with each other's hair. The pupils are very purposeful; the majority of them know exactly what they should be doing, and are working very well in small teams, each pupil fulfilling their designated role. Working within their own space as a group, each pupil is working within a clearly defined space within that larger space. There seems to be an awareness of where one's own space ends and another's starts, something that most adults are acutely aware of. The times they touch each other are when they put their arms round each other, suggesting an element of complicity rather than the 'free-for-all' touching that happens among the younger pupils; and when someone is upset. The issue of touch between children is the subject of this final commentary.

> Mrs Atkins claims that she has 'never, ever worked in a school where this (see below) happens so much!' She feels that a lot of them are 'streetwise' and their play is 'mature . . . what they say to each other is very much what you'd expect from older children. They're like year sixes in year twos' bodies. Their language is very sexualised which I suppose comes from TV and older brothers'. She talks about how the children behave in the playground and how the hugging and hand holding seem almost 'adult'.

(research notes)

During interview Mrs Atkins talked about one incident at carpet time[1] when one boy had his hand in another boy's lap holding on to his 'willy' 'like you would hold a pencil'. They were smiling at each other. Mrs Atkins: 'I clocked them, frowned at them, I didn't say anything so all the other children were waiting for the story to begin again. I just waited for them to look at me and stop. It took about 30 seconds'. She informed the head about what had happened and both boys are now closely watched. This incident made her think about: 'What am I comfy with? What do I allow? What don't I allow? For me they should sit with their legs crossed, hands in their laps, and you don't invade other people's personal space'.

From her account it would seem that the boys were neither embarrassed nor uncomfortable but Mrs Atkins plainly found the situation very difficult. She did not speak to the boys about the incident either at the time or afterwards but instead went to the head teacher who decided that the boys should be 'watched'. Mrs Atkins' attempt to deal with the issue is interesting. She is clearly disturbed by what she has witnessed and she obviously feels this is unacceptable behaviour yet she chooses to deal with it using silence, not even telling the boys to stop what they are doing but waiting for them to notice that she has seen them. Presumably she decided to deal with it this way because she assumes that once the boys see that she is watching they will realise that what they are doing is wrong and stop. However, we do not know why the boys stopped – whether it was because they knew their behaviour was inappropriate, or whether they simply stopped because of the look on Mrs Atkins' face. The head also decided to adopt the 'silent surveillance' approach, most likely because she too feels that if the boys are being watched they will not behave in a sexual way whilst at school. Their silence both accepts and denies the boys' sexuality. Their behaviour is perceived and labelled 'sexual' yet the school appears to deny it by not confronting the issue with the boys themselves. Moreover the purpose of watching them is not clear. In hindsight there were a number of questions that I could have asked but I was infected by her embarrassment. For example, how could she tell what the boys were doing; what exactly happened; why does the school feel that watching the boys is the way to deal with this; are they worried that the touching might somehow escalate into something worse?

As we are about to go out into the playground she points to some of the children to illustrate what she's been talking about. In one corner a boy has placed his arms round the shoulders/neck of a younger girl. They are facing each other; she has her hands round his waist and is leaning her head on his shoulder. He has his face buried in her neck. Having just had a conversation about children's sexuality, they appeared perhaps more like teenagers, than five- and eight-year-olds. She says she feels something about it 'isn't right' and asks me what I think. It's a strikingly adult pose for children so young and I find it discomfiting, but does it mean anything? If we hadn't just been discussing children's sexuality I don't think I would have thought anything of the incident at all, or may just have thought 'how sweet'. Are they just copying what they see on TV, or how their older siblings act? It is interesting that at first Mrs Atkins described the way the boys touch the girls as 'an ethos of caring for younger children', a perception that would fit nicely with the school's family approach as articulated by the head teacher. However her tone of voice and demeanour suggest that this is not at all what she thinks. Rather she feels uncomfortable with the amount of contact that occurs between the pupils and particularly about the overt display of young children's sexuality.

These observations raise some interesting issues. All those interviewed had a particular view on touch and pupils. Although it was felt that not to touch children could be detrimental to their emotional and physical well-being, there was no agreement on the parameters of touching. Some teachers used controlling touch far more than others as part of their disciplinary method, where others used their voice and other forms of non-physical touch. Some teachers had no qualms at all about using reassuring touch whereas for others touching a child, who is merely seeking comfort and reassurance, is a mine-field, even in a school which promotes a caring and family ethos.

Chapter 8

Case study
Secondary schools

Helen Bowen

The secondary school case study necessitated a consideration of touching practices between teachers and young people who are neither child nor yet adult. The teachers, parents and pupils all struggled to negotiate the meaning of touch in this borderline context. As discussed throughout, our involvement in the research had forced us to question our own contribution to the 'contamination' of this issue. This concern was reinforced and extended by one head teacher who feared we were likely to 'open a can of worms'. Our assumed ability to 'open a can of worms' suggests that merely by talking about touching practices we would find things out that were 'inappropriate', that should not have happened, but which are best left unspoken. By introducing 'touch' as a topic for discussion and troubling concepts and practices that were generally taken to be self-explanatory or tacit, we would be stepping into space that defines what is spoken and unspoken, the inferred meaning, and the suggested 'other' meaning of the word itself.

Gaining access

The brief questionnaire sent early in the research process had invited schools to take part in later stages of the research. In the secondary school context many had replied in the affirmative, but this initial interest, which had usually been expressed by a deputy head teacher, was soon lost when the head's permission was sought.[1] In retrospect, most head teachers decided they would rather not be involved in our study. This inaccessibility was reflected by the fortress style of many of the secondary school buildings. Most were combined schools or colleges – centres of excellence that taught in excess of a thousand pupils. Their inaccessibility, high walls, jagged gates, locked doors and secure windows, seemed to offer a visual representation of their inaccessibility. The restricted access defined the space and the world of the teenager, and seemed to symbolise the division we were researching. So the troubled concept – the problematics of touch – informed the whole research experience. It wouldn't fit or flow and it had the habit of making us question our motivation.

In order to resolve the access difficulty, we approached secondary schools that were already known to us in some capacity, and asked teachers we knew to act as gatekeepers. In addition we made contact with groups of young people through different networks. We needed an in-between place that would allow entry, and in gaining access we would be able to see the fortress institutions which appeared to be keeping us out, or teenagers in. In the event these defining boundaries were not as fixed as they appeared, but were constantly being negotiated by students, pupils and parents alike. Finally and after much persistence with friends, colleagues, teachers, parents of teenagers, youth workers, we were able to gather data on this age group. Through these contacts a school was identified where the headteacher had been recognised as a bit of a 'maverick' and who was considered to work 'out of the box' (*Times Higher Supplement* (*TES*) 11/07/03) and fortunately he agreed to our involvement.

Entry at last

The school had around 1,700 pupils on roll aged between 11 and 18 years, had above average GCSE and A Level results and was located in the Greater Manchester area. It had recently been awarded specialist media arts college status. There was a strong message from the headteacher that he wanted the school to be 'pro-student' and that his style of teaching was relaxed. He claimed that 'many teachers fear kids and hide behind their role, but you can only teach if they understand there is a real person behind the teacher. You have to give of yourself' (*TES* 11/07/03). It became apparent during visits to the school that the influence of the headteacher was strong, that he had obviously 'given of himself': 'the rules aren't there to be rigidly interpreted, the rules are there to be used . . . kids will go, "that's unbelievably fair", they don't go away thinking he's a soft touch, they go away thinking he's alright'. Some teachers agreed with his perspective and others did not. Some teachers felt that he gave the pupils the impression they had 'too many rights' which encouraged them to use these rights against the teachers. His office space reflected his 'maverick' status. Students' paintings were on the wall, with notes attached and with his nickname added. This was quite surprising but did make the room cheery and gave the impression that pupils had a presence here. His manner was very flamboyant, but despite his theatrical leanings he helped clarify the role teachers' play when teaching, and the idea of touch being a form of communication which is intrinsically linked to the way some pupils learn and some teachers teach.

Visits to the school allowed touch to be considered from two different positions. The interview with this head was very 'light' and entertaining. He raised concerns about 'opening a can of worms' with children, and how talking about touch with some pupils would be wholly inappropriate as it may bring up issues they would rather not talk about. Although I assured him that we were aware of the difficulties some children will have experienced in their past and that I would endeavour to keep the conversation related to the school setting, I was aware of the fear attached to talking about 'touch' which could make teachers and pupils apprehensive, and empathised with his position. At the same time, given the difficulties in 'getting into' a school, and the unease about the whole topic, I didn't want to press too hard, so a subsequent visit took place some months later. During this time many changes had occurred. Not only was the deputy head now acting headteacher (the previous head was reportedly 'off sick'), but there had also been allegations made against a young male teacher by a group of girls. The story had been in the local news, and the police had arrested the teacher.

With hindsight it was probably good that interviews with pupils had not already taken place prior to this event, as fears that the research process might 'open the can of worms' would seemingly have been confirmed. Discussions about touch would have been perceived as raising awareness of a topic which had previously lain dormant. Although this was a relief it also provided a good opportunity to learn what it had been like working in a school where a fairly high-profile incident had occurred. However, the situation meant that the pupils were now 'out of bounds' as interviewing them was thought to be inappropriate in the circumstances, but interviews with teachers and observation of interactions during lessons and break times were able to go ahead as planned. Pupils were still accessible via their other networks, i.e. their families, local youth groups, etc.

The contrast between the visits to the school under the different headteachers' leadership enabled a consideration of the influence a head can have. Whereas the first head's office was informal and colourful, the deputy quickly transformed the room into a business-like area. There was no evidence of pupils' art work. No funny letters on the notice board. The style of the office was serious and straightforward. This change appeared to signify a message relayed by some of the teachers: that the first head had been too informal, and his flexible boundaries had led staff to become confused. The allegations were partly blamed on his informal approach as this had left staff open to both abusing and being abused: 'We have to make children aware of the conventions of touch, what people expect and what people allow . . . all which the [absent] headteacher breaks completely' (male secondary teacher aged 50). But, such a need for control, for policy and guidelines, could also be regarded as a response to the crisis situation, and the absent head provided a suitable scapegoat. Given this head teacher was not typical of secondary heads in our experience, and other schools have also experienced similar allegations, it seemed possible that the accusations had little to do with the attitude of the head at all. On the other hand, it is always possible that this attitude meant that the girls felt able to voice a serious incident with some confidence. Yet this view was not articulated.

The first head had referred to a Vulcan mindset when attempting to describe interactions between him and his pupils. He was very aware of the performative nature of these interactions, also in how pupils interact with teachers. He thought the process of developing an understanding should be the basis of whether to touch or not, and that this cannot be covered in a policy:

A lot of my staff I think misunderstand it because all they can see from a distance is what looks like me being excessively nice to kids and cuddling them even when they've been really bad . . . Now it's very much like . . . the Vulcan mind link . . . that actually what happens is you touch somebody like that . . . it's an exchange. Nothing really happens but as far as they are concerned you are very very close to them and that makes all the difference in the world . . . There are lots of kids who want an affectionate pat, they want to be stroked, they want to be patted on the head . . . they want somebody to actually make that link.

Types of touch

While there are many different types or ways of touching there appears to be a general consensus that the act of touching defines an interaction, provides a demarcation, a boundary. But the meaning is fluid and changes, depending on who is touching, who is receiving, and who perceives the touch. There are a multitude of meanings depending on: who you are; how old you are; what gender you are. Also where you are: inside a building; outside a building; which building; and of course what you are 'used to', and what 'feels right' to you, whether your family touch and whether you are a 'touchy-feely' person. Some of these differences were expressed in interviews:

Girls give hugs.

(girl, 13)

Boys touch . . . only if they are gay.

(boy, 13)

Some teachers can't help it . . . they are 'touchy-feely' people.

(girl, 14)

It's different though . . . because we wouldn't want to be touched . . . at our age.

(boy, 14)

These things are intuitive and instinctive . . . I sweep their body subconsciously to see how tense they are.

(first headteacher)

Touch is shaped by the roles people perform and roles can define interaction:

I think it's a relationship I've built up with them . . . over the seven years that they are here. And all sorts of people expect me to do things like that, as I am sort of very fatherly . . . some of the kids say I'm grandfatherly and that's how they see me, and I'm the head . . . and I'm very formal, and I'm very informal, and the kids understand easily. My colleagues don't.

(first headteacher)

As this headteacher is keen to make clear, the role being performed at the time of the touch can define the action. For example, teachers constantly referred to their role as being *in loco parentis*. Yet as this was acknowledged, there was a qualifier which led them to explain that this meant that teachers have their pupils' best interests at heart, but this did not mean that teachers would touch or hug their pupils as parents might, except in exceptional circumstances. An example of exceptional circumstances arose during interviewing as a pupil had died. Under these circumstances it was felt that it was appropriate for teachers to hug pupils because at times like this pupils needed to feel comforted:

> You have to have the blanket policy and then it's the guidance of wise men . . . and fools . . . people have to judge the situation themselves. We had a death, one of the year ten children died just before the holiday and people were very upset and there were many incidents where staff were just putting their arms around kids and saying it's OK you can cry and it was perfectly acceptable and proper. But you can't as a general rule go around doing that, it was an exceptional situation that required exceptional measures I guess.
>
> (male teacher, 50s)

> We have a lot of vulnerable children in the school . . . because of the inclusion policy, we get children who have very difficult home lives and they are looking for parental figures and you're doing that and giving them hugs . . . but it isn't always advisable and can put you in a very difficult position, one you shouldn't be in because you're not there to be that role.
>
> (male teacher, 50s)

> Some people's touch can be perceived inappropriately when it isn't inappropriate, and I certainly think there's a gender divide that women get away with it so much more than men because they're the nurturers.
>
> (female teacher, 20s)

There is a sense that how a touch is perceived depends on the gender of the person, and whether the situation is friendly or unfriendly. It also appears that although there is a general understanding that there should not be any touching – there generally is. It can be used to demarcate a situation, to add meaning to what is being said, or to offer support. In some ways the teachers seemed to be saying they use touch as a way of communicating more:

> Equally when a kid's not focused, a little touch . . . a little 'Come on, back to it' on the back, gets them back and focused. Sometimes a reassuring hand on the shoulder when a kid's working can be lovely . . . I think teachers primarily say 'Oh I never touch people, I follow all the codes that you're supposed to follow' but I'm sure that they do. I know I do.
>
> (female secondary teacher, 30s)

So, a touch can give a little extra meaning to a situation or an interaction. In addition to the gender of the person, it also seemed to make a difference what age the person doing the touching is. Not only in terms of how the touch is read and whether it is fatherly or motherly (or grandfatherly), but also how long the teacher had been teaching, and how comfortable they were in their 'style', and what their experiences with pupils had been like:

> When I trained it was no touch at all that was appropriate, since then there has been a slight change in that it says now you can touch if you are restraining, so long as it's restraining and not applying pressure, that's obviously intervening in a fight . . . But equally there are kids, and again it's usually the lads who cross the boundaries to make you feel uncomfortable sometimes . . . I've got a year 11 lad who is hilarious and I do find very entertaining, he's extremely intelligent, when I have a go at him and tell him off, he'll crack jokes and say: 'Come on Miss, you need a hug, don't you' and he gives you a hug and I'm like: 'Get away, this is the middle of the lesson in front of the class' and the class are like: . . . 'Oh gosh, how's she going to react?' . . . It's one of those scenarios where you want to kill him but you end up laughing because it's funny.
>
> (female teacher, 30s)

It is clear this teacher uses her discretion (in spite of what 'it' says) and recognises that pupils will play on notions of acceptable touch. Although attitudes towards touch change over time, the influence of policy is apparent as teachers and pupils recognise the significance of whether a touch is perceived 'allowable' or not. The underlying message is very much related to gender, with male teachers perceiving their role in terms of a general sense of 'un/acceptable' masculinity. Such a sexualised definition carries the implication that it is inappropriate for men to be in a situation where they cannot be 'observed'. Male teachers cannot be in a room with a female without having a security measure in place to protect them – like windows in doors for example:

> With boys especially, male teachers can easily get into confrontations.
>
> (male teacher, 50+)

I think it's more difficult for them, I sometimes think being a mum may make things easier, if you've got children of your own perhaps that helps at times . . . we've got very conscious of windows and doors and male staff in particular not being alone with females and yet you get to the point where you draw the line because you're still a teacher and have to teach them, but I think for men that situation is . . . very difficult and it's difficult for me to put myself in a man's shoes, whereas rightly or wrongly it wouldn't bother me so much if a lad came in here and I'm a female teacher but should it . . .? Is that because I've got two children of my own and they're both lads . . .

(female teacher, 50+)

It depends how fit [slang for attractive] the teacher is.

(boy, 15)

In the last quote the pupil is playing with a sexual subtext. He is suggesting that touching would be allowable or understandable (from his perspective) if he found the teacher attractive. At the same time the 'motherly' teacher shows how her social position outside the school influences her behaviour within. As a mother of two teenage boys herself she is perhaps more comfortable with this age group than someone else might be. For her, a maternal analogy displaces the possible suggestion of any sexual register in the relationship. Implicitly, she invokes the ghost of an 'incest taboo': she would not think about her own 'lads' sexually, and she transfers that taboo to the school kids. The roles of teachers outside the school therefore can shape pupils and fellow teachers' perceptions of their behaviour in school. For some male teachers who had reached a certain age and remained unmarried, their sexuality could be called into question. The inferred suggestion appears to be that as he is unmarried he may be homosexual, and if he is homosexual then it is assumed he may be interested in 'grooming' male pupils, and which also reiterates a comment made in an earlier chapter about the likely sexual predilections of a lesbian teacher. This reflects a general acceptance of societal homophobia which is played out in schools on a regular basis and was a view expressed by both teachers and pupils alike.

The only time touch can be fully expressed as permissible or understandable is when the pupil is young or upset and in exceptional circumstances. At these times physical comfort is recognised as something that is required, needed, and is justifiable:

When you're little you need more of that sort of thing, comforting, protection and stuff. I remember in nursery the reason I wanted to sit on their knees [was] because I didn't want to be away from you [mum present] so I needed someone to be like my mum . . . but as you get older you don't.

(girl, 14)

I would find it a bit strange if they came up to you and put their arm around your shoulder, I wouldn't feel comfortable, it's not the relationship you have with your teacher, they're there to teach you . . . not to be . . . your friend.

(boy, 14)

I don't like a teacher sitting next to me . . . if they put their hand on your leg or something . . . It depends if it was a male touching a male . . . I don't know . . . I just don't like it . . .

(boy, 15)

Both teachers and pupils appear to want to have clear boundaries of what is acceptable or not. That some teachers, in a special role, will use more touch than others is acknowledged, but the most important thing seems to be a need for a shared understanding and understanding requires a general consensus that everyone is ascribing to. Acclimatisation into the school culture begins with primary education and develops through to secondary school, and is eventually 'learnt' by the majority of young people. The 'culture' of the school is reinforced by the attitude of the head and general discipline offered by teachers:

Although I'm a fun teacher, I like to know where the boundaries are.

(female teacher, 25ish)

The teacher may say 'this way now' and put their hand on your back . . . but there are mentors and things and they are specially trained if you get upset or whatever, and they can hug you if you cry and they will do that.

(girl, 14)

The idea that pupils can receive hugs from specially trained people in special circumstances is interesting. It is of note that pupils did not like teachers who invade their personal space and overstep the boundary, putting their face up too close; although this isn't strictly 'touching', it is nevertheless perceived as overstepping the boundary. Touch is not just a physical act; it is a spatial relation between bodies, measured in an emotional rather than a physical register:

I've seen teachers on the corridor when they're shouting at someone they go right up to their faces . . .

(girl, 13)

I work with kids who always talk about that, how they hate it if a teacher comes up to their face and they've got smelly breath and spit in your face.

(female youth worker)

There are kids that answer teachers back and I have been in classes where the teacher would go up to their faces and say something and they'd say: 'Get out of my way, get out of my face'.

(girl, 14)

It depends who the teacher was . . . because there are some teachers who I am just creeped out by.

(girl, 13)

Generally pupils seemed to be aware of the others' roles and boundaries and negotiated this flexibly according to the situation and personality of the teacher. The headteacher suggests that touch is a form of communication, which can define a situation. But at the same time, he suggests it must be reciprocal:

What is your space? What is my space? Now I take the view that within reason I'm prepared to let you into my space and I expect to be able to go reasonably into their territory and then I would regard that as on a par, as equal, so I will have this conversation with the kids. Kids have got my mobile number. They leave me messages . . . It just gives them that one more piece of trust. I think that's what it's all about, this two-way thing. I am prepared to let them into my space which includes coming to me at home at night . . . I think it's all about giving contact . . . and you have to be willing to do the same for me . . .

(first headteacher)

Yet giving of one's self and giving personal information was not popular with all staff:

One of my colleagues . . . gave her mobile number to her sixth form students for course-work and things, and she would text them to say: 'Where are you and why aren't you in?' Now that's inappropriate, that's crossing the line . . . I think there should be boundaries because they're to protect the students and protect the teachers because you don't want to be in a position where either of you could be questioned for your actions.

(female teacher, 30s)

For the interaction between teachers and pupils to work, the rules of engagement need to be understood by both sides. Some schools define a rigid framework for controlling touch; some schools present a more flexible approach. In some ways this is dependent on the leadership of the head and the policies that are established and adhered to – not the same thing, of course. At the same time each individual teacher and pupil defines their own framework that fits best with their needs, but this can be informed by a sense of unease that forms a backdrop to the situation. All teachers and pupils are aware of the power each holds over the other: 'by choosing to touch they then have the control of the situation they're imposing on that child whether they want it or not' (male teacher, 50s). The teacher fears the allegation, and the pupil uses this power to protect and maintain some power for themselves: 'and that's the way the law works, so if a child makes an accusation it has to be investigated and even if you are innocent your teaching career's ruined' (female teacher, 30s).

Touch inducing fear

Fears include the fear of being accused; a general fear of litigation; and the fear of being judged as inappropriate. It may help to consider how these fears work in shaping behaviour. How does the fear of touch inform actions and shape the relationships between teachers and pupils? And how can this interplay be better understood so that teachers and pupils can begin to develop a positive learning environment?:

> There are occasions where you touch them on the sleeve just to make a point or even put your arm around them at times when people are upset but you have to do that with an awareness of how that can be mistaken . . . if you're alone with a student and in a touching situation it can be easily misinterpreted.
>
> (female teacher, 40s)

> But a lot of it is to do with not putting yourself in compromising situations where you're having confidential discussions with students and they do come and tell you very distressing things about themselves . . . and you have to go through procedures – you can't sort of take it on an 'I'll solve all your problems' type attitude.
>
> (male teacher, 50s)

> Kids will pick up on anything they can to put the teacher in the wrong . . . blow things up out of all proportion . . . in a conflict between a teacher and a kid then the kid will use whatever they can to put the teacher in the wrong.
>
> (female teacher, 40s)

The teachers shape their behaviour to the possibility of accusation, at least in the back of their minds. The comments also highlight the suspicion they attach to pupils' accusations when they suggest that 'kids will use whatever they can' to put the teacher in the wrong. It is almost as if the pupils are abusing their rights or have too many weapons to use against the teachers who feel held to ransom. Most teachers had previously worked at a school where some form of allegation had been made, and, whether the allegation was true or not, all teachers were aware of the impact this would have on their careers:

> There was a fight between two girls, and the teacher just stepped right back and didn't go anywhere near them in case she got prosecuted, whereas other teachers will get right in there and separate them.
>
> (girl, 13)

> Kids can come home from school saying something about a teacher that could ruin their career, and they can do it as a comment that's just because they think he's weird . . . it seems to be a problem more with men than women.
>
> (male deputy head, 50s)

Situations can be informed by an underlying sense of teachers being fearful and pupils being aware that the teachers are fearful, all of which can lead to a general sense of unease. The fact that an allegation was made at the school helped feed a fear that had already shaped perceptions of touch in school. This uneasiness is also felt by pupils and teachers outside this particular school, so societal attitudes and perception of social roles will shape how any behaviour is read. The 'motherly middle-aged' teacher has more freedom to touch pupils than an 'unmarried childless man'. There is less of an abusive social script available to her circumstances of age and gender. Any man over a certain age who isn't married and doesn't have children is deemed suspicious whether in school or outside. The fears change in different settings and over time. With sensationalised stories in the press feeding parental prejudice, any comment made by pupils about an unwanted gaze could be followed up by a phone call to the head. All accusations have to be treated seriously as the school cannot afford to be seen in retrospect to have been careless about the possibility of abuse. Of course times have changed and children are now listened to in relation to abuse, and their rights protected, but teachers fear that attitudes have swung too far and they can be held to account on the whims of a teenager with a grudge. They are guilty until proven innocent, and with a tendency to base innocence on marital status.

Touch can communicate

Touch then is a form of ambiguous communication. A physical gesture can enhance or confuse meanings that are spoken and unspoken. The physicality of the relationship between teachers and pupils can help define a learning environment and help form a teaching relationship. This physicality also includes the distance between teachers and learners:

You've got to respect everybody's space and that can vary as well, the mood you're in that day . . . some people want that cuddle and some don't.

(female teacher, 50s)

. . . particularly PE teachers have that instinctive way of dealing with kids and it's not just about touching, it comes down to everything, they know when to challenge a kid, when to talk about something . . . when to touch when not to touch . . .

(female PE teacher, 40s)

The headteacher's comment that situations with pupils need to be reciprocal is also important. If he is informal with pupils, then they in turn must be allowed a level of informality with him. Touch then conveys more than the act. To isolate 'touch' as a separate entity from talking, teaching and communicating sets up false boundaries, and this is a problem with guidelines which try to shape behaviour in minute detail:

I think there's a difference between teachers, some of my teachers are really nice . . . the other day I was in drama and I've got a really nice drama teacher and he called me darling or something . . . and someone said as a joke . . . 'You're not allowed to say that to her sir, it's against the law' . . . we just laughed.

(girl, 14)

Although they laugh, they recognise that these things can be misinterpreted. Teachers and pupils are aware of the complexities of the context and will adapt and utilise the situation accordingly. In each situation, with each inter-action, the rules of engagement are redefined and performed differently as pupils and teachers engage in a power struggle to protect and establish their position. As is evidenced from many of the quotes, there is much energy spent on this complex interplay of 'no touching' situations – which in reality are full of interactions which involve touching of one kind or another. Each situation is loaded with expectation and responsibility from all sides. It would appear that any 'no touch' guidelines which do not recognise touching as an option are only paying lip service to protecting both teachers and pupils alike.

Chapter 9

Case study
Considering disability

John Powell

Observing differences in touching patterns between professionals with disabled children can provide an example which destabilises the 'rules' by a consideration of how we sometimes transgress them. Here, a different operational practice comes into play – a 'needs must' approach is adopted, which can result in placing some children in a very different situation from others. For example, communicating through touch is considered quite normal when working with children who are either blind or deaf (Miles 1999). Adults and other children frequently use touch in order to gain each others' attention, and/or engage in a conversation. Generally children with a variety of physical difficulties will be touched so that routine dressing and toileting can take place. Miles describes the importance of hands for the person who is deaf–blind, and notes that hands serve as sense organs. Workers are advised to watch a child's hands for cues; use their own hand under the child's hand to express feeling; and to make their own hands available for the child to use as he or she wishes. Touch is similarly recommended for children with autism as a way of helping prevent an orienting to irrelevant sounds and other stereotypical behaviours (Kazuka in Field 2002), although some also claim that children with autism prefer not to be touched at all (see Chapter 7). Yet why some children should be assumed less likely to make false allegations of physical or sexual harassment just because of their disability; why others who police our behaviour would question our motives less in such a situation; and why some professionals have until recently felt less need to police themselves in these circumstances, is less clear. However, as noted below, fears have now spread to those working with disability and their comments probably bear too many similarities to those in earlier chapters.

Research in the area of disability also often emphasises the positive aspects of touch:

> A study involving 48 hearing mothers and their two-year-old children with and without hearing impairments found mothers of children *with* hearing impairments touched each other more and that, unlike hearing

dyads, the presence of maternal hostility was related to a decrease in . . . maternal and child touches.

(Yoshinaga-Itano 2001)

Mothers of children with a hearing impairment would withdraw touch as a form of punishment. So while maternal hostility of hearing children may result in mothers shouting and in some instances smacking their children, mothers of children with hearing impairment ostracise and punish their child by a withdrawal of touch (yet both responses can result in silencing and disempowering their child). We have a classic double bind – for disabled children touch is regarded as 'good', and they are punished by its withdrawal, yet this simultaneously reinforces notions of their victim-hood. For other children, as we have seen, touch is considered risky; they must do without its developmental benefits, keep an eye out for abusers, and be aware that others tend to assume them capable of making false allegations (see Piper *et al*. 2005).

The setting

This chapter focuses on touching practices within a residential school where all the children have a Statement of Special Educational Need. The range of complex disabilities includes autistic spectrum disorders, in addition to communication and hearing difficulties, and many exhibit severe behavioural problems. The school is situated in a semi-rural location in extensive grounds in the North of England and is an independent non-maintained residential establishment for pupils/students aged 5 to 21 (a few are even older). Some young people are accommodated 52 weeks of the year, and some of these are 'looked after children', under the Children's Act Legislation. The 65 residential children/young people are accommodated in one of the eight units. In addition there are some pupils who stay one or two nights per week and in addition a number are day pupils. The school has (in many cases) a need to communicate through direct touch particularly where the student also has additional difficulties with limited or no vision. The school has developed a range of policies aimed at informing practice so as to enable staff to respond to the needs of the children and young people in 'appropriate' or approved ways. These policies have been influenced by the ways in which touching is constructed through wider societal discourses (see earlier chapters and above). The residential school requested total anonymity; consequently the pseudonym Springbrook is used throughout. Children and young people are represented mainly through observations, as speech often represented a significant aspect of their disability; where possible young people were interviewed with the help of signers so that their perspective could be incorporated alongside the views of others. The research at Springbrook involved exploring both the educational and residential aspects of community life, which reflects the multidisciplinary and interprofessional relationships and practices that run hand in hand.

Springbrook could not operate as a 'no-touch' zone as the nature of the disabilities of many of the young people mean they use touching as their main mode of communication. Yet, touch is 'dealt' with by close management, and via the creation of policies which advocate that less touch, not more, is a better or at least safer option. Discourses influencing Springbrook's policy include human rights: 'We have, blind, deaf, paraplegic, and these people have a lot of care done for them by other people, we have to make them aware that it is not OK for people to touch their bodies without permission' (head of residential care). These and other issues make any policy writing particularly difficult when aimed at young people with the range of disabilities referred to above. However, there is evidence that the ethos at Springbrook does involve recognising the rights of the many young people in its care.

Selected history and the development of rules

Springbrook's senior management group devised a number of internal policies that lay out the rules and guidance for the application of touch in a range of contexts including intimate and social situations. However, all such policies are open to personal interpretation. The policies relating to touch are intended to make all touching less likely to be misunderstood by any passerby. One influential point in favour of touching policies is revealed in the following extract:

> I think policy and procedures are a good idea. About ten years ago residential care [i.e. in combined educational and residential settings] was seen as the poor relative. The education was seen as being good, but when they went into the residential home in my opinion this was seen as very poor. Over the years it has been recognised that the residential/social care they receive is given by professional people, and this is a professional career.
>
> (head of residential care)

The extract suggests guidelines and policies as one means by which the perceived professional binary is presented as a division between the relatively 'well off' educators and their 'poor' professional relatives, the social care staff. It is believed that through such policies professional standards can be raised particularly for care staff. In this sense the presence of a set of professional policies is part of a strategy through which equality amongst practitioners is attempted. Policy is offered as a way of bridging the gap between the different practitioner identities by reinforcing a discourse of 'professionalism', although it cannot do this convincingly when there are still wide disparities in career opportunities and salary levels.

The policies also suggest an internal approach which anticipates touching practices so they can be managed through internal mechanisms and agency-approved ways. There is a recognition that the initiation of touch is often from the student rather than a member of staff. This leads to a further strand of policy (see later), i.e. that concerned with training students how to behave in public situations, and how they might avoid problems, such as receiving undesirable attention from members of the public. The focus of such policies is to educate, so difficulties may be avoided, and embarrassing or even harmful situations be prevented, or if not entirely prevented, then at least 'outsiders' will know that there was a strategy in place – so that if practice failed, it was not for the want of proper procedures.

This policy of prevention/anticipation is delivered through educational sessions which focus on 'appropriate' touch for students attending the school. New members of staff are introduced to issues relating to touching, and to the policies which they then follow through as rehearsal in training sessions. From the point of view of carers and teachers these strategies have the potential to lead to two different practitioner outcomes: those who use policies defensively and those who do so reflectively. Banks (2001) is one amongst others who argues that to 'follow the book', means surrendering the option to act ethically if this brings conflict with the rules. She suggests that reflective practitioners are more able to accept personal accountability and respond to contradictions as far as the policies and the rules are concerned, and so are more able to act in the best interests of both service users and the institution:

> For various practical reasons some touching is necessary as part of the education and care of children/young people with complex needs. It is used to gain attention, to accept nursing, caring and changing, and is a means of guiding, feeding and safeguarding. Touching is a form of communication and socialisation, and is an aid to instruction. Intensive interaction is a therapeutic strategy used with many of our children/ young people . . . When touching a child/young person, staff should consider where on the body is most appropriate and be conscious of the intention and purpose of touching. It is imperative that touching is always carried out with courtesy and respect, recognising that each child/young person has the right to dignity and self esteem. Only if children/young people are shown respect will they learn respect. All touching should be positive and performed in the best interests of the child/young person.
>
> (Springbrook's 'Intimate Care Policy')

This is articulated through the following set of management expectations:

> We do not encourage people to hug students; we do not want to give the wrong messages to people who have complex needs. It is more difficult

with younger children but we try to discourage staff from putting distressed children on their knee but to sit them to the side of them, and if necessary give them a [sideways] hug.

(head of residential care)

The rules or guidance detailed above are both descriptive and prescriptive and give a clear impression of a formal approach influenced through the implementation of the rules, which requires a reduction in certain kinds of touching such as hugging, whilst simultaneously recognising the touching practices which are important to caring and education. Such an approach may seem baffling but according to Banks, contradictory messages are more likely to lead to reflection and discussion. However, the extract also raises questions as to whether the young people understand why they should not be hugged, and why they should not hug others.

One aspect of the 'culture' of Springbrook is its holistic and coherent set of discourses which includes a set of practices which suggest consistency and uniformity. There are also other strands of Springbrook's culture that are likely to be less predictable. It seems clear, however, that historical events and the attitudes of managers have been influential in the development of policies relating to touch. Children with disabilities including sensory deprivation, and who attended school, were historically excluded from the rest of society, especially if they were the children of relatively poor families. However, the development of schools to meet the needs of children with sensory disabilities has led to an education geared to providing children with a 'means of maintaining themselves by their own industry' (Borsay 2005: 95). Non-sectarian moral and religious instruction was a cornerstone of the training and offered a way of introducing the disabled person into the world of 'normal' everyday life, often by offering the chance to work through a handicraft 'so that on leaving school a child is able to take advantage of any suitable opening that offers' (ibid.: 97). The present context is one where many children and young adults with complex needs both live and are educated at Springbrook, and there are many different practitioners involved who provide this overall care and education, albeit with different working assumptions. There is however, considerable overlap particularly amongst the managers, who hold a wider range of responsibilities.

A specific aspect of Springbrook's history which is particularly relevant to current attitudes relating to touching practices was a child protection investigation following allegations:

We had an NSPCC investigation about five years ago, and one of the things they brought up was that they did not feel there were enough guidelines for staff. We have now increased the staff induction from one day to six weeks. The course now is much more professional. Staff now have a one-week course followed by shadowing another member of staff.

The staff has much more support and it is all much more structured. They have the guidelines to follow.

(senior care manager)

Part of the concerns arising from the investigation has led to Springbrook's management team recognising that it needs to be more transparent to a range of external practitioners and parents:

Our practice needs to be open and we need to be confident in what we are doing. We need to be confident with what works. It's bad enough being brought up in care and restricted by your disabilities and your needs to be tactile, it should be open. If staff felt uncomfortable they know they should go and speak to somebody about their feelings.

(chief executive)

The above extracts highlight a position that developed out of anxieties lived through during the 'investigation', which recognises the needs of the children and young people, yet which also implicitly acknowledges that 'touching' is no longer spontaneous. The investigation also made staff recognise the need to set up systems that would reduce the possibility of a repeat investigation. Going through the investigation was a 'baptism of fire', as one family link worker puts it: 'It was an awful time, terrible, we came through it and it was fine, but at the time it was terrible'. It has left emotional scars which serve as reminders to the management group, particularly of the consequences of the disapproving attention that the school may receive from outsiders. This then can be viewed as Springbrook urgently attempting to reassure the wider practitioner community that their practices are acceptable and appropriate and in line with everyone else's. Touch is not just significant from the point of view of meeting needs, but also of preventing scenarios that could be interpreted as questionable. Staff also need protecting from any external negative scrutiny emanating from the gaze of external practitioners and parents along with the reputation of the establishment.

Touch and risk taking

Touch in Springbrook has become understood as a set of risk practices that need to be planned for and carefully managed and reflected on. This in turn has resulted in a system of surveillance where everyone becomes sensitive to the ways that touch operates, and which touch is 'appropriate' and which 'inappropriate'. On the other hand, Springbrook is also involved in taking what it perceives to be calculated but necessary risks and has consequently developed some progressive thinking around practices that support young adults in exploring their sexual identity, for example:

> We have beautiful 18-year-old girls who to the outside world look able-bodied apart from their communication disorders; [they] cognitively appear a lot younger, this results in attracting more attention. We have to make people here understand sex within a loving relationship. This is a difficult task. We show them videos, books, etc. and this has to be done in an educational way.

> (head of residential care)

The suggestion is that young adult females with learning disabilities seem unaware of the excitement they may generate in public spaces in the 'outside world', and so they need to learn about appropriate sexual relationships through a programme of PSHE. Staff are similarly concerned that young people might initiate an 'inappropriate' form of touch:

> A student may touch a member of staff's or a fellow student's genitals . . . [Is it fairly common?] No, it's regular enough, there is a repeated pattern, there are other issues about touch I think, and the type of touch that would be appropriate in different social settings or even in residents, it's really hard for our students to understand that feeling an idea that they have isn't automatically the same for the person concerned.

> (PSHE coordinator)

Staff members were generally anxious about the potentially predatory nature of others who may wish to exploit the young people's lack of understanding and draw them into inappropriate sexual relations. This may be compounded by young people responding to their own needs without attempting (or being able) to control their touching behaviour, or being able to understand the consequences of not doing so. Young people from Springbrook may also respond or initiate inappropriate touching as part of their expression of personal desire, rather than seek out more meaningful relationships where it may be more appropriate to channel sexualised touching behaviour. These messages are reinforced through policy statements which offer guidance and advice to practitioners to consider social touch with children and young people in relation to their development. For example, whilst spontaneous touching might take place within a family or friendship context they are to be discouraged between staff and young people as unprofessional and open to misinterpretation. This official rationale is concerned with treating young people with respect, by not assuming that they necessarily want to be touched.

As one young person, a 16-year-old female, explained through sign language, which was interpreted by one of the carers who works closely with her (this reads as if in the third person as a result of the literal translation of the signer):

If she gets stressed or angry then her touch gets harder. She doesn't like people touching her when she's angry or stressed. With some deaf students to get their attention she will tap them or try and get their attention. [So tap them on the leg?] Yes or the shoulder. [Sometimes are there other kinds of touch she would use? For instance if she felt very happy or very sad, would she want to touch then? . . . Sometimes then it's OK to touch you on the shoulder and it's OK to touch you on the knee, but what about other places?] No, she'll get angry if you touch her anywhere else, she knows where she likes to be touched, shoulder, knee, arm, not private places.

This young woman appears to be clear about what is acceptable or not and this appears to be clearly linked to her feelings and the ability of those around her to be able to relate to them. This may be difficult for other young people who may act on their own feelings rather than responding to others around them, and which could result in angry exchanges. Equally this young woman has determined where the boundaries exist on her body, identifying private places as out of bounds. Her awareness of touch boundaries is consistent with the PSHE programme at Springbrook; the following is taken from an observation of a session:

The teacher was going through a presentation at the front of the class. She was signing and at the same time speaking as each presentation picture was shown to the group. The session was dealing with personal relations and in particular the inappropriateness of certain forms of touching. The first of the overhead displays was of a man approaching a woman in a park setting, no one was around and the woman was sitting reading a book, the man proceeded . . . to go towards the woman and then to hug her. The young people were asked about their opinion of this, and there was strong feeling that this was not the most appropriate way to introduce yourself to a stranger.

(observation notes)

The unease about touch felt by managers and articulated through policies and guidance documents which supports training is closely linked to concerns about the risk of inappropriate behaviour either by a practitioner or one of the children/young adults; or even appropriate but misinterpreted actions, which could come to the notice of external visitors including social workers and members of the inspectorate. This in turn could impact on the school's reputation and affect recruitment. 'Inappropriate' touch can take place in both intimate and/or social settings as the Vice Chair of Governors comments:

The friendly cuddle can be misinterpreted and it is important for there to be an appropriate touching policy. Touch is very important but there are worries in today's PC atmosphere. For example, if you walked with your arm around a child this can be misconstrued, and particularly if this happened a number of times with the same child. Colleagues in other schools have been the subject of disciplinary proceedings and have been suspended pending investigations whilst complaints about them appearing to have inappropriately touched a child have been looked into. In a way what we have to do is to place ourselves under a form of surveillance because of this sense of the possibility of having touch behaviours misconstrued.

At Springbrook, practitioners are likely to be involved in developing and reforming perceptions of risk on a regular basis within the situations in which they are working. The following extract illustrates an informed level of anticipation and awareness of the likely response when the speech therapist wishes to extricate herself from the unwelcome touch of a young person:

> I was working with a student, actually working on transition, helping a student to go from one place to another, emotions go very high and they go very low and the student sometimes likes to walk along and put her arm round you. Now I could say: 'No, you don't do that' but if I said 'No' then we'd have a massive, massive scene so I gave her gentle face feedback; a pat on the back and then I gently withdrew and she withdrew so it was short and it was manageable, it didn't become me rejecting her socially. Don't forget she can't initiate it very much through language so it's her bit of expression: 'I'm happy now, I'm comfortable with you being with me' and she was communicating that to me so I communicated back to her: 'Yes, I'm happy with this, we're fine here, we're OK, that's it now, we've done our bit of communication' and me knowing that I don't want to be walking around with my arm around a student. I then withdraw, but she was quite happy with that, we'd had our moment of communication and now we're carrying on walking.
>
> (speech therapist)

This shows very clearly the need to manage touch sensitively from the practitioner's perspective but also illustrates the need children with disabilities have to communicate through touch as it is an important part of their repertoire and one that aids relationships. Touch is therefore central for these young people and their experiences of relating to the world, and when understood and responded to sensitively should lead to positive feelings about touch. However, as referred to earlier, some of the young people may be perceived by those outside the school as vulnerable. At first sight many look able-bodied apart from their communication disorders. As a result of regular affirmation through touch they are more likely to feel respected, but this is an insider experience, and once outside the school they are more likely to be treated as sexual objects. Practitioners therefore need to help negotiate the moves between developing identities from 'vulnerable children' to that of emergent 'sexual beings' (also vulnerable) and who also need to be protected from the outside world while still allowing for their needs to be met, but not in such a way that they are exploited. However such complex judgements of these moments will always be problematic:

> On holiday with Springbrook we had volunteers. We had taken a young man of 19 from here who was playing by the ball pool. A girl of 18 (a carer) who was showing all her midriff then jumped into the ball-pool, the young man in his sexual way jumped on top of her and he then had to be taken home. The girl claimed that she did not look at him as a sexual object and therefore did not think she was leading him on. Because the student was disabled she was not counting him as being a human being. Sometimes young people do not see disabled people as having sexual needs like the rest of us. So you should dress accordingly, then you will not give off the wrong vibes.
>
> (senior care manager)

This extract represents a real dilemma that is at the heart of any attempt to be inclusive and raises issues about what appropriate behaviour looks like in relation to students with complex disabilities. The manager is clear that the female carer was behaving in a sexually provocative way by revealing all her midriff which resulted in the incident. The accusation that she viewed the young man in question as less than human because she had not taken into account his sexual identity was followed by the young man being sent home because of his inability to articulate or control his feelings. This raises issues that challenge the ability to manage moments in the outside world when misunderstandings occur, and the immediate response appears to be a defensive one which underlines the vulnerability of the young person, and reasserts his label as disabled. This incident raises questions about the policy that guided staff into their 'reactive' response rather than a 'reflective' one as suggested by Banks (2001), and which reinforced the young person as 'vulnerable' and disabled. The situation also reinforces the previous extract from the speech therapist which implied that students were unlikely to receive the same sensitive responses outside the school, as they did inside.

Innovative practice: introducing Spencer

Running alongside the discourses of control, prevention and protection (both to the young people and staff) is a parallel discourse which acknowledges needs as part of young people's human rights, and which recognise their development into adulthood. This is partly addressed through the PHSE programme referred to above. Springbrook has also developed innovative, unorthodox practices, where not to do so could disadvantage the young people. For example, a doll known as Spencer is used to illustrate masturbation to the students:

> Somebody might come to me and tell me that a student is acting out his sexual frustration. We don't know what to do then, so I will bring the team together, invite parents in, discuss what strategies we can use, then the programme in college or school can be put in place to – maybe we do a programme on sex education – reintroduce that or, I can think of one student who maybe targets male members of staff so strategies would have been put in place around that to make sure that the staff are aware of it, that they know if a male member of staff is nearby then there would be more support for the student.
>
> (family link worker)

A part of this strategy might be to use Spencer to introduce the topic of masturbation:

> We have to teach the students about masturbation etc., when the young men who are aged 14/15 become very challenging. They don't understand what is going on. They begin rubbing their penis and genitals against radiators and hurting themselves. This is why Spencer the masturbating doll was brought in; the students need this kind of information.
>
> (senior care manager)

In this way Spencer is used to augment the existing programme of sex education:

> If they (care practitioners) have somebody who is maybe sexually frustrated then we would try and guide them to be private and to go into another room in the house or go in the bedroom, so it's guiding them really.
>
> (family link worker)

The use of this doll represents a pragmatic method for clarifying acceptable and necessary ways of dealing with sexual frustration which is very difficult to explain:

> Spencer is highly symbolic because he is at the extreme edge of what's permissible, which essentially is masturbation. Some students because of their physical or cognitive or other disabilities cannot achieve satisfaction through masturbation, they don't understand it, and cannot actually manage it.
>
> (educational psychologist)

However for young people at Springbrook who are able to achieve satisfaction through masturbation Spencer offers an approved means of rehearsing personal sexualised touch which can be viewed as helpful. On the other hand Spencer appears to be an exception to the policies in as much as it represents an aspect of touch that may be misinterpreted (interestingly 'anatomically correct dolls' were popularised in the sex abuse scandals, e.g. Orkney, a few decades earlier). The extracts referred to above indicate that the use of the doll is part of a considered policy/strategy which has included communication with appropriate practitioners and parents, so this practice can be better understood outside Springbrook.

Concluding thoughts

The chapter has raised a number of important issues that have influenced the current touching culture at Springbrook, and in particular the development of policies as the means by which practice is guided. The interpretation of policy recommendations into practice outcomes is often sensitive and fragile and managed via the relationships between a practitioner and a child. Reverberating throughout the policies is an overriding concern to minimise risk and thereby avoid investigation and potential censure and the consequences this would have on the reputation of Springbrook. However, an important consideration relates to the management of sexual development as it affects the young people, and in this area there are some interesting innovative and daring exceptions to the constraints imposed by too narrow a reading of policy, these are intended to provide a meaningful life experience for Springbrook's children and young people.

Chapter 10

Case study

Summerhill School – an exception to the rule

Summerhill school was founded in 1921 by A.S. Neill, whose work on education and child development was of international repute especially in the 1960s and 1970s when it became a 'transatlantic cult' (Skidelsky 1969: 15). The school is fee-paying, has charitable status and is now located on the edge of a small town in rural East Anglia. Spatially, the grounds of the school comprise several acres of woodland, some open grassy areas, a large house, and a number of single-storey classroom blocks. The school is divided into five age-related houses: Cottage, San, House, Shack, and Carriage, in ascending order of age. Most staff live in. The School currently describes itself as 'the oldest child democracy in the world' (www.summerhillschool.org) and remains unchanged in its ways of self-government since Neill's time. It is a predominantly residential 'free' school, one much inspected and criticised down the years by the relevant government inspectorates in England. In 1999 Her Majesty's Inspectorate tried to close down the school, lodging a series of objections that the school was forced to resist in court in order to remain open and true to its principles (Stronach in Vaughan 2006). Ending the policy of voluntary attendance at lessons has been the government's enduring target. The government failed, and since then the school has prospered. Indeed, a recent Social Services Inspection report praised the school's 'very high' levels of pupil satisfaction (CSCI 2005). The current roll (*c*.90) includes children from age 4 to 16, from countries as varied as the UK, US, Germany, Holland, Japan, Taiwan and Korea. The core of the school is the Meeting, where pupils and staff, on a one person–one vote basis, decide how the school will be run.[1] Summerhill was selected as a case study site because we anticipated, on the basis of previous research experience in the school (Stronach *et al.* 2000; Stronach 2002b), that Summerhill could be seen as being at one end of a continuum, a school generally thought to be less 'regulated', where children could choose whether they wished to attend lessons, and where pupils were part of a self-governing community. The original intent to explore 'touch' at Summerhill was quickly affected by the recognition of touch per se as a banal issue. The unique characteristics of Summerhill made it obvious that 'touch' was merely one aspect of other social, organisational, cultural, and ethical features of the environment in which it occurs. We could only understand 'touch' if we explored Summerhillian practices of the self, the other, the community, the culture – and the reproduction of all these.

Getting into Summerhill

The easiest way to interpret Summerhill is to succumb to its difference. It is democratic while schools are generally autocratic. There is an egalitarian relation between adults and children. It rejects compulsion in relation to attendance at lessons, examinations, assessment, and even report cards to parents. It is exotic and so we read it, easily or uneasily, against our prejudices. Our own unease on our first visit to the school as part of the research was triggered by a newspaper we chanced upon. 'Jacko's Lair: Bed where he "groped" teen Gavin' (*Daily Mirror* 4/3/05) read the headlines of the marked 'school' copy. It lay in the dining room and was flicked through by teachers during breaks, while we grew increasingly anxious about our questioning in relation to 'touch' at Summerhill. We observed children throwing snowballs at each other, giving each other a piggy-back across the snow, occasionally hugging, play-punching a teacher on the arm, writing sponsorship amounts on a sheet propped against a teacher's chest, and so on. But as we asked about adults touching children, children touching each other, adults touching adults, it felt a bit 'pervy' as a subject for conversation, an attempt to unnaturalise what the subjects regarded as absolutely normal.

Our discomfort surfaced in our field notes: 'how do you say they "rubbed against one another" (two Taiwanese girls) or "he put his hand on her thigh" ... without immediately being in a sexual register?' What was the overall source of our uneasiness? It seemed that asking such questions carried a sexual innuendo that became more prominent as the field-work continued. In a 2001 mini-inspection of the school, the Government Inspector had drawn attention to 'inappropriate touching' as a teacher gave a piggy-back to a small child. When asked what touching *was* appropriate, the inspector's answer was unequivocal: 'no touching'. What we were doing as researchers felt like another case of 'inappropriate touching', and asking questions about touching in Summerhill felt contaminating. The *Daily Mirror* headlines about Michael Jackson provoked a Kafkan dilemma. They symbolised the contaminating guilt that preceded 'offence' and stood as an analogy for our own research headlines about 'touching', however differently we might want to place our own allegiances. Purity and prurience kept changing place. They posited 'touch' precisely in its moral panic terms, which is where the potency of our research question comes from: adult power over child innocence = 'groping' = sexual perversion = Michael Jackson personified, if only as presented in the tabloids. Summerhill (both adults and children), in contrast, seemed to deal with bedtime arrangements in a different sort of way – pragmatically: Law

13: 'For House and below BOs [Beddies Officers] have to check with Houseparent before people can sleep in each others' rooms', and Law 17: 'If you are camping out you have to come to bedtime, tell your houseparent/BO where you are, and who you are with'.

There is a contrast here between the practical management of risk of whatever kind (most likely to be nuisance or petty theft in Summerhill situations) and the inspector's anticipatory prohibition of the very possibility of error or even mistaken perception, always conceived as implicitly sexual in nature (i.e. 'no touching'). It was interesting that when we presented those sorts of 'outside world' scares (e.g. no adult and child together in an otherwise solitary situation) and explained the rationale to older Summerhill pupils, they looked astonished, and said: 'If they don't trust in the teacher to actually be on their own with pupils then that's just pathetic'. Yet the staff nevertheless receive obligatory 'child protection' training and inspection days, and consider some of it irrelevant to what goes on in Summerhill (e.g. 'What would you do if a parent came up to school smelling of alcohol?' – in a boarding school not a very relevant example, as a teacher pointed out). But teachers in Summerhill tend not to wonder too much how things might be perceived elsewhere. One houseparent considered what 'boundary' might be appropriate to her dealings with the youngest children in the school. The notion of 'not touching' was inconceivable, but she obliged us by finding a boundary: 'I wouldn't take them into the bath with me, as I would my own kids'.

Another major difference from other schools is that pupils propose and police laws to ensure the proper running of the school, privacy and the rights of individuals. These laws are decided democratically, with each child and teacher having one vote. They address specific problems as they arise, rather than envisaging possible problems in terms of universal prescription. Even the School Laws have numerous specific exceptions. For example, Law 48: 'Freddy can have a stick bigger than him'. In the wider social context as evidenced in other case study sites, however, policy and practice is highly affected by real or imagined media concerns and it might be argued that both the morality of the media and its simultaneous pornography are reliant on each other. However, in Summerhill 'touch', is not a sensitive issue – and indeed appeared a ridiculous intrusion when we brought it up. And as the bringers-up, we became unwilling agents of the same sexualised culture of 'risk' that we were committed to investigate impartially, even though there was no impartiality out there for us to adopt as a stance. We came away from our first field trip feeling in parts both guilty and silly. As outsiders, we felt contaminating, but that was part of the data: we were subjects in transit across Summerhillian boundaries that we could begin to feel in terms of their difference, but not yet understand.

Summerhill outside-in

Summerhill is an almost perfect panopticon, incapable of secrets: 'There are no secrets here, they all come out. The children believe that there are *some*, but actually there are no secrets' (houseparent), and 'there are no secrets, so it [abuse] couldn't happen . . . everything goes to the Meeting and is spoken about and sorted out' (teacher). Or as one pupil put it, 'you're around people all the time, and you kind of live here, and it's like a big family and you know everybody'. It is a total institution with boundaries both invisible and powerful – school pupils/'downtowners',[2] locals/Summerhill cosmopolitans,[3] limits to parental visits,[4] and hidden definitions of normal/abnormal. As another pupil informed us: 'there's other people who have been teaching in *normal* schools but they find it a really big jump but they do in the end settle in just fine, and are just *normal*' (pupil, our stresses). No one is locked in or out, but the borders are not often crossed. Staff members are seldom off-duty in reality; there is a problem of 'getting time on your own'. Pupils visit them at will: 'sometimes you just randomly turn up and say "hi" and have a cup of hot chocolate or something' (pupil), and 'you know them as well as you know another child' (pupil). So without intending anything negative, we suggest that Summerhill is a very precise and reliable mechanism for the social manufacture of selves.

The Meeting scrutinises breaches of the democratically agreed laws, and legislates for and against transgressors. All adults and children are equally entitled to participate in discussion, criticism and voting. On the occasions we attended the Meeting, around two-thirds of the pupils were present. At that time, there were extant 174 laws which had been voted in over time, including individual and minute prescription of behaviour: 'BAN. Victor not allowed rubber band gun until he appeals', 'Law 48: Len can have a lighter that doesn't light but sparkles'. The Meeting has the power to make law, and indeed to abolish any or all laws. As we watched in March 2005, an 11-year-old sought permission to light fires in the woods. Law 79 says she is too young: 'Only Shack and over are allowed matches and lighters'. Her claim was that 'I'm good with fires; it's a nuisance to find someone who's older'. The meeting decided that she was responsible enough, but had to undertake that she would not light fires for others of her age or younger and/or leave them in charge. Even those deemed less responsible in that particular ruling voted in her favour. The elected laws cover everything from bedtimes, bath-times, and bikes, to more arcane matters, this next one seemingly straight from Harry Potter: 'Law 37: You can't swap, sell or buy Magic Cards without someone from the Swindling Committee'.

Each law is the product of debate and voting, and can be unmade at any time. This is self-regulation with a vengeance. Each alleged transgression is considered in its own right. In June 2005, Tom was brought up at the Meeting for urinating from a tree and splashing an older girl who was passing by. Some laughed; one said, 'that's evil'. The Chair interjected: 'It's one thing pissing people off, another pissing on them'. Much hilarity. But he was told not to do it again. In each case, and in the Summerhillian's accumulation of cases over time, there are questions of right and wrong, serious or piddling, appropriate or not. In ways such as these, the school – though it is a community more than a school in the conventional sense – invites and receives an all-embracing allegiance from its membership which is unheard of in state schooling. It manufactures Summerhillians whose loyalties may transcend those of country and home: 'my life is more kind of here and not at home . . . I would call this [Summerhill] home instead of back in [county]' (pupil), and a teacher notes: 'he finds it an alien nation really for him [when going home to SE Asia] and he finds himself being very lonely . . . it's missing that wholesome relation that you bond with many individuals on a deeper level, I think'.

When 'being yourself' and 'having your life' proves problematic, the Meeting not only makes laws but is there to advise and adjudicate. Disputes or complaints may be dealt with informally, or by Ombudsmen, who are older students of either gender appointed to be a first point of assistance. Unresolved or serious complaints may lead an individual to 'bring up' whoever has offended them at the Meeting. Any child or adult, in any combination, may do so. An 11-year-old girl explains:

> The point about the meeting is to make . . . *me* feel [our stress] that it was totally wrong, this is a strong warning. But if you do it again, we will fine you. If you make contact [violence] you won't get a strong warning, they will probably fine you some odd random things like 'Bully's List',[5] no television, no screens, no social games.

She offered a judicious view of its effectiveness:

> Bully's List is one of the fines *we* use [our stress – see later] if someone has made physical contact or bullied someone like mad, like really harassed them, bullying someone by harassing them, and that tends to work for some people and not for others because you get a trouble-maker in every school and we've had a few troublemakers and Bully's List has worked and hasn't worked, like every fine might work, might not work.

But the real force of the sanctions is social rather than financial. The Meeting teaches the anti-social that they 'can't get away with this stuff because everyone thinks *I'm* a right twit now and *I* [our stresses] have to calm down and build relationships . . . the more they go to the Meeting [and are 'brought up'] the more fed up and vocal the Meeting gets . . . so it [the problem] does turn itself around'. There is a clear element of persuasion, and also of public shaming in these arrangements, but no signs of scapegoating. It is held, even, that those 'brought up' seldom resent their accusers, although we did come across a pupil who felt that was not the case for her. Basically, the Meeting disciplines by instilling a sense of right and wrong in pupils by a practical, case-based approach. Through repetition, the more general, moral development of a sense of fairness and responsibility is fostered. The internalisation can be vivid:

> but it's not laws like *you* can't run in the corridors and you have to pick flowers at this time, it's nothing like that, so you really have to use your head and think 'Oh, can *I* do this?' like if you were about to carve *your* name in a wall, you'd think, 'Oh, do *I* think that *I* can do this, no, *I* probably can't'. [our stresses]
>
> (student)

It seems to us significant that Summerhillians shift between 'I', 'you', 'we' and 'them' in the way that they do. The speaker above hypothetically incriminates herself as an 'I', envisaging herself considering an infringement. The tendency to regard self as I, we, you, them, interchangeably was also observed in the case of Garry, a boy who reported to the Meeting other boys who owed him money. Everyone was unsympathetic as lending money was against the laws. He ended up voting against himself in agreeing he wouldn't lend money to them or anyone else again. While this may well have been the outcome he had hoped for (saving him future embarrassment in saying 'no'), the situation was nevertheless dealt with both dispassionately and impersonally. In a similar act of self-distancing, Summerhillians sometimes also referred to the 'I' as a first name, 'Katie', 'Vicki': 'I wasn't the real Vicki when I was in state school, you're not yourself'. Transgressors were seldom discussed in terms as simple as an impersonal 'he', 'she' or 'them'. Such thinking was deliberative, empathic and agentic, rather than recriminatory: 'unless one does it for one's self, it isn't thinking' (Dewey 1966: 303). This kind of consideration was extended to their treatment of their interlocutors. It is not often that a schoolchild says to a researcher, 'Have you had a good experience so far?'

We have been trying to show how structured and structuring Summerhill is. We invoked the panopticon, although a paradoxically plural one available in large measure to all the participants. We used a rather dark language of mechanism, laboratory and total institution. The strength of boundaries makes the Summerhill 'community' almost the opposite of the conventional school-as-community. In the latter case it is the weakness of school-community boundaries that defines the ideal (Carspecken 1991). Far from the 'free' image with which we started this account, Summerhill school has invisible boundaries, powerful inspections, binding agreements and redemptive rituals, as well as a set of public punishments that prompt and enact acceptable ways to live together. These all act as an 'outside-in' pressure that frames and disciplines interactions while developing identities and relationships, yet always with the possibility of change or resistance. We have suggested something of the 'total' nature of pupils' engagement with these structures. Summerhill is a powerful mechanism, generating discipline from within, and without the coercive relations of a 'normal' school. The school orchestrates a vortex of engagements, from which there is no 'backing away', as one pupil put it.

Summerhill inside-out

At the same time, the 'school' has weak boundaries where conventional 'schools' have strong ones. There are weak boundaries between different pupil age groups: 'In Summerhill a five-year-old could be best friends with a 16-year-old and that would not be a problem' (pupil), and 'every time a new kid comes you help them more and more and more and feel better about yourself' (older pupil). Similarly, boundaries between staff and pupils are minimal in comparison with a conventional school. Pupils visit staff in their caravans, as we've seen – 'it's just like visiting a friend in their room'. They do so informally and indeed can be shoo-ed away in like manner. The first thing the Principal looks for in recruiting new staff is 'nice people'; a central focus is on relationships. Within the school, there are also many weak distinctions between public and private spaces:

> They [the youngest kids] don't feel they have to stay out of the staffroom or keep out of your room. [So they would come to your room?] Yes, they do, but I don't always let them in, as I've usually had enough of them. I tell them I need time on my own and they're quite good about that because in a similar way they wouldn't want me to hang about their rooms all the time.
>
> (teacher)

Another weak boundary is spatial. The classrooms are inside but the outside woodland is accepted as an equally important learning area – how to play, make things. Pupils come and go as they will, unlike movements 'down town'. Inside or outside, whatever the season, male and female pupils often dress in similar clothes, big jumpers and loose trousers (a phenomenon noted by other observers more than 40 years ago). The strong boundaries are for outsiders like us, who can't climb the trees, can't go to the bedrooms, or upstairs in the House. We need a vote of the Meeting even to attend. There is also a reciprocity theme here. Weak boundaries are places of negotiation rather than prohibition or permission and so Summerhillians are good at reading each other, as well as being experts on 'themselves'. This, as we will see, is integral to the practices and interpretations of 'touch' at the school: 'Each teacher is different, a different person takes a different amount of time to settle in, the same as students' (pupil) and 'for everyone it's different, and as long as everyone is respectful and isn't interfering with someone else's space and how they feel about that, there's no problem' (pupil).

This contrast between strong invisible boundaries round the school, and weak boundaries within aspects of its social activity means that pupils themselves can be relatively unaware of the former, and see themselves as completely unfettered:

> But when ex-pupils come back they sense that they didn't know how complicated a job it is to be an adult here. They didn't know about the responsibilities and roles we have and I think that's brilliant. I think it's brilliant that they don't know because it shows that what we're doing is right because they're really unaware of the stuff that we have to worry about and think about. So I think, 'Well that's a good sign', because it means we're doing it well, and I think that's important for the kids, that they can get on with their life.
>
> (principal)

How do the participants make overall sense of this interlaced world of weak and strong boundaries? The pupils' metaphors of association centre on notions of 'home', 'family', 'brother' and 'sister', with the teachers most often portrayed as 'friends really', 'like visiting a friend'. Asked what the weirdest thing about Summerhill was, one of the oldest pupils replied: 'I think it's that we all get on'. The adults noted the 'enormous attachment' pupils had to the place, 'it's astonishing really', but were more likely to refer to the 'tribe' or 'community' of Summerhill, a 'community based on the rights of the child with some constraints about ownership and about property and things like that . . . a community based on friendship rather than a family based on friendship' (teacher). Both staff and pupils pointed to a central value of 'trusting people', with pupils more often claiming that the relation is an equal one – 'we're all like equal' while some of the adults shied away from the 'family' images, and noted that the relation was pretty equal, but not entirely: 'I'm not sure it would be such a good thing if they knew as much about me as I know about them' (teacher) and 'so in spite of anything that leads towards equality there is definitely a distinction between an adult and a child and I think any of the adults here would have to acknowledge that' (teacher, reinforcing a related point made by the principal, above).

Those qualities of trust, equal rights, responsibilities, commitment, honesty and confidence in pro-Summerhill accounts can take on a *Swallows and Amazons* romantic flavour, and we would prefer to stress that these are not so much the *qualities* of the inmates or the community as the *work* of the school in the construction, and reconstruction, of selves. For example, a teacher stressed that: 'the kids are confident with adults, they're not coy. It's [teaching at Summerhill] not for someone who's a prima donna. I don't care if a kid says "fuck off"; I don't care what the kids say to me actually, I think the honesty of it all is very good'. There is a *dispassion* within Summerhill, as well as a passion for it. As a teacher put it to us, 'there's none of the anger that underpins it [swearing, etc.] at other schools', and at that point we began to make sense of another teacher's enthusiasm for Summerhill. Having said familiar things about seeing 'the emotional difference between living in a place like this and living back out in a kind of atomised family structure, and it hits you quite profoundly when you've been here a while', he went on to point to the 'sense of community and connectedness'. At the time of the interview, he puzzled us: 'the kids are completely *neutral* about what they are doing' (our stress). We now interpret this in terms of that 'dispassion' we noted above. That is, it isn't personal; there is a system that delivers consequences for actions. Your friend may 'bring you up' but it is the Meeting that delivers judgement. The Meeting is not *them*, it is *us*. It's connected to the phenomenon of the 'floating pronouns' that we noted earlier – the grammar of empathy, as it were. We began to see that theme as a thread through the numerous conversations we had with pupils and teachers. The Meeting was clearly central to the 'neutral' functioning of the school as a learning experience for the pupils, as well as a demonstration of 'equality' in relation to adult as opposed to child power. As one teacher commented: 'it's good for the kids to see you can "bring up" adults', while another commented on the confidence that even little kids showed in the Meeting:

> it's amazing sometimes how the little kids speak in the Meetings and the respect they get from everyone. Everybody is really quiet to be able to understand them so they really get heard and I think for the little kids that must be amazing to see these much bigger people all listening to what *I'm* [our stress] saying, it must be an amazing confident feeling.

One of the oldest girls commented that Summerhill was 'a different way of life and a different way of education'. We were struck by that coincidence of 'way of life' and 'education' in the social mechanisms of the school. The notion of 'living your own life' was a dominant aspect of the culture. The older girls told of the arrival of a young Japanese girl, when they too were young:

> we actually taught her English. She didn't go to any lessons till a later stage . . . you bond better because you know who they are, so even though she couldn't speak any English we still managed to get on with her completely fine, and still play like little girls do, because we were young then. [later adding] I always thought in some way you learn more life skills than you would anywhere else because of sharing and learning to get on with each other, being patient kind of thing.

This pattern of social learning within little groups, often of different ages, was very apparent in the data: 'I always tend to have friends who are older than me because when I mix with kids my own age I don't learn anything, whereas if I mix with kids younger, I teach, er, give skills to the younger kids and the older kids give skills to me. So it's a win–win situation' (female pupil). The avoidance of the word 'teach' may be significant. It's a little too directive for the culture. In fact, to understand 'education' at Summerhill you have to be ungrammatical: the pupils *learn each other*, in more than one sense. And the teachers are *part* of that.

Summerhill also appeared to staff and pupils as a place of necessary risk. The grounds were open to the pupils, tree-climbing was permitted, and – to pick out the feature that would probably most alarm the 'risk culturalists' – older children were allowed to carry 'machetes', defined by Summerhill Law as blades over six inches (Law 94), and controlled by the likes of 'Law 85: You have to be Shack or over and can only have a machete in the woods and are not allowed to carry it around – have to keep it in your room', and 'Law 80: No sheath knives down town (UK law)'. Note the strength of the boundary implicit in Law 80. The 'outside' is the UK, and by implication Summerhill is somewhere else – another country seemingly. Most concerns about safety were not about sexual threats of any kind; they concerned injuries caused by play, mainly skateboarding. Pupils were adamant about the value of 'risks' such as swinging from the Big Beech tree: 'if you didn't do that sort of thing you'd never have the chance to grow up', and 'whatever you do there's a chance you'll hurt yourself and if you can't have chances like that, you can't live'. Teachers agreed, and the Principal identified both the necessity of risk to learning, and the dangers it posed for the school as the risk culture expands:

> I see that this whole safety issue and the insurance and the accountability and the whole thing that goes on out there is going to seep into us . . . I don't see how they [pupils] can have access to these huge high trees just whenever they want . . . and that we can get away with it. I don't know how it will come about, whether somebody will actually get injured and there'd be a huge litigation thing, or whether our insurance company will eventually say we're not going to insure you any more unless you make these restrictions. I don't know, but I can see it coming and I think that's very frightening because the whole issue of risk-taking is so vital to Summerhill – because that is what Summerhill is all about . . . so the whole child protection issue comes under the same bracket really, we have to keep going because we believe that what we do is fine and we believe it's good to be able to cuddle children and we believe that physical contact between kids and adults is absolutely fine and should be happening and if we believe that, then we have to keep doing it, because it's OK.

Finally, it is important to link these experiences to perceptions of the 'outside'. Many Summerhillians are familiar with conventional schools. Indeed, for quite a few, it is their 'failure' at these schools that has taken them there. A dominant theme is that adults in such institutions 'distance' themselves from the children: 'I find it very strange when I see people distancing themselves away from other people'; 'all the teachers there [state school] stayed very distant . . . and didn't give hugs' (Kent), 'the teachers used to stay in staffrooms and kids stayed out of staffrooms in my school' (NE England), and 'when I came here it was such a relief. I felt like there was this weight off my back. I didn't have to go to the state school any more. I didn't have to be bullied for the rest of my life and I didn't have to pretend to be something I'm not'.

A further dominant theme concerned their sense of themselves referred to previously, and the emotional ethos of the school they had attended, including issues of bullying and harassment. Summerhill, perhaps above all else, was somewhere where you did not have to pretend: 'trying to act cool in a certain way to get people to like you', 'you can just totally be yourself and don't have to act or try to get people to like you because if you're yourself and they harass you or make fun of you, you can bring them up in the Meeting' (pupil). They noted the absence of sexual harassment and name-calling at Summerhill, contrasting that with their earlier experiences: 'If someone of the same sex gives each other a hug there, they'd get harassed loads and thought to be gay or lesbian', and 'if you're a little bit different then you'll be classed as a freak and they won't go near you. But here, it's OK, they don't care'. Again, that same, *neutral* 'don't care':

> Here you get freedom, you're allowed to speak in the Meetings. You can deal with people bullying you. If someone comes up to you and says you're a squashed nose person, I could take it to the Meeting and they would do something about it pretty quick.

Summerhill: touching on inside-out and outside-in

It's taken us a long time to return to 'touch'. Just as well because it is the wrong focus; it became apparent that 'touch' made no sense without locating it within the culture of relationships that constitutes Summerhill's production of selves. Recall the inspector's injunction: 'no touching!' In terms of our research focus, we had to retreat from 'touch' in order to locate it in a more contextual way. *Relational touch* contained physical touch, in ways foreign to 'outside' institutions where an accountability and risk culture determines touching practices in more rigid ways. In Summerhill, 'touch' (and its embodying relationships) was constituted by both the 'outside-in' and the 'inside-out' features of the culture. It was a question of the nature of the flows between these two surfaces. We prefer to call Summerhill a 'culture' rather than an 'organisation' because it effected itself in more tribe-like ways: it *governed* itself, and in doing so produced a distinctive citizenship, one that we find difficult to name happily as 'pupils' or 'students' or 'kids', given the range in ages (4 to 16), and stages of development. That active citizenship in turn was the generator of identity. It was active and self-formative, in that participants *chose* what to take an interest in, and in choosing learnt something of their own desires, responsibilities and identity. As a Summerhill teacher from North America explained it to us: 'if you're a child you expect some guidance, but the basic raw thing is: do you or do you not have the right to choose what you do from morning to evening, to stand or fall on the choices. And here you *do*'.

The outside-in boundaries of Summerhill constructed the features that we earlier noted as 'dark' – panopticon, total institution, self-regulation and surveillance, all of which made Summerhill a strong as well as a benign society. It is also a highly intuitive and tacit one. The Principal spoke of Summerhill's community as a:

> . . . family or a tribe, I think it's like a tribe, but it's more than that, it's just a life area. It's an area where everything happens and it's definitely not a school. [Are you a tribal leader then?] No, I'm not a leader. No, because I'm not really a leader anyway, I'm just here, I kind of monitor things and keep an eye on things – people sometimes sort of want me to be – I don't really think of myself as a leader, I'm just a bit bossy that's all.
>
> (principal)

But at the same time, these strong and bounded relations were interlinked with, and helped generate weak boundaries between age cohorts, learning spaces, and across teacher–child relationships. The strong boundaries ensured things like social and personal identity, safe spaces, effective government and social redress. At the same time they enabled weak boundaries that provoked relationships based on self-knowledge and negotiated spaces that were potentially learning-rich in all sorts of social ways. People learned to read each other, and hence themselves in a kind of social dialectic: in such interaction varying degrees of 'relational touch' were negotiated. And the panopticon features were available, more or less, to all.[6] Of course, the opposition of 'strong' and 'weak' is inadequate in itself, because the 'freedoms' of Summerhill could also be breached in the strong sense – that's what all the laws and Meetings were for. Such breaches, however, were part of how the school worked as an organism; they were how people learned, in important ways. The Meeting was a place of conflict just as much as it was of consensus. The Meeting has been portrayed in utopian terms, but it would be more useful perhaps to see it as a 'working dystopia', as part of the 'organic moving space' (Principal) of the community. It is maybe not too much of a paradox to say that one way the School worked was by breaking down and mending itself, rendering problematic social relations *explicit* as a moral, emotional and rational curriculum for communal and personal living as well as learning. Issues central to 'relational touch', then, were an inherent part of these disputes.

In addition, these processes were fed by a series of informal learning sets, based on a myriad of relationships – teacher–pupil, pupil–peers, mixed-age groupings, and so on. This was Summerhill as a learning-swarm.[7] In most organisations or institutions strong links mean constraint and coercion, but in Summerhill the strongly bounded features – like the Meeting, or the social circumferences of the school, the school as community – seemed to create spaces for people to feel that they could 'be themselves', 'live their own lives', 'recover' themselves from damaging earlier experiences, live without 'harassment', successfully seek redress for whatever injuries befell them in the school itself. In that latter sense, the 'outside' was also at the core of Summerhill, as a set of learning and living experiences that pupils had to work on – hence the many comparisons by pupils of 'state school' with conditions in Summerhill. Hence too, in a weaker sense, the same core/periphery relation existed for the teachers at the school. Summerhill dealt with the real world outside as well as inside, constantly turning the inside out and the outside in. Nor did Summerhillians fear their future 'outside'.[8]

> Researcher: You could say you live in this happy little bubble when you're young and growing up and stuff and then suddenly you are in the big, bad, cruel, jealous, possessive, ambitious world.
> Pupil (f): It's good if it teaches you how to make friends when you get into the big jealous bad world.

Our conclusion was that the school enabled its pupils to be Summerhillians, and to call that 'themselves'. Each sought, in an oft-recurring sentiment, to 'get on with their lives'. An experienced teacher at the school, familiar with free schools internationally, commented that there is 'an accepted individuality and agency that I have not experienced happening anywhere else'; 'a very, very definite personal narrative'. We see this vividly in the data: 'if you don't act like yourself, you can't get true friends' so 'you're just yourself'. That was both the autonomy and conformity of the school. In such an relational circulation, policed in such a 'neutral' way, physical 'touch' was neither here nor there. You do it if you feel like it, and if not, you don't. Another stereotype bites the dust – Summerhill was some way from being the 'touchy-feely' school it is sometimes portrayed to be.

Relational and physical touch

As we've seen, the 'outside' experiences of school were typically reported in terms of 'distance', of being 'pushed away' by adults; the 'inside' perceptions were of a place where you could not 'back away', where you were always in touch with others.[9] The pushing/backing/distancing/closing metaphors suggested the notion of 'relational touch', provided we define that 'touch' as also a calculation of distance. Children at Summerhill were in relational touch with each other and with themselves. That particular touch was an odd mixture of *passion* (about the place) and *dispassion* about others, in a governmental sense. Inspection agencies had no brief for relational touch, but as we've seen they were intent on proscribing physical touching. In a previous inspection Tim (teacher) had attended a Meeting with inspectors present, and he reported to us:

> So I'm sitting there and Karen comes up and says: 'Can you massage my shoulders?' I know the inspector is behind me, I know it's an issue, but I thought: 'Well, I'm not going to change my behaviour because an inspector is behind me', so I massaged her shoulders and then at the end of the two-day inspection, I'm part of the curriculum advisory team, so I was asked to go in with the inspectors and listen to feedback and then they said: 'You can leave now because we've got something to talk to [the principal] about', and they basically said that a member of staff had been inappropriately touching a young female student and they were going to report it to Social Services.

Tim had known the student for around four years. 'Shoulder massage' was a familiar activity between them and within the community more generally, as we observed ourselves and were also told: 'it's not unusual to see one man giving another a massage at the Meeting'. Those who were deemed good at it amongst the children sometimes had queues waiting for attention. The practice of massage is part of the school culture: some do it; some don't, and it varied according to national cultures, backgrounds and dispositions of both staff and students.[10] At a follow-up visit the same thing happened a second time as the girl hadn't been informed: 'they're sitting behind me, exactly the same as before, and I'm thinking "what do I do" so I thought I'm not going to say "no" so I repeat the massage'. Tim was later questioned by the Social Services inspector:

> . . . and so we had this 20-minute argument about touch and culture, and why was it wrong, and where was it appropriate . . . he basically said: 'Do it, it's OK, but don't do it in front of me'. Now you can't have a Social Services inspector saying that because they're basically condoning saying you're doing something against the values of Social Services and against their advisory statements and guidance and everything else, but that's what he did say in the end.

There was a similar variety in relation to other forms of touch, such as hugging, play-fighting, and so on. Anything that got out of hand – as sometimes play-fighting might – could be resolved at the Meeting, if not more informally. Generally, staff and pupils felt that touch was not an issue and were incredulous at practices 'outside'. Typical comments included: 'never crosses my mind', 'not a real problem for us', it's 'natural', 'part of the ethos', 'it's really a matter of trust'.

As part of a more general aspect of Summerhill governance, issues of touch were not decided by universal prescriptions, any more than were relationships and lesson participation. Each case of 'touching' or 'not touching' was decided on its own merits. There were also examples given of touch as a kinaesthetic approach to writing and other skills, and also of the need to wean any 'clingy' kids into a better understanding of other people's 'space', without making a fuss about it. But both of these were considered 'inappropriate' in our other case study schools where, in contrast, 'needy' was rescripted too risky, while 'touch defensiveness' implied emotional damage. There were some predictable age and gender differences as well, but which add little to our purposes here.

We could cut short this account of 'touch' by saying that Summerhill generally regarded it as a fuss about nothing. Where new children seemed particularly needy the Principal would alert staff. In accordance with government requirements, paper policies had to be produced and guidelines were issued to members of staff. These were regarded as a bureaucratic imposition and much less important than the social processes of the community. But there was a further cost to the school in the state's obsession with sexual and other forms of abuse. These 'external forces' which had completely changed the behaviour of those in our other case studies still had *some* effect on the strong boundaries of the school that the Principal and others had noted. The first of these was the relatively explicit imposition of policies and audit requirements, and the extension of regulations to cover 'risk', or its audit twin, 'safety'.

The second was more insidious, and suggests a risk that the strong boundaries of the school could be undermined by a more existential uncertainty. Reflecting on his encounters with the Inspectorates (Educational and Social), Tim (see above) pointed to a number of successive states of mind. First, he could be spontaneous, and offer a massage to whomever, or give a piggy-back to small children. He had done that for over eight years. But as soon as the inspectors drew attention to such behaviour, he had to make a conscious decision to maintain his behaviour or desist – live the 'lie that you can do it as long as they're not there'. Then there followed a sort of backwash effect from that process: 'that lie then makes you conscious of you doing it when they're not there in some ways'. The intrusion was experienced as a kind of pollution that made spontaneity less possible. We might add that the inspectors' concerns that staff know 'where the *boundaries* are' suggested a 'beyond' to these boundaries that constituted 'abuse'. Thus abuse, never on the agenda before, was then never entirely absent from professional calculations. The inspectors' boundaries thus invaded the school's very different boundaries with a possibility of what Tim called the 'corrupt', and this trace of corruption takes us back to our initial concerns that our own endeavours to research and interrogate 'touch' were similarly corrupting.

Chapter 11

Bonfire of the insanities

Our concluding chapter ends with a call for a more ethical practice, one that encourages professionals not to slavishly follow 'no touch' guidelines, but to put touch back into context (i.e. relationships) and take account of trust and friendships. It is argued that we need to think through notions of 'free touch' just as much as we would 'free speech'. This is no call for licence, but it is a call for recognition that any system that prioritises bureaucratic constraint over 'freedom' introduces a regime of unfreedoms that then develop – through a series of 'ratchet effects' – a kind of creeping totalitarianism, not to mention a galloping fatuity.[1] However, arguably such appeals are more easily made than translated into action in the social contexts which have already fostered the moral panic evident in practice. We have sought to trouble the isolation of touch as a discrete phenomenon, and questioned the use of such metonymic philosophising (and practice). Simultaneously, and perhaps somewhat paradoxically, we pointed to an under-theorisation of touch compared with other senses (and behaviours), most specifically 'sight' (which we attempted to begin to rectify in Chapter 5). Through the practice of taking touch as a discrete phenomenon and out of context, it has become fetishised and therefore very much part of any problem which it seeks to redress.

The original premise for our research (i.e. that touching practices were becoming problematic) was reinforced both within and beyond the boundaries of the research process, through wider social events including the researchers' everyday lives and even their acquaintance with television soap operas. Although the main focus of the research was teachers' and carers' reluctance to touch children in our selected settings, media publicity surrounding the research resulted in contact from a much wider group of adults including stepparents, family friends, 'other' children's parents. They expressed concern with a much broader group of behaviours such as looking 'funny' at girls, texting teenagers, and concern about talking to unrelated young children in playgrounds. Those adults and professionals who behaved in less defensive ways (or 'naturally' as it was frequently referred to) were conscious of taking some 'risk':

If you're not careful you put yourself in a situation where you become suspicious of yourself, you don't trust yourself . . . and I was determined never to get to that point because otherwise I can't get onto a bus where there's a single female, I can't go into a coffee shop, can't do anything.

(male secondary teacher)

As we embarked on the project, defensive and over-cautious practice led many gatekeepers to fear our potential contaminating effects when we sought permission to interview young people about touch in a particular setting. Some headteachers feared that we might encourage tales of abusive behaviour that would open a 'can of worms' that we (or they) would not be able to manage. This response was especially prevalent in secondary school contexts (as Chapter 8 indicated) where reluctance to engage in the research process was mainly a result of this fear. On a number of occasions a deputy head (as initial contact) would express interest: 'I'd love to be involved in that, the head is bound to agree, s/he gives me a free rein in this respect', only to stop returning phone calls and eventually admit that the head had said 'no'. The phrase 'opening a can of worms' would be offered by way of an explanation implying that there was bound to be something going on that was best avoided because 'knowing' would mean having to deal with it according to child protection procedures. The word 'touch' seemed to carry with it the power to open the can of worms, and the firmly closed 'can' was seemingly all that stood between a quiet ordered life, and chaos. But, as we have seen, the worms had long escaped from the can, as acknowledged by all sides – each aware of the significance of touch in repositioning vulnerability and power. 'Touch' then was already problematic.

The word touch itself appeared to hold within it the inference of inappropriateness ('looked after' children for example, discuss 'good' and 'bad' and/or 'appropriate' and 'inappropriate' touch with their key workers), and inappropriate inferences have spread beyond professional discourses. Therefore, asking about 'touching' raised the possibility of the unwanted – whether sexual, physical or verbal. It opened a space for inquiry, simultaneously innocent and complicit. It is innocent in that it can be represented as a deliberative, moral space where questions could be asked on one side or the other and where moral decisions could be reached (e.g. what forms of touching exist in this situation; how they are sanctioned; what boundaries exist, and how they are argued). But that even-handed possibility is contained within a linguistic and cultural space that already admits the possibility of the transgressive or illicit. So the space is innocent in relation to the adjudication of content, but complicit in terms of its form, place and quality. This was the basis of a concern that our enquiries (alongside the current 'no touch' discourse) could serve to reinforce the idea that some behaviours are suspect (or taboo), and therefore potentially the focus of desire.

As a result the research also helped us to extend previous understandings of the 'moral panic' prefaced on the Other – the mugger, the pervert, for example (Hall *et al*. 1978), where policy hysteria was its flip-side. That moral panic also faced generalised Others, such as global economic competition, and lone parents. However, the issue of touch raised an important new variation, as it became apparent that this new manifestation of moral panic articulates the *Self* as an Other. It faces inwards, constructing *self*-mistrust and *self*-regulation (Foucault 1979). The outside comes in, producing 'petrified selves of audit' (Stronach *et al*. 2002) and the inside goes out, in a part-surrender of professional autonomy which actualises both a new inhumanity of care, and a new insanity of the professional self. In Foucault's terms, we might regard it as the *rebirth* of the clinic, but this time as a criminalisation rather than a medicalisation of the gaze. At the same time, the ridiculous is inoculated against laughter, because to laugh is to fail to take the danger seriously and to do so would condone the ever-present risk of perversion. In short, the case studies confirmed that professionals and carers have learned how not to trust themselves, and to call that damaging condition 'safety'. Yet we are reminded of the 15-year-old boy (in Chapter 8) who when asked whether he thought it was OK for teachers to touch him, said: 'It depends how 'fit' [slang: good-looking] the teacher is'. He was playing with the sexual subtext and making a joke by suggesting that touching would be allowable or understandable if he found the teacher attractive. He uses the sexual register to playfully displace the hierarchic relation; a kind of joking that deliberately and for comic effect 'misreads' the dominant register. He constructs himself in jest as a sexual agent rather than an educational subject, a joke that only works in a context where a teacher touching a pupil is considered odd in the first place.

We also became interested in the notion of 'grooming' which has now entered the child protection discourse (a notion clearly founded on the metaphor of 'touch'). It operates in two ways, as a form of touch that is in itself not necessarily illicit but which is likely to lead to more illicit touching practices (perhaps undoing the top button in singing lessons – see below). It is imported from the paedophilic child abuse panics as a central practice of contamination. It is 'danger' personified, gradual and insidious. Through its ubiquity it has the effect of denormalising ordinary practices of touch by (a) making the touched person suspicious, or (b) arousing suspicions among peers that have to be allayed by reporting practices and detailed specification of touch allowances and prohibitions, and/or (c) arousing self-suspicion in a double kind of way. First the professional thinks the unthinkable: if I say 'undo your top button' they will think I'm suggesting this for some sexual reason. Then the individual has to cope with a gaze that is thereby sexualised by the very fact of having to think of such possibilities (cf. Chapter 10). The internal application and external practice of such accountability simultaneously makes the arena of concern pornographic. Finally, to stay sane the individual then has to obliterate the possibility of guilt by relegating such machinations to a necessary but regrettable compliance with the audit culture, where pupils in singing lessons sit cross-legged with their buttons fastened and ties firmly in place. In these ways the concept of grooming acts within that expanding circle of contaminations and suspicions that characterise the risk society.

'Grooming' turns up elsewhere in panic discourses. In *Promoting Good Campus Relations: Working with Staff and Students to Build Community Cohesion and Tackle Violent Extremism in the Name of Islam at Universities and Colleges*, the DfES (2007) posits Islamic extremists as 'grooming' innocent students first by targeting them and then befriending them. So the practice – a largely illusory fear in 'touch' contexts – is discursively disseminated as a metaphor for putative terrorist practices, whereby by the innocent are defiled by 'Violent-Extremism-in-the-Name-of-Islam' (a new compound noun). This is appreciated in terms of a similarly perceived 'threat' ('a real, credible and sustained threat to the UK' ibid.: 4). This is a violation of the social rather than the sexual body of the individual, but the former is interesting in that 'grooming' implies not a social movement so much as an individual seduction/contamination. The individual separated out by college from 'family and old friends' (ibid.: 7) is vulnerable to contamination by 'charismatic radical speakers' (ibid.: 8) who are 'forceful, persuasive and eloquent' (ibid.: 8). Therefore, precautionary ethics demand close and informed relationships between 'educational institutions, Students' Unions, societies, security officers and police' (ibid.: 10). HE providers are asked to clarify response procedures, such as identifying 'who should decide whether to inform the police' (ibid.: 11). These 'reporting mechanisms' (ibid.: 14) are much invoked in the text. The cure is also familiar: 'Developing an institutional *Standard*' (ibid.: 15). The publication proposes a five-stage escalator of responses – ending in 'Enact the decision including bringing in the police if and where necessary' (ibid.: 15). This is portrayed again in the universal rhetorics of 'good' government. The HE/police should utilise in a 'partnership approach' (ibid.: 16) that operates in a preventative way: 'A partnership approach between police and HE providers may enable early intervention to take place that could negate a later need for enforcement' (ibid.: 16). This implies that the concern is not just for 'existing' but also for 'emerging' instances of 'violent extremism' (ibid.: 16). It is suggested that the police can train HE to 'recognise signs of violent extremism' (ibid.: 16), much like heads can presumably train their staff to recognise paedophiles.

Many hold 'risk society' (Beck 1987, 1992) responsible for polluting touching and other behaviours (including campus relations). Risk has been described as 'a container for a bundle of issues that are not readily disentangled' (Mythen 2004: 54) and which focus on the eternal theme of damage and disgrace (Douglas 1985). As a result, schools are enjoined by the state to understand themselves and become sites of generalised risk, with the effect that managing risk mismanages opportunities to learn. The 'risks' are managed not by managing and distributing the 'goods', but by managing and distributing the 'bads'; performance is very much focused on danger. To invert Law and Mol's taxonomy of utopianism (2002), this is 'dystopian absolutism'.[2] However, such accounts offer only a partial reading of 'expert–lay' relations and 'fail to recognise that the "done to" lay public are at one and the same time "doers" working within the relations of definition' (Mythen 2004: 60). In other words, both professionals and lay public share an experience of helping to create particular labels and definitions which in turn provide sets of relationships that derive from them. In a situation where the 'non-risky' population now view themselves (and are viewed by others) as at equal risk with the 'risky' population, powerful elements of self-fulfilling prophesy begin to circulate. Those whose aim is self protection 'appear to create risk categories and hierarchies of risk themselves, that is, to make up risk cultures' (Adkins 2001). Such over-scripted protocols for practice inevitably lead to a kind of defensive professional reaction, through which central aspects of professionalism (e.g. relationships, values such as trust, empathy, responsibility, individuality) are over-written by defensive prescription and proscription.

(Mis)guidelined

It was frequently and wrongly assumed by many respondents that actual legislation prohibits physical contact between adults and children and young people in their charge (as we saw in Chapters 3 and 4). This impression was reported and documented as being privileged by authoritative figures, including a number of Ofsted inspectors, quality auditors and child protection advisors, and similar, who issued verbal or written statements, explicitly or by implication to this effect. Professional development and training programmes were in some cases acting on this advice, and in turn privileging defensive responses and encouraging cautious touching practices in the majority of professional settings. Practices which had been routine for the past 30 years or more (e.g. loosening a tie for singing lessons) became the subject of internal inquiries (e.g. where an LEA adviser was brought in to adjudicate):

> And that is me saying . . . you loosen your tie because it gives you a little bit more freedom . . . you might want to undo the top button and sit in a relaxed way, don't have your legs crossed, don't flop, and don't sit rigid, because it's putting it in context. If the implications weren't so serious it would be quite funny . . . once a rumour has been discussed and documented it's there in print. There's no smoke without fire.
>
> (retired music teacher)

Although this teacher was eventually found 'not guilty' of sexual misconduct following enquiries by school managers, he chose early retirement after some pupils greeted him each morning with calls of 'pervert'. To be subject to investigation carries with it in almost every case a stigma that managers are powerless or unwilling to combat.

We have noted throughout the ratchet effect of these 'informal' guidelines and policies. A further aspect of this effect is that 'perfectly innocent' acts now have to be legislated against. Such precautionary ethics are naturally defensive in nature and emphasise the negative. We found that most Behaviour Policies were Bad Behaviour Policies. More generally, the nature of the 'don'ts' was absurd and redundant as advice and instruction (e.g. not employing known abusers, not touching pupils in an indecent way, etc.) conveying imperatives that only a serious pervert would need to be told (and in which case would obviously ignore). They therefore address, in this particular sense, the professional as pervert. At the same time the list of 'dos' offer procedures that are often unrealistic, weirdly over-detailed, bureaucratic and excessive, this time the professional is addressed as idiot. They normalise and universalise perversion as something that good professionals should be thinking about all the time they are with children, or even in the company of other professionals. This situation may be conceived not just as madness, but a category of excessive madness that knows itself to be mad. Once again, better safe than sane. Incidentally it also creates a situation in which any professional or researcher who suggests alternative approaches to the issue may find themselves at risk on a number of levels.[3] The verbal asides of professionals indicate exactly this, making clear that it is 'sad' that things have come to this, and so on. As a result good relationships, expressed as authentic, or in terms of affection, become the 'danger' of things going wrong. And so proper 'care' becomes not-caring (about 'care' as previously understood) and caring about 'care' as risk and danger. This is a world of moral and professional topsy-turvy, where the inauthentic self is a legislated necessity and the professional arena is reconstructed as a matrix of cautions, prohibitions and procedural alibis (we ticked all the boxes).

If we take the fear-based discourses evident in the majority of our sample to their logical conclusion, we would have to conclude that many potential (or actual) paedophiles look after our children. Yet paradoxically when questioned, respondents 'knew' that professional abuse was extremely rare (we were made aware of a single current instance in our case study sites during the 12-month period of the research), 'knew' that most abuse takes place in families, and 'knew' that their defensive behaviours were suspect and unhelpful to children and young people in their care. As such in general it could be read that we oppose guidelines and guidance relating to touching behaviours per se. However we do not conclude that *all* guidance in *all* situations is necessarily bad. Indeed, we recognise that re/negotiated guidance on how to deal with (for example) children with autism, those with sensory deprivation, or those considered to be too 'needy' or too 'difficult', for whatever reason, is part of what being a professional entails. Guidelines may be particularly appropriate when a consistent approach is essential, and *confident* professionals should be capable of such negotiation on the basis of their training and experience:

To introduce formal guidelines on this matter would begin to break down the relationship between professional, parent, and child by removing the power of decision from the professional. As a result of this, many children should suffer in an attempt to legislate against very rare instances of unprofessional behaviour which should be dealt with through adequate training and supervision for all staff working with young children – and is covered by child protection procedures.

(parent of preschool child)

However, a practice which requires the same amount of negotiation for even common 'everyday' interactions leads to the odd behaviours evidenced throughout the book, and arguably could serve to obscure the rarer but real incidence of abuse, while everyone is distracted in 'watching their own backs'. Yet professional touch and the very possibility of such touch are now policed by the perfect panopticon where legislation is superfluous. We police ourselves and each other while blaming Others for our actions: 'It's just a shame that society is coming round to this' (headteacher primary school). We do not propose to set the pendulum swinging to the opposite extreme, where child abuse is neglected, but to encourage professionals (and their trainers and inspectors) to *be* 'professional', and to make professional judgements:

You know yourself as an adult those children who prefer a bit of distance, after years of training, I suppose you just know when not to encroach on their space. If you are a confident teacher, you know when the touching and cuddling is OK.

(teacher primary school)

and: 'now you can't do that with everybody, you just have to know which girls, which boys are very introvert and don't like anybody touching them, and you *just, must,* not do that' (headteacher secondary school).

Our examples all featured different emphases of 'touch' accountability, expressed across a range of contexts and concepts, and generating different mixes. For example, the Summerhill case is foregrounded on a notion of relationship emphasised through the Meeting, which polices the quality of interactions. It is an instance of the 'free touch' philosophy we earlier developed in Chapter 5. The school also offers vivid illustration of the ways in which moral and pornographic discourses feed off each other. A recent example: *The Sunday Times* (Scottish edition) offered half-page coverage to a proposal by two senior academics in Scotland. It was to set up a 'Scottish version of Summerhill'. The account offered some pros and cons, citing both the current Principal Zoë Readhead, and the views of the former Chief Inspector Chris Woodhead, who had tried to close it down. So far so good. But the illustration, taking half of the space is instructively different. There is a colour picture of one of the academics, and a picture (undated but of some antiquity) of Summerhill kids, at their swimming pool, most of them naked. The subtext is in this way sexualised, indeed implicitly made pornographic. The caption reads: 'Doyle, left, plans to bring to Scotland a version of Summerhill, where pupils could bathe naked'. (In fact, even the name was wrong. It should have read Boyd, not Doyle.)

Even so, it would not be true to say that Summerhill ignores background 'precautionary' audit. It too goes a little mad in order to stay 'compliant' with regulations. However, other contexts stress much more severe notions of restraint, compliance or precaution, exhibiting the 'ratchet effect' we earlier noted:

> We try to ensure that that there are always two members of staff present with children e.g. toilets/nappy areas, or nursery room, to back each other in case of accusations. We have a behaviour book where we record any incident of when we have had to touch/restrain a child . . . We write down a short account and date it and put which staff were present and at what time, we then explain it to the parent and ask them to read and sign it . . . We constantly draw attention to each other so that if any issue crops up we have a witness that can protect us.
>
> (manager preschool)

No single example from our case studies, of course, is entirely one thing or the other, and most comprise a constellation of different foci, some reinforcing, others contradictory. In this way, issues of touch are expressed within a taxonomy of concerns which are irreducible to any idea of homogenous demand or response. Nevertheless, the audit regime often appears to insist on this kind of universalism. Nor are these taxonomies comprehensive in the sense that they successfully cover all activities and eventualities. There is always a residue of activity that is not amenable to accountability in the discursive senses in which it is implemented (as prescribed in principles, procedures or practices). In other words, audit always aspires to an impossible reality.

Summerhill revisited

In Summerhill School however, such concerns had rarely crossed anyone's mind, or were not even conceivable in a cultural context where 'Ombudsmen' and the 'Meeting' empowered children to represent any misgivings and seek clarification or redress. As a teacher said during our visit: 'Summerhill would be a paedophile's nightmare' – there were no private places, no adult powers of sanction over the child, children were in charge in ways that were not tokenistic. This made us feel particularly contaminating (and contaminated) because we introduced illicit possibilities in the form of our enquiries about touching. In other case studies this contamination had already occurred and elsewhere the language and practice of 'care' already carried with it the burden of abuse. Taking Summerhill School as a point of comparison risks making it the 'Other' and therefore exotic. However, this is inevitable, and is in any case a game the school turns on its head (in relation to 'down-towners') and is also proud of (when marketing itself for example). Summerhill is a 'free' school, locally known as the 'do-as-you-please' school. Yet we found Summerhill to be structured in ways that were almost always neglected by inspectors, media accounts and academic comment (Chamberlin 1989).[4] It had strong boundaries and many laws, as we were reminded by a 'dinner lady's' reference to the idea that it is a rule-free school as 'completely wrong really, because there's more rules here than anywhere I've ever been'.

It will be recalled that there were 174 laws extant at the time of our field-work. We used the analytical language of Foucault (1977) to express these strengths, i.e. the language of the panopticon, self-regulation, discipline, boundary, confession, orthodoxy, and consensus as an outcome – the moral factory of Summerhill, and the processes through which it manufactured selves. But these structures enable rather than disable in the ways that might be anticipated by those familiar with Foucault. So Summerhill is a *benign panopticon,* within which various forms of learning are promoted as a result of the weak boundaries between staff/students, and also age cohorts in the community. It is helpful to consider how the plural and paradoxical panopticon works for the good, or at least for certain kinds of good, and how that connects with the notion of 'emotional or relational touch' that we identified in a previous chapter. Our feeling is that the efficacy is not psychological so much as anthropological, much as Neill argued when he concluded that the school worked as a social organisation that allowed the pupils 'freedom to be themselves' (1971: 16).

As we saw earlier, the notion of 'touch' as an issue of 'safety' or 'protection' was widely regarded as absurd at Summerhill. Summerhillians learned to relate to themselves, to others, and to intuit boundaries. As we saw from the 'floating pronouns' in their talk about the rights and wrongs of 'cases', they were culturally adept both at putting themselves in other minds and, more importantly, putting other minds in themselves. We were reminded of the distinction between a liberal expression of difference ('they are just like us') with a more radical insight ('we are just like them'). We also noted how democratic mechanisms within the school ensured a visibility of practices that was far more 'effective' than any conceivable transparency of procedures. The Meeting filled the gap between what Law and Mol (2002) call 'managerialist' control (as it were, the very limits of audit) and the still excessive flow of complex, embodied interactions that characterise any organisation. The prospective or retrospective rhetorics of audit were merely 'staging accountability' (ibid.: 100–1) – as prevention or blame – while the agonistic realities of resolving real conflicts and injustices enacted responsibility *in the moment* and *for the moment.* Of course, this practical/procedural dichotomy was breached continuously in Summerhill by the creation of new laws and adjudications in respect to members. But these latter regulations were part of the practical flux, open to adaptation, extension or repeal. They were not a fixed, abstract and universal template for measuring compliance so much as a situated and shifting search for resolution that regarded its short-term failures as ultimately productive: they approximated self-government, not governmentality.

The extended reference to the Summerhill case study does not imply that we believe that all educational or child care contexts could or should operate on this basis. However it is significant because it indicates principles and practices which are far from prevalent in more mainstream settings and which appear to obviate concerns regarding touching. The beneficial impact of a primary commitment to individual integrity and agency, for both pupils and adults, reinforced by organisational practices and a jealously guarded culture, is highly suggestive to any consideration of how the current pathological situation might be combated at the level of individual schools, classrooms and care settings.

Conclusion

We have argued that policy and practice which essentialises 'touch' as a discrete phenomenon, and disconnects it from other bodily and discursive practices is far too narrow, and renders interaction incomprehensible and unmanageable. As we have seen, individuals in our case studies claimed they do not like the way 'someone looks at me', or how a teacher throws paper on the floor 'so he can look up my skirt', or a particular member of staff 'gets into my space', or 'is in my face'. Others are offended more by harsh words (or ostracism), or intimate text messaging, than by any form of touch. Yet touch is now taken as a discrete phenomenon where the part (touch) stands for the whole (all human interaction). Adopting touch metonymically depends in part on the use of aphorisms: 'talk, don't touch'; 'use your words'; 'leave the door open'; 'watch your back'; 'cold sores', etc, all of which contribute towards the separation of the issues into meaningless fragments, seemingly dredged from some more coherent or alternative narrative. And so it would appear that aphorisms have displaced personal responsibility and professional discretion. The snappy one-liners have removed the necessity for ethical considerations. But to focus on touch as a form of metonymy and to rely on one-liners has wider ramifications, and we are reminded by Nochlin (1994) that once we've taken everything apart, it could conjoin in ways we did not intend.

Meanwhile in the current climate, the professional who is subscribing to the 'no touch' rhetoric, and who adopts the snappy one-liners, is generally considered to be behaving as a responsible practitioner. The child is safe, the professional is safe from accusation, and the organisation (school, nursery, etc.) is taking all the necessary risk precautions and so cannot be blamed if/when something does go wrong. If professionals ignore the guidelines then the reverse must be true, children will be abused . . . However, we have argued that the guidelines and 'no touch' rhetoric when deconstructed serve to fetishise touch via the invisibility of an action that hasn't happened and in all probability never will:

> I can feel though, with . . . my stepdaughter of 12, a definite hesitation and suspicion of myself that's very much an implanted awareness . . . Potentially more serious though is a feeling that this implanted awareness alerts any proclivity I have towards 'the taboo'; that it might awaken otherwise non-existent desires. It feels like this awareness acts like a carrier of an 'infection' to abuse . . .

> (email respondent)

Coren recently (2007) suggested that the banning of chastity rings (a current trend among teenagers who wish to publicly declare their intention not to have sex before marriage) serves to make what we don't do more interesting than what we *do* do. (Like the boy scout in reverse – Mum! I've earned my 'didn't-snog' badge; ibid.: 42.) She suggests this will inevitably lead to a contrary swing where the fragment (the ring) conjoins with a different scenario which popularises the wearing of promiscuity rings in the teenage population. Once again, there are cross-overs between morality and immorality – they are often in uneasy generative relation with each other. The result is not so much 'fitness for purpose', 'safety' or 'compliance' as an infantilisation of professional discourses.

Such a scenario is also anticipated in our account of Tim's 'guilt stages' (see Chapter 10) in massaging a girl's shoulders in front of the inspector, and of our own initial uneasiness about our 'pervy' questioning when conducting this research. Policing leaves actions and presences behind, and looks forward *in panic* to the possible interpretations of possible future actions. The presumption of innocence preceding any precaution is rendered irresponsible. The fetishism focuses on the least relevant aspect of touching, i.e. not touching at all. Yet the fetishism serves to re-inscribe no touching with the whole history of incest and titillation. The very prohibition thus inadvertently privileges abusive behaviours. This is performed through what Derrida terms 'the phenomenological "conjuring trick"' (1994: 126–7). There could be no fetish in the first place without the ghost of actual titillating (and in the contexts discussed throughout, abusive) touching. The obscuration therefore has to attend to the spectral nature of the fetish, and this awareness is the ghost which continually reasserts its presence. But the ghost cannot remove the magic of the fetish: 'A conjuring trick in fact multiplies itself . . . and is unleashed in a series' (ibid.: 127). We find ourselves in a situation where 'no touching' advice is fiercely protected by its bodyguard of fetishes and ghosts which cannot be exorcised. Our responsibility then is to readthrough the fetishes rather than slavishly multiply their effects.

We argue then that the notion of touch in itself is inadequate, and lists of 'dos' and 'don'ts' (and it is usually the don'ts) serve little useful purpose. Any attempt to legislate in advance for what will and will not count as 'moral' conduct undercuts the interpretive procedures that people use to 'read off' morals and intentions from behaviour. Touch policing disables the sociocultural resources that people would otherwise have mobilised in order to deal with these issues on a case-by-case basis. So touch needs to be regarded in terms of relationships, which take place in spite of, as well as because of, the discrete variables where touch is not really the point. It's not so much touch that we should be concerned with but motive and context: 'I was thinking then . . . in this specific case I did actually touch a girl and everybody saw the context of it, there wasn't any problem from anybody at all' (the secondary school teacher reporting on putting his arm round a girl whose grandparent had died). Professional (and all other) activity should be based on a sophisticated judgement of motive and context which is guided partly by 'good sense'. 'Touch' then is not really the point. It's not so much *touch* that we should be concerned with but *motives, context* and *values*. Yet motive, context and positive values are missing from 'accountability' policy and guidelines. We propose therefore, that we all need to adopt a more 'inside-out' ethical way of thinking for ourselves. Over-scripted professional protocols inevitably lead to a kind of defensive professional reaction, whereby central aspects of professionalism (relationships, trust, responsibility, individual judgement, etc.) are over-ridden by defensive prescription and proscription. We suggest an urgent need for a significantly different operationalisation of professionalism, and a return to notions of professional trust and agency. This return is not proposed in a spirit of nostalgia. In the past there was neglect as well as licence. What we propose is a sensible thinking through of 'freedom' for the child as well as the adult, rather than a retrospective based on the assumption of horror, harm and abuse. To do otherwise is to provide a licence for the incremental erosion of all civil and caring interaction between adults and children, as well as positive factors such as professionalism in education and child care settings. The general context in which our particular focus of study is situated has been discussed by others (Strathern 2004; O'Neil 2002), including Power who comments:

> The risk management of everything reflects the efforts of organisational agents . . . to offload and re-individualise their own personal risk. The result is a potentially catastrophic downward spiral in which expert judgement shrinks to an empty form of defendable compliance.

> (2004: 42)

We must not conform with such 'compliance' if our children are to be educated as opposed to trained, valued rather than protected, and taught to take creative risks. If our professionals are to work to their best ability, then we need a climate founded on trust, responsibility, and only hedged with precaution where necessary rather than where conceivable. In that sense, issues of touch are a touchstone of a far greater malaise in our current systems of governance: they operationalise a fear of freedom against which we must all fight.

Notes

1 Problematics of touching

1 A different version of this chapter appeared as Piper, H. and Smith, H. (2003) 'Touch in Educational and Child Care Settings: Dilemmas and Responses' in the *British Educational Research Journal*, 29: 6, 879–94; this version is included with the expressed permission of the editors.

2 Relationships: ethics committees and research

1 The authors of this monograph can also confirm that such zeal from ethics committees is common in the UK. In their experience, a six month contract to involve a Sure Start initiative was subject to two ethics clearance procedures (one for each of the sponsoring bodies). The earliest clearance might be given, assuming no hitches, was four months into the research process – which could not be delayed because of changes on the ground that meant that the evaluative object would have disappeared with the introduction of yet another new initiative. We sought a different remedy to that reported here from Australia – binning the paperwork and doing the work anyway. Needless to say, the world did not collapse on itself, and the ethics committees simply forgot about the research (although it was their organisation that had commissioned it!).

2 During and since the ESRC funded research discussed throughout, there has been a proliferation in the number of research ethics committees in the UK context.

3 While opportunities were in theory increased by this deregulation, risks were also privatised. We are now more responsible for our failures as well as our successes, so that more choice in, say, how our superannuation is invested may lead to increased wealth in old age, or, if most know as little about such matters as I, then it could just as easily lead to destitution. Similarly, many have vigorously promoted 'school choice'. Should the choice prove poor and the child suffers, however, it is the parents who are to blame. Research has demonstrated that this endless proliferating of choice does not lead to more contentment and increased well-being but often the reverse, and that the citizens of contemporary Anglophone cultures are drowning in a sea of often unwanted decision-making (Schwartz 2004).

4 Anyone who has ever attempted to argue with an ethics committee about an unfavourable assessment of his or her research has probably experienced the uneasy feeling of being among the damned, whose every word and act are further proof of the evil lurking within. Attempting to talk sense does no good, as sense is not something that comes from the lips of the wicked, only lies, selfishness and deceit disguised as other things.

3 The Criminal Records Bureau: policing access to children

1 Vetting and CRB checking has been considered by Josie Appleton, and we are grateful for her agreement that we could use her data for this chapter. This data has resulted from documentary analysis (websites, newspapers, government documentation, etc.) and interviews with a wide range of individuals. We refer readers directly to The Manifesto Club's (2006a) 'The Case against Vetting' and 'How the Child Protection Industry Stole Christmas' (2006b): these can be accessed via http://www.statewatch.org/news/2006/oct/THE%20CASE%20AGAINST%20VETTING.pdf and http://www.manifestoclub.com/files/CHRISTMASREPORT.pdf respectively.

4 Guidelines and dangerous bodies: the half-closed door

1 Elsewhere, 'there is no universal prescription regarding what is appropriate, safe or legally justifiable'.
2 Note the discursive similarities with an earlier quote about 'fit' persons. This illustrates the recurring phenomenon of similar or same phrases and sentences being used, as a result of a version of policy borrowing that extended to literal if unacknowledged citation.

5 Saving touch: private parts and public wholes

1 Damien Hirst works such contradictions in his art, claiming: 'I try to say something and deny it at the same time' (1997: 48). Anthony Gormley, perhaps more interestingly, plays with the simultaneous materiality and immateriality of the body, especially in his more recent 'matrices' (2006–7) where the body emerges rather than presents itself to the gaze (Foucault 1975, 1977; Vidler et al. 2007). His bodies are both there and not there – above all, they lack skin, boundary. Gormley's interest is in the space and the spacing, not the body as object. He sculpts the spaces that bodies inhabit – and ex-habit.
2 Absence/presence is probably not the best way of thinking about that relation or set of relations. It's a bit like asking if the 'economy' is absent or present. It just is, even if it isn't ever 'that'.
3 Andy Williams, 'You're just too good to be true' ('Untitled' c.1967). (A postmodernist rendering of that song would prefer a reversal: 'You're just too true to be good', etc.) Note also how the lyrics in the very next line obey the conventional privileging of the gaze – 'Can't take my eyes off you'.
4 'One' can always be more than 'one' and less than 'one', provided we allow it the metaphorical status that it both has, and denies. 'Each, halting, print, of, individual word on paper inserts and withdraws meaning, giving a 'one', more or less, and taking away an infinity of not-said in the lop-sided arithmetic of writing' (Stronach 2002a: 293).
5 There is a tendency for theorists to favour the word 'haptic' as a marker of the sense of touch (e.g. Deleuze and Guattari, Derrida). We resist it because the notion of touch and its surrounding associations of tact and the intangible offer a rich and dense field of associations that we want to play with and explore.
6 Mead criticises prevalent sexual training in these terms: 'All the chief flaws in our fatal philosophy of sparing children a knowledge of the dreadful truth' (Mead 1928/43: 177). See also Autton 1989 on the 'drift towards minimizing personal encounter' (x). Zur and Nordmarken also note that 'sexualization of innocent touch has a long history' (2004: 8).
7 We neglect the historical dimension here, but note that cultures of touch do change over time. Erasmus did not find the English cold and distant: 'Oh, Faustus, if you had once tasted how sweet and fragrant these kisses are, you would indeed wish to be a traveller . . . for your whole life in England' (Classen 2005: 26).

8 Mairal sees the RPS as a 'geocultural area' (2003: 185) which 'activates uncertainty, disorder, social disarticulation and conflict' (ibid.: 186).

9 And that was pretty hard. '"Libertinage", Durand put in, "is a sensual aberrance which supposes the discarding of all constraints, the supremist disdain for all prejudices, the total rejection of all religious notions, the profoundest aversion to all ethical imperatives"' (de Sade 1797/1968: 1115).

10 Starting from the assertion of 'it is', 'that it is' – i.e. the event, happening, that is 'surprise', Nancy adds that it is 'to leap into nothing . . . the articulation of the difference between nothing and something' (Nancy 2000: 172).

11 Nancy argues somewhat like Derrida in terms of 'its offering and withdrawal' (Nancy 1993b: 152).

12 Arguing that presence is never pure presence, and 'comes apart in order to be itself *as* such' (Nancy 2000: 2, his emphasis), he posits separation where others might claim the generalisation of a collectivity, but in order to argue back towards 'a singularly plural existence' (ibid.: 3), wishing to go beyond Marx's alleged failure to 'think being-in-common as distinct from community' (ibid.: 24). Nancy concludes that we are 'contemporaries of ourselves, contemporaries of the stripping bare of being-in-common' (ibid.: 63). Images of naked/stripped bare/'right at' point to his desire to assert a something performative beyond discourse, in what Hutchens wants to call a 'hybrid empiricism' (Hutchens 2005: 157). Nancy aspires in this way to a 'tact of reading that I know discourse is unable to provide' (Nancy 1993a: 198).

13 These are very much our interpretations and developments of Nancy's thought, particularly in *Being Singular Plural* and the *Experience of Freedom*. These are early days yet, in this line of thinking, but the essential unpredictability of social life is a recurrent 'disappointment' of the social sciences, in previous and current articulations of prediction and control. We might want to regard 'complexity' theory as the most current of these fantasies, rather than setting it up as the corrective to more simplistic social sciences of prediction and control (like 'What Works?' 'Value for Money', 'Best Practice', and other half-witted fantasies of control and prediction, e.g. *Promoting Good Campus Relations: Working with Staff and Students to Build Community Cohesion and Tackle Violent Extremism in the Name of Islam at Universities and Colleges* (DfES 2007).

14 Nancy lists some of these in the Preface to *Being Singular Plural*. They include Bosnia, Rwanda, Somalia, Shining Path, Iraq, Liberia, Afghanistan, Chechnya, Tutsis, Huta, Tamil Tigers, Afghanistan, and a lot more besides. There is no question that 'horror' can safely be relegated to the monstrous Other, although of course that is precisely why it must be. And as we've known, at least since Conrad, 'the horror, the horror' is much more what we deal out than we are dealt (Conrad 1904/94; Stronach *et al.* 2006).

15 The cure is also a bit familiar. There must be institutional 'Standards', close cooperation between Higher Education and the police ('partnership', of course), and a five-stage escalator of appropriate responses.

16 Contrast with the decorous niceties of the Cold War or with the IRA campaign. But also contrast with the ways in which the ending of the Cold War licensed wholesale and massive attacks of Afghanistan and Iraq that would not otherwise have been dared. Tough on terror, of course, but tough on the causes of terror? Not so far.

7 Case study: primary and junior schools

1 Carpet time is when all the children are brought together to sit on the carpet in one particular area of the classroom. It is an opportunity for teachers to carry out whole-class activities with whole-class input. This might be stories and singing, games and exercises, but also maths, English, geography, and PSHE lessons, so children have the opportunity to develop skills such as listening and communication and emotional literacy.

8 Case study: secondary schools

1 This is a common avoidance strategy in this urban area. Another ESRC project studied teenage gangs, which required researchers gaining access to young people and to their families. The only group that would not talk to them were the headteachers. This circumstance is not unconnected to the audit culture and its precautionary ethics. To discuss the problem in general is to imply that there is a problem in the particular circumstance of the school. Such problems reflect badly on the image of the school and so their acknowledgement is to be avoided.

10 Case study: Summerhill School – an exception to the rule

1 In addition, younger children may also appeal to older children who act as mentors and are called Ombudsmen (of either sex). A series of committees and pupil-appointed functionaries run aspects of the school – for example, bedtimes are decided by the Meeting, and supervised by 'Beddies Officers'.

2 This is the term used to describe people in the local village. School Law 42: 'You can't go to local kids' houses unless you have been invited by an adult and they have contacted the school'. The School Laws are more restrictive outside the school than inside – there is 'no swearing' down town, for example.

3 The school intake is international – the staff is mainly but not exclusively British.

4 The Principal had no concrete limit, but visits were usually 'about twice a term' on agreed days. Otherwise, 'it disrupts the whole life of the community to have people coming and going'.

5 An adult explained elsewhere: 'the Bully's List, that's a really harsh fine. So that could just be given because he's been a pain in the arse [discussing a particular case] and won't listen to the Meeting so you could give Bully's List. But a big fine doesn't mean that you are a bully, it's just the harsh fine. You can't watch screens; you can't go down town, [you have to go to the] back of all the queues'. There were no pupils on Bully's List at the time of the field-work.

6 The classic panopticon disciplines by making the mass visible to the master (Foucault 1977). Hence its blueprint for schools, prisons and factories in the nineteenth century – as the all-seeing eye of power. But in Summerhill, the term can be radically distributed, in that each member has a perspective on the others which they hold to be complete, or almost so. Hence the repetition of the 'no secrets here' theme. Of course, the adults think they know more than the kids, and the kids don't know what they don't know, and so on. But it is clear that perspectives on the other are unusually mutual, unmediated and visible in the Summerhill community. Hence our use of the term 'benign'.

7 It was this aspect of the school that the government inspectors most consistently neglected. In the last full inspection of the school (1999) by HMI/Ofsted only one data-recording sheet (out of 54 lodged by the inspectors) addressed learning outside the classroom. Inspectors regarded what happened outside the classroom basically as a kind of truancy, hence their obsession with the question 'How often do you attend lessons'?

8 A survey of ex-Summerhillians conducted in 1999–2000 supported such a conclusion. The oral history of Lucas and Lamb (2000) would mainly support that conclusion, although a few ex-Summerhillians felt that they had been disadvantaged in terms of an increasingly credentialist economy.

9 We acknowledge that as researchers our relation was an 'outside-in' one. But there were elements of the 'inside-out' in that one of the researchers had helped with a school evaluation that was part of the school's defence in the 1999 Tribunal case, and was appointed by the school as their 'expert witness' as a condition imposed on Ofsted as a result of the Tribunal agreement. As some of the data above suggest, the Summerhillians tended to

treat us in terms of the 'weak boundaries' – although a group did report us to a teacher on the grounds that they were not sure where our questions about relationships were leading. The school is rightly sensitive to outside representations, which have often taken the 'school for scandal' line as a typical media starting point. Readers nevertheless need to consider the impact of that relation between researchers and school in interpreting *this* account.

10 As one member of staff put it, there were a number of children from UK, Korea and Japan – all of whom had cultures that were more inclined to avoid touch.

11 Bonfire of the insanities

1 Milosz noted what sounds like a very similar 'ratchet effect' in Stalinist contexts. The cadres seek to over-produce in order to demonstrate compliance to 'the Center' (Milosz 1953/90: 125).

2 In analysing situations where risk is managed, Law and Mol point to a common kind of 'utopian absolutism' (2002: 90) where justifications are offered of the kind: if human life is beyond value, then precaution X is necessary whatever the cost. In our inversion, 'the bad' is foregrounded and all forms of precaution are then necessary, whatever the costs.

3 See example provided by Catherine Scott, author of Chapter 2:

> In recent years I have been interviewed on Australian radio stations on a number of occasions on the subject of my research on perceptions of risk and the rise of the victim identity as discussed in Chapter 2. In early 2004 I was interviewed on a programme that also included an interview with a researcher who was investigating the consequences of child–adult sexual contact. On returning to my home town I received an email from a colleague at my university who also worked as a clinical psychologist. It was a long email, self-righteous in tone, containing grave charges against me, and it had been copied to my Head of School. The sender informed me that he had been contacted by patients who had seen my name on the radio network's website in connection with the interview on the consequences of child–adult sexual contact, and that he was disgusted by my condoning of child rape. He informed me that a number of his patients had contacted him to report that my remarks had increased their pain and suffering intolerably. He noted that he had previously read about my research in this area in the local press. He also indicated that my attitudes gave solace to sex offenders with whom he had worked, who had apparently reported they felt vindicated by my words. He also demanded that I make a full account of myself and explain why I held such vicious beliefs.
>
> I was upset by his email on a number of levels, personal and professional. Any whiff of condoning or accepting sexual assault of children would result in my exclusion from schools as a researcher. I am also a mother of a small child and the resident of a country town. I reasoned that I would be quite easy to locate, and the thought that convicted criminals may now be interested in me or my family was frankly terrifying. Over the next few days I received worrying anonymous telephone calls at work, which only increased my fear and concern.
>
> I sent the man an email explaining that he was mistaken, that I did not do the type of research he was condemning but that I had been interviewed on radio with someone who did. There was obviously some misunderstanding, as I had certainly never appeared in the local paper as someone who researched that topic. I received a reply from him that demonstrated that he had not accepted my explanation and he repeated the various accusations against me and his demands that I explain my vicious attitudes to the victims of sexual abuse. It was like talking to the proverbial brick wall, or pleading innocence to the prosecutor of a witch trial. My supposed attitudes had placed me in the category of 'evil' and there was to be no talking myself out of that. In some

considerable distress I contacted senior members of the university administration to explain what had happened and my consequent professional and personal fears. At first there was some insistence that I prove my innocence, for instance by showing that I had never appeared in the local press as a researcher interested in child–adult sexual contact. Proving a negative is of course extraordinarily difficult, but fortunately the immoderate tone of the accusatory emails, and my own record, told against the person, as did my having received the worrying phone calls. We were both required to attend a mediation session, chaired by his Dean and mine, and the University subsequently disciplined him. During the session I spoke of my fear for my family and myself from the disturbed people with whom he had shared his wrongful opinion of me. I asked that he contact the sex criminals and set straight their ideas. He revealed that only one sex offender, and one or two other patients who were unlikely to be able to harm my family, had contacted him. So distorting the facts to promote his case was fair game. His emails had given a clear impression that I had an army of disturbed people bent on exacting retribution for my imagined heretical beliefs.

4 Chamberlin's philosophical account of education and freedom takes individual autonomy at Summerhill to be just that: she neglects its social construction and the prevalence of 'adult suggestion' (1989: 108), at least as we found it in our data. Accordingly she takes Neill to be an 'extreme' libertarian, and offers the usual disclaimer: 'The freedom to choose what line of study to pursue and how best to pursue it is inappropriate for children whose intellectual skills are relatively underdeveloped' (1989: 110).

Bibliography

Adkins, L. (2001) 'Risk Culture, Self-Reflexivity and the Making of Sexual Hierarchies', *Body and Society*, 7: 1, 35–55.

Andrews, L.V. (1981) *Medicine Woman*, London: Penguin Arkana.

Apple, M. and Beane, J. (1999) *Democratic Schools: Lessons from the Chalk Face*, Buckingham: Open University Press.

Atlanta Project (2002) *Teaching Sexual Abuse and Abuse Prevention: Atlanta Good-touch/Bad-touch Project*, online available www.goodtouchbadtouch.com/Atlanta_project.html (accessed 6 March 2006).

Autton, N. (1989) *Touch: An Exploration*, London: Darton, Longman and Todd.

Bakhtin, M. (1968/84) *Rabelais and his World*, (trans.) H. Iswolsky, Cambridge, MA: MIT Press.

Bakhtin, M. (1975/81) *The Dialogical Imagination*, Austin: University of Texas Press.

Banks, S. (2001) *Ethics and Values in Social Work*, 2nd edition, Houndmills, Basingstoke: Palgrave.

Barthes, R. (1975) *The Pleasure of the Text*, (trans.) R. Miller, New York: Hill and Wang.

Bauman, Z. (1995) *Life in Fragments: Essays in Postmodern Morality*, Oxford: Blackwell.

Bauman, Z. (1997) *Postmodernity and its Discontents*, Cambridge: Polity.

Baumeister, R.F. (2001) *Evil: Inside Human Violence and Cruelty*, New York: Owl Books.

Baxter, C. (1997) *Burning Down the House: Essays on Fiction*, Saint Paul, MN: Graywolf Press.

Beck, U. (1987) 'The Anthropological Shock: Chernobyl and the Contours of the Risk Society', *Berkeley Journal of Sociology*, 3: 153–65.

Beck, U. (1992) *Risk Society: Towards a New Modernity*, (trans.) M. Ritter, London: Sage.

Belk, R. (1985) 'A Child's Christmas in America: Santa Claus as Deity, Consumption as Religion', *Journal of American Culture*, 12: 87–100.

Benjamin, J. (1986) 'A Desire of Her Own', in T. de Lauretis (ed.) *Feminist Studies/Critical Studies*, Bloomington: Indiana University Press.

Bernstein, B. (1971) 'On the Classification and Framing of Educational Knowledge', in M. Young (ed.) *Knowledge and Control, New Directions for the Sociology of Knowledge*, London: Collier-Macmillan.

Boholm, A. (2003) 'The Culture Nature of Risk: Can there be an Anthropology of Uncertainty?' *Ethnos*, 68: 2, 159–78.

Borsay, A. (2005) *Disability and Social Policy in Britain since 1750*, Basingstoke and New York: Palgrave Macmillan.

Brettingham, M. (2006) 'Safety Clause Slays Santa', *Times Educational Supplement*, 15 December 2006, online available http://www.tes.co.uk/search/story/?story_id=2318766 (accessed 20 December 2006).

Carspecken, P. (1991) *Community Schooling and the Nature of Power: The Battle for Croxteth Comprehensive*, London: Routledge.

Caulfield, R. (2000) 'Beneficial Effects of Tactile Stimulation on Early Development', *Early Childhood Education*, 27: 4, 255–7.

CCPAS (2002) *Issues Churches with Safe Guidelines for Santa Claus*, Churches' Advisory Protection Service, Kent Press Release 20.11.02, online available http://www.ccpas.co.uk/Press%20releases/20%20Nov%202002.htm (accessed 20 March 2007).

Chamberlin, R. (1989) *Free Children and Democratic Schools: A Philosophical Study of Liberty and Education*, New York: Falmer.

Charlton, B. (2002) 'Audit, Accountability and All That', in S. Prickett, and P. Erskine-Hill (eds) *Education! Education! Education: Managerial Ethics and the Law of Unintended Consequence*, Thorverton: Imprint Academic.

The Children Act (1989) London: HMSO/DfES.

Classen, C. (ed.) (2005) *The Book of Touch*, Oxford: Berg.

Clastres, P. (1987) *Society Against the State: Essays in Political Anthropology*, (trans.) R. Hurley and A. Stein, Cambridge, MA: MIT Press.

Cohen, S. (1972) *Folk Devils and Moral Panic: The Creation of the Mods and Rockers*, New York: St. Martin's Press.

Colt, G. (1977) 'The Magic of Touch: Massage's Healing Powers Make it a Medicine', *Life Magazine*, August 52–62.

Conrad, J. (1904/94) *Heart of Darkness*, Harmondsworth: Penguin.

Coren, V. (2007) 'Be a jewel personality', *The Observer*, 22 July 2007: 42.

Crossley, N. (1995) 'Merleau-Ponty, The Elusive Body and Carnal Sociology', *Body & Society* 1: 1, 43–63.

CSCI (2005) 'Boarding School: Summerhill School', London: Commission for Social Care Inspection, HMSO.

Csikszentmihalyi, M. and Rochberg-Halton, E. (1981) *The Meaning of Things: Domestic Symbols and the Self*, Cambridge: Cambridge University Press.

Curtis, B. (1995) 'The Strange Birth of Santa Claus: From Artemis the Goddess and Nicholas the Saint', *Journal of American Culture* 18: 4, 17–32.

Deleuze, G. (1969/90) *The Logic of Sense*, (trans.) M. Lester; C. Boundas (ed.) London: Continuum.

Deleuze, G. and Guattari, F. (1988) *A Thousand Plateaux: Capitalism and Schizophrenia*, London: Athlone Press.

Derrida, J. (1992) 'Force of Law: The Mystical Foundation of Authority', in D. Cornell, M. Rosenfeld and D. Carson (eds) *Deconstruction and the Possibility of Justice*, London: Routledge.

Derrida, J. (1994) *Specters of Marx: The State of the Debt, the Work of Mourning, and the New International*, (trans.) P. Kamuf, London: Routledge.

Derrida, J. (2005) *On Touching – Jean-Luc Nancy*, (trans.) C. Irizarry, Stanford, CA: Stanford University Press.

de Sade, M. (1797/1968) *Juliette*, (trans.) A. Wainhouse, New York: Grove Press.

Desjarlais, R. (1996) 'Presence', in C. Laderman and M. Roseman (eds) (1996) *The Performance of Healing*, New York: Routledge.

Dewey, J. (1962) *The Child and the Curriculum*, and, *The School and Society*, (first published 1900, 1902, respectively) Chicago: Chicago University Press.

Dewey, J. (1966) *Democracy and Education: An Introduction to the Philosophy of Education*, New York: The Free Press.

Dews, P. (2002) 'Uncategorical Imperatives: Adorno, Badiou and the Ethical Turn', *Radical Philosophy*, 111: 33–7.

DfES (2007) *Promoting Good Campus Relations: Working with Staff and Students to Build Community Cohesion and Tackle Violent Extremism in the Name of Islam at Universities and Colleges*, online available http://www.dfes.gov.uk/pns/pnattach/20060170/1.txt Department for Education and Skills (accessed 25 January 2007).

Diprose, R. (1998) *Generosity: Between Love and Desire*, online available http://www.iupjournals.org.hypatia/hyp13–1.html (accessed 20 February 2007).

Disclosure Scotland (2005) *Sample Policy on the Secure Handling, Use, Storage and Retention of Disclosure Informationm*, online available http: //www.disclosurescotland.co.uk/SamplePolicyHandling.htm (accessed 20 March 2007).

Dolby, N. (2003) 'Popular Culture and Democratic Practice', *Harvard Educational Review*, 73: 3, 258–84.

Douglas, J. (1978) 'Pioneering a Non-Western Psychology', *Science News*, 113: 154–8.

Douglas, M. (1984) *Purity and Danger: An Analysis of the Concepts of Pollution and Danger*, London: Routledge.

Douglas, M. (1985) *Risk Acceptability According to the Social Sciences*, New York: Sage.

Douglas, M. (1994) *Risk and Blame: Essays in Cultural Theory*, London: Routledge.

Douglas, M. (1996) *Thought Styles*, London: Sage.

Elias, N. (1939/2000) *The Civilizing Process: Sociogenetic and Psychogenetic Investigations*, (trans.) E. Jephcott, London: Blackwell.

Felman, S. (1997) 'Psychoanalysis and Education: Teaching Terminable and Interminable', in S. Todd (ed.) *Learning Desire: Perspectives on Pedagogy, Culture, and the Unsaid*, New York: Routledge.

Field, T. (1998) 'Massage Therapy Effects', *American Psychologist*, 53: 270–81.

Field, T. (1999) 'American Adolescents Touch Each Other Less and are More Aggressive toward their Peers as Compared with French adolescents', *Adolescence*, 34: 753–8.

Field, T. (2002) *Touch*, Cambridge, MA: MIT Press.

Field, T., Harding, J., Soliday, B., Lasko, D., Gonzalez, N. and Valendeon, C. (1994) 'Touching in Infant, Toddler and Preschool Nurseries', *Early Child Development and Care*, 98: 113–21.

Fitzgerald, M. (2005) 'Punctuated Equilibrium, Moral Panics and the Ethics Review Process', *Journal of Academic Ethics*, 2: 4, 1–24.

Foucault, M. (1975) *The Birth of the Clinic*, New York: Vintage.

Foucault, M. (1977) *Discipline and Punish: The Birth of the Prison*, Middlesex: Peregrine Books.

Foucault, M. (1979) 'Governmentality', *Ideology and Consciousness*, 6: 5–21.

Foucault, M. (1980) *Power/Knowledge: Selected Interviews and other Writings, 1972–1977*, in G.C. Gordon (ed.), New York: Pantheon.

Furedi, F. (2001) *Paranoid Parenting: Abandon Your Anxieties and be a Good Parent*, London: Penguin.

Furedi, F. (2002a) *The Culture of Fear: Risk-Taking and the Morality of Low Expectation*, (2nd edition) London: Continuum.

Furedi, F. (2002b) 'The Silent Ascendancy of the Therapeutic Culture in Britain', *Society*, 39: 3, 16–24.

Giroux, H. (1992) *Border Crossings: Cultural Workers and the Politics of Education*, New York: Routledge.

Giroux, H. and McLaren, P. (1984) 'Teacher Education and the Politics of Engagement: The Case for Democratic Schooling', *Harvard Educational Review*, 56: 3, 213–38.

Glaser, B.G. and Strauss, A.L. (1967) *The Discovery of Grounded Theory*, Chicago: Aldine.

Goffman, E. (1990) *Stigma: Notes on the Management of Spoiled Identity*, (first published 1963), Harmondsworth: Penguin.

Goldacre, B. (2006) 'Bad Science: It's not so Easy to Predict Murder – Do the Maths', *Guardian*, 9 December 2006: 16.

Grace, D.J. and Tobin, J. (1997) 'Carnival in the Classroom', in J. Tobin (ed.) *Making a Place for Pleasure in Early Childhood Education*, New Haven and London: Yale University Press.

Guardian Offer (2002) *Practical Art of Baby Massage Video*, Littlemead, Surrey: JEM Marketing.

Hall, D. (1984) 'The Venereal Confronts the Venerable: "Playboy" on Christmas', *Journal of Popular Culture*, 7: 63–8.

Hall, S., Critcher, C., Jefferson, J., Clarke, J. and Roberts, B. (1978) *Policing the Crisis: Mugging, the State, and Law and Order*, New York: Holmes and Meier Publishers.

Hansard (2006) *Safeguarding Vulnerable Groups' Bill, 2nd reading*, Baroness Morris of Bolton, 28 March, online available http://www.publications.parliament.uk/pa/ld200405/ldhansrd/pdvn/lds06/text/60328–29.htm (accessed 1 March 2007).

Hirst, D. (1997) *Damienhirst*, London: Booth-Clibborn.

HMI/Ofsted (1999) *Report on Summerhill School*, Ofsted, HMSO: London.

Holden, C. and Clough, N. (eds) (1998) *Children as Citizens: Education for Participation*, London: Jessica Kingsley.

Hooks, B. (1994) *Teaching to Transgress: Education as the Practice of Freedom*, New York: Routledge.

Hutchens, B. (2005) *Jean-Luc Nancy and the Future of Philosophy*, Chesham, Bucks: Acumen.

Johnson, R.T. (2000) *Hands Off! The Disappearance of Touch in the Care of Children*, New York: Peter Lang Publishing.

Jourard, S.M. (1966) 'An Exploratory Study of Body Accessibility', *British Journal of Social and Clinical Psychology*, 5: 221–31.

Kafka, F. (1919/61) 'The Penal Settlement' in F. Kafka *Metamorphosis and Other Stories*, Harmondsworth: Penguin.

Kamuf, P. (1997) 'Deconstruction and Feminism: A Repetition' in N. Holland (ed.) *Feminist Interpretations of Jacques Derrida*, Pennsylvania: Penn State University Press.

Katz, D. (1989) *The World of Touch*, (trans.) L.E. Krueger, Hillsdale, NJ: Lawrence Erlbaum Associates.

Kidsco Projects (2006) *Children's Entertainers, Fun Activities, Entertainments and Childcare Services Providers*, online available http: //www.kidsco.co.uk/Father_Christmas.htm (accessed 20 March 2006).

King, J.R. (1997) 'Keeping it Quiet: Gay Teachers in the Primary Grade', in J. Tobin (ed.) *Making a Place for Pleasure in Early Childhood Education*, New Haven and London: Yale University Press.

Kroker, A. and Kroker, M. (1988) *Body Invaders: Sexuality and the Postmodern Condition*, London: Macmillan.

Laderman, C. and Roseman, M. (eds) (1996) *The Performance of Healing*, New York: Routledge.

Lave, J. and Wenger, E. (1990) *Situated Learning: Legitimate Peripheral Participation*, Cambridge, UK: Cambridge University Press.

Law, J. and Mol, A. (2002) 'Local Entanglements or Utopian Moves: An Inquiry into Train Accidents', in M. Parker (ed.) *Utopia and Organisation*, London: Blackwell (Sociological Review).

Leavitt, R. and Power, M. (1989) 'Emotional Socialization in the Post-Modern Era: Children in Day Care', *Social Psychological Quarterly*, 52: 1, 35–43.

Leavitt, R. and Power, M. (1997) 'Civilizing Bodies', in J. Tobin (1997) *Making a Place for Pleasure in Early Childhood Education*, New Haven and London: Yale University Press.

Lévi-Strauss, C. (1952/93) 'Father Christmas Executed', in D. Miller (ed.) *Unwrapping Christmas*, Oxford: Clarendon Press.

Lindon, J. (2004) 'Is it Alright to Cuddle? Supporting Young Development and Good Practice in Child Protection', *Early Years Educator*, 6: 1, 1–7.

Lions Clubs International (2004) *Policy Concerning the Protection of Vulnerable Persons Including Children and Young Persons*, online available http://www.lions105d.org.uk/Downloads/vunrbl_apr04.pdf (accessed 22 December 2006).

Lorde, A. (1984) *Sister Outsider: Essays and Speeches*, Trumansburg, NY: Crossing Publications.

Lucas, H. and Lamb, A. (2000) *Neill's Diamonds: An Oral History of Summerhill School*. (mimeo).

Lupton, D. (1999) *Risk*, London and New York: Routledge.

McDermott, N. (2007) 'Parents Take Parenting Far Too Seriously', *Spiked Online*, online available http://www.spiked-online.com/index.php?/site/earticle/3699/ (accessed 3 August 2007).

McWilliam, E. (2000) 'Foreword' in R.T. Johnson, *Hands Off! The Disappearance of Touch in the Care of Children*, New York: Peter Lang Publishing.

McWilliam, E. and Jones, A. (2005) 'An Unprotected Species? On Teachers as Risky Subjects', *British Educational Research Journal*, 31: 1, 109–20.

Mairal, G. (2003) 'A Risk Shadow in Spain', *Ethnos*, 68: 2, 179–91.

Manifesto Club (2006a) *The Case against Vetting*, online available http://www.statewatch.org/news/2006/oct/THE%20CASE%20AGAINST%20VETTING.pdf (accessed 20 November 2006).

Manifesto Club (2006b) *How the Child Protection Industry Stole Christmas*, online available http://www.manifestoclub.com/files/CHRISTMASREPORT.pdf (accessed 17 January 2007).

Marwick, M.G. (1964) 'Witchcraft as a Social Strain Gauge', *Australian Journal of Science*, 26: 263–8.

Mazzei, L. (2007) *Inhabited Silence in Qualitative Research: Putting Poststructural Theory to Work*, New York: Peter Lang.

Mead, M. (1928/43) *Coming of Age in Samoa*, Harmondsworth: Penguin.

Merleau-Ponty, M. (1990) *Phenomenology of Perception*, (trans.) C. Smith, London: Routledge.

Miles, B. (1999) *Remarkable Conversations: A Guide to Developing Meaningful Communication with Children and Young Adults who are Deafblind*, Watertown: Perkins School for the Blind.

Milosz, C. (1953/90) *The Captive Mind*, (trans.) J. Zielonko, New York: Random House.

Montagu, A. (1971/86) *Touching: The Human Significance of the Skin*, (3rd edition) New York: Harper and Row.

Morean, B. and Skor, L. (1993) 'Cinderella Christmas: Kitsch, Consumerism and Youth in Japan', in D. Miller (ed.) *Unwrapping Christmas*, Oxford: Clarendon Press.

Morris, M. (2001) *Rethinking the Communicative Turn: Adorno, Habermas, and the Problem of Communicative Freedom*, Albany, NY: State University of New York Press.

Mueller, J. (2006) 'Do No Harm', paper presented at the Law and Society Conference, Baltimore, 8 July 2006.

Mythen, G. (2004) *Ulrich Beck: A Critical Introduction to the Risk Society*, London: Pluto Press.

Nancy, J.-L. (1993a) *The Birth to Presence*, (trans.) B. Holmes, Stanford, CA: Stanford University Press.

Nancy, J.-L. (1993b) *Experience of Freedom*, (trans.) B. MacDonald, Stanford, CA: Stanford University Press.

Nancy, J.-L. (2000) *Being Singular Plural*, Stanford, CA: Stanford University Press.

Neill, A.S. (1939) *The Problem Teacher*, London: Herbert Jenkins Limited.

Neill, A.S. (1971) *Talking of Summerhill*, London: Gollancz.

New Opportunities Fund (2002) 'Massaging Rubs out Anger', *Initiative*, 11, 6 May 2002.

Nochlin, L. (1994) *The Body in Pieces: The Fragment as a Metaphor of Modernity*, London: Thames and Hudson.

Nolan, J.L. (1998) *The Therapeutic State: Justifying Government at Century's End*, New York: New York University Press.

O'Brien, R.M. (2006) 'The Institutional Review Board Problem: Where it Came From and What to Do about it', *Journal of Social Distress and the Homeless*, XV: 1, 24–46.

Ofsted (2006) *Safeguarding Children: An Evaluation of Procedure for Checking Staff Appointed by Schools*, June, online available http://www.ofsted.gov.uk/publications/2647 (accessed 20 March 2007).

Oken-Wright, P. (1992) 'From Tug of War to "Let's Make a Deal": The Teacher's Role', *Young Children*, 15–20 November 1992.

O'Neil, O. (2002) *Autonomy and Trust in Bioethics*, Cambridge: Cambridge University Press.

Osler, A. and Starkey, H. (2005) *Changing Citizenship: Democracy and Inclusion in Education*, Maidenhead: Open University Press.

Perry, L.-A. (2006) 'Risk, Error and Accountability: Improving the Practice of School Leaders', *Educational Research Policy and Practice*, 5, 149–64.

Phelan, A.M. (1997) 'Classroom Management and the Erasure of Teacher Desire', in J. Tobin (ed.) *Making a Place for Pleasure in Early Childhood Education*, New Haven and London: Yale University Press.

Piper, H. (2002) 'Touch Me Touch Me Not: In Search of Guidelines on Touching Behaviour', Unpublished Research Report, Manchester: Manchester Metropolitan University.

Piper, H. and Smith, H. (2003) '"Touch" in Educational and Child Care Settings: Dilemmas and Responses', *British Educational Research Journal*, 29: 6, 779–894.

Piper, H., Powell, J. and Smith, H. (2005) 'Parents, Professionals and Paranoia – The Touching of Children in a Culture of Fear', *Journal of Social Work*, 34: 2, 151–67.

Powell, J. (2001) 'Making Contact', *Community Care*, 12 April 2001: 22.

Powell, J., Gould, A., Knibbs, C. and Wolstencroft, M. (2004) *The Early Years Practitioner and Practices of Touch: A Touch Too Much?* Manchester: Stockport EYDCP and the Manchester Metropolitan University.

Power, M. (1994) *The Audit Explosion*, London: Demos.

Power, M. (1997) *The Audit Society: Rituals of Verification*, Oxford: Oxford University Press.

Power, M. (2004) *The Risk Management of Everything: Rethinking the Politics of Uncertainty*, London: Demos.

Probyn, E. (1995) 'Lesbians in Space: Gender, Sex and the Structure of Missing: A response to Bell *et al.* (1994), *Gender, Place, and Culture*, 2: 1, 77–84.

RGBI (2006) *Protection Policy – Advice for Christmas Activities*, Rotaract in Great Britain and Ireland, online available http://www.rotaract.org.uk/info/download/rgbi_protection_adviceforchristmasactivities.pdf (accessed 20 March 2007).

Roman Catholic Diocese of East Anglia (2004) *Staff Recruitment Procedures, Child Protection Handbook – Recruiting Volunteers*, online available http://www.Catholiceastanglia.org/family/files/uplink/ch6_volunteers1_13.pdf?565682c098e024566ba67dd312a9a25f=68faff7c9e6a41989801f3543078fe76 (accessed 20 March 2007).

Rose, N. (1990) *Governing the Soul: The Shaping of the Private Self*, New York: Routledge.

Sale, G. (nd) *The Koran: Commonly called the Alkoran of Mohammed* (first published 1734) (trans.) G. Sale, London: Frederick Warne & Co.

Sanders, A. (2006) House of Commons Hansard debates, 19.6.06: Column 1139, online available http://www.publications.parliament.uk/pa/cm200506/cmhansrd/cm060619/debtext/60619–0551.htm (accessed 20 March 2007).

Sartre, J.-P. (1943/56) *Being and Nothingness: An Essay of Phenomenological Ontology*, (trans.) H.E. Barnes, New York: Simon and Schuster.

Scheffler, I. (1984) 'On the Education of Policymakers', *Harvard Educational Review*, 54: 2, 152–65.

Schildkrout, E. (2004) 'Inscribing the Body', *Annual Review of Anthropology*, 33, 319–44.

Schwartz, B. (2004) *The Paradox of Choice: Why More is Less*, New York: Harper Perennial.

Scott, C. (2003) 'Ethics and Knowledge in the Contemporary University', *Critical Reviews in International Social and Political Philosophy*, 6: 4, 93–107.

Scott, C. (2006) 'A Little Knowledge is a Dangerous Thing', *Spiked! online*, 2 March 2006, online available http://www.spiked-online.com/index.php?/site/ article /224/ (accessed 15 March 2006).

Silin, J.G. (1997) 'The Pervert in the Classroom', in J. Tobin (ed.) *Making a Place for Pleasure in Early Childhood Education*, New Haven and London: Yale University Press.

Skidelsky, R. (1969) *English Progressive Schools*, Harmondsworth: Penguin.

Slunt, E.T. (1994) 'Living the Call Authentically', in M.E. Lashley, M.T. Neal, E.T. Slunt, L.M. Berman and F.H. Hultgren (eds) *Being Called to Care*, Albany: SUNY.

Smith, H. (2000) 'Touch in Childcare Settings: Investigating the Conflict between Policy and Practice', Unpublished dissertation, Manchester: Manchester Metropolitan University.

Spradley, J.P. (1980) *Participant Observation*, New York: Holt, Rhinehard & Winston.

Stake, R.E. (1978) 'The Case Study Method in Social Inquiry', *Educational Researcher* 7: 2, 5–8.

Stanley, J. and Goddard, C. (2002) *In the Firing Line: Violence and Power in Child Protection Social Work*, Chichester: Wiley & Sons.

Steadman Rice, J. (1998) *A Disease of One's Own: Psychotherapy, Addiction and the Emergence of Co-dependency*. New Brunswick: Transaction Publishers.

Stoller, P. (1996) 'Sounds and Things: Pulsations of Power in Songhay', in C. Laderman and M. Roseman (eds) *The Performance of Healing*, New York: Routledge.

Strathern, M. (2004) 'A Community of Critics? Thoughts on New Knowledge', *The Huxley Memorial Lecture*.

Strauss, A. and Corbin, J. (1998) *The Basics of Qualitative Research: Techniques and Procedures for Developing Grounded Theory*, Thousand Oaks: Sage.

Stronach, I. (2002a) 'This Space is Not Yet Blank', *Educational Action Research*, 10: 2, 291–307.

Stronach, I. (2002b) *The OFSTED Response to Summerhill's Complaint: An Evidence-Based Appraisal*, Manchester: Manchester Metropolitan University.

Stronach, I., Allan, J., MacDonald, B., Kushner, S. and Torrance, H. (2000) *Report on the Evaluation of Summerhill School*, Manchester: Manchester Metropolitan University for the Nuffield Foundation.

Stronach, I., Halsall, R. and Hustler, D. (2002) 'Future Imperfect: Evaluation in Dystopian Times' in K. Ryan, and T. Schwandt (eds) *Exploring Evaluator Role and Identity*, Greenwich, CT: IAP.

Stronach, I., Frankham, J. and Stark, S. (2006) 'Sex, Science and Educational Research: The Unholy Trinity', *Journal of Education Policy*, 22: 2, 215–35.

Stronach, I., Garratt, D., Pearce, C. and Piper, H. (2007) 'Reflexivity, The Picturing of Selves, and the Forging of Method', *Qualitative Inquiry*, 13: 2, 179–203.

Stronach, I. and Piper, H. (2008) 'Can Liberal Education Make a Comeback? The Case of "Relational Touch" at Summerhill School', *American Educational Research Journal*.

Strong, T. (2002) 'Kinship between Judith Butler and Anthropology? A Review Essay', *Ethnos*, 67: 3, 401–18.

Tanesini, A. (2001) 'In Search of Community, Mouffe, Wittgenstein and Cavell', *Radical Philosophy*, 110: 12–19.

Tassoni, P. (1998) *Child Care and Education*, Oxford: Heinemann Educational Publishers.

Taylor, J. (2005) 'Surfacing the Body Interior', *Annual Review of Anthropology*, 34, 741–56.

Thompson, A. (1998) 'Not the Colour Purple: Black Feminist Lessons for Educational Caring', *The Harvard Educational Review*, 68: 4, 222–554.

Thompson, W. and Hickey, J. (1989) 'Myth, Identity, and Social interaction: Encountering Santa Claus at the Mall', *Qualitative Sociology*, 12: 4, 371–89.

Tobin, J. (1997) *Making a Place for Pleasure in Early Childhood Education*, New Haven and London: Yale University Press.

Todd, S. (ed.) (1997) *Learning Desire: Perspectives on Pedagogy, Culture, and the Unsaid*, New York: Routledge.

Travis, D. (2006) 'Treating volunteers like criminals will kill community sport', *Spiked online*, 23.10.16 online available http://www.spiked-online.com/index.php?/site/article/1975/ (accessed 1 December 2006).

Vance, C. (1984) *Pleasure and Danger: Exploring Female Sexuality*, Boston: Routledge & Kegan Paul.

van den Hoonaard, W.C. (2001) 'Is Research-Ethics Review a Moral Panic?' *The Canadian Review of Sociology and Anthropology*, 38: 1, 19–36.

Vasseleu, C. (1998) *Textures of Light. Vision and Touch, in Irigaray, Levinas and Merlau-Ponty*, London: Routledge.

Vaughan, M. (ed.) (2006) *Summerhill and A.S. Neill*, London: Open University Press.

Vidler, A., Stewart, S. and Mitchell, W. (2007) *Antony Gormley: Blind Light*, London: Hayward Gallery.

Vygotsky, L.S. (1978) *Mind and Society: The Development of Higher Mental Processes*, Cambridge, MA: Harvard University Press.

Wainwright, M. (2004) 'Fears of Abuse put Santa on Camera', *Guardian Online*, online available http://www.guardian.co.uk/christmas2004/story/0,,1365451,00.html (accessed 19 December 2006).

Ward, A. (1990) 'The Role of Physical Contact in Childcare', *Children & Society*, 4: 4, 337–51.

Warner, M. (1990) *Fear of a Queer Planet: Queer Politics and Social Theory*, Minneapolis: University of Minnesota Press.

Watney, S. (1987) *Policing Desire: Pornography, AIDS and the Media*, Minneapolis: University of Minnesota Press.

Weiss, G. (2000) 'Écart: The Space of Corporeal Difference', in F. Evans (ed.) *Chiasmus: Merleau-Ponty's Notion of Flesh*, Albany: New York State University Press.

Winnicott, D. (1953) 'Transitional Objects and Transitional Phenomena', *International Journal of Psychoanalysis*, 34: 89–97.

Witz, A., Halford, S. and Savage, M. (1996) 'Organized Bodies: Gender, Sexuality and Embodiment in Contemporary Organizations', in L. Adkins and V. Merchant (eds) *Sexualizing the Social: Power and the Organization of Sexuality*, New York: St Martin's Press.

Yoshinaga-Itano, C. (2001) 'The Social-Emotional Ramifications of Universal Newborn Hearing Screening, Early Identification and Intervention of Children who are Deaf or Hard of Hearing', Proceedings of the second International Paediatric Audiology Amplification Conference (Sound Foundations), Chicago, Illinois.

Zur, O. and Nordmarken, N. (2004) *To Touch or Not to Touch: Exploring the Myth of Prohibition on Touch in Psychotherapy and Counselling*, online available www.drozur.com/touchintheraapy (accessed 5 April 2007).

Index